THE
CREATIVITY
CURE

Carrie Barron, MD, and Alton Barron, MD

Scribner

New York London Toronto Sydney New Delhi

153.35

SCRIBNER
A Division of Simon & Schuster, Inc.
1230 Avenue of the Americas
New York, NY 10020

The names and details of some individuals in this book
have been changed and some individuals are composites.

Copyright © 2012 by Carrie Barron and Alton Barron

First Scribner trade paperback edition August 2013

SCRIBNER and design are registered trademarks of The Gale Group, Inc.,
used under license by Simon & Schuster, Inc., the publisher of this work.

For information about special discounts for bulk purchases, please contact
Simon & Schuster Special Sales at 1-866-506-1949 or
business@simonandschuster.com.

The Simon & Schuster Speakers Bureau can bring authors to
your live event. For more information or to book an event, contact the
Simon & Schuster Speakers Bureau at 1-866-248-3049 or
visit our website at www.simonspeakers.com.

Designed by Ellen R. Sasahara

Manufactured in the United States of America

1 3 5 7 9 10 8 6 4 2

Library of Congress Control Number: 2012007163

ISBN 978-1-4516-3679-6 (pbk)
ISBN 978-1-4516-3680-2 (ebook)

For our children:
Chloe, Nicholas, and Caroline

And our parents:
Florence and Joseph L. Vigilante
Arlene and Jim Barron

Contents

Contents

Introduction

F ROM THE TIME I was a small child I reveled in creativity, and
therapy was a big part of the conversation in my house—my parents were both therapists—so this book, which combines the two, feels
like a natural extension of the way I live, and have since I was a young
girl.

Creativity was held in high regard in my entwined extended family.
We were eight cousins, and several of the eldest, plus their significant
others, were established artists. I was not among this elite, though I
did sing for many years, but I enjoyed listening to them talk about the
world of art and I always wanted to be a member of their club.

My fascination with psychological ideas and healing as well as creativity started early. When I was nine, I would pretend I was a therapist and act out treatment scenarios with ideas from the Ann Landers
column. At twelve, I wanted to be a psychoanalyst because after two
sessions with a child analyst, I felt a weight had been lifted off my
shoulders as I left the room. She asked about what I liked to do, what
my nighttime dreams were, and whether I would rather be seven or
seventeen. After seeing her, I stopped getting into trouble and started
getting good grades.

However, when I underwent my own four-days-a-week-on-the-
couch treatment (a requirement for psychoanalytic training), I did

not find it to be the humanistic enterprise I had imagined. It seemed to me that more was needed for wellness than the pursuit of insight. Not being able to buy in, latch on, be subsumed, believe, and belong was disappointing, and it took me a long time to come to terms with this.

Over the years I have met many people, analysts among them, who felt that their psychoanalytic treatments were subpar, too expensive, and even "traumatic" in the words of three who had trouble with the classical analyst who "never said anything." They felt a lack of support and seemed to be searching for something else. So during my twenty-three years of practicing and teaching psychotherapy I have strived to figure out how to combine the powerful, beautiful, nuanced, effective ideas of psychoanalysis with scientifically validated forms of treatment, and to have it be affordable and accessible. I have tried to integrate creative thinking in my work both by helping clients to uncover and develop their own creative possibilities and by encouraging them to be curious and nonjudgmental about what pulses through the self, however surprising or unsettling. For many people, a partner is necessary for one's own creative growth, and Alton has been that person for me.

Alton has been with me every step of the way for the last twenty-five years. We met in 1985 on the day we interviewed for Tulane Medical School. We had one of those long conversations where we talked about so many things—writing, music, and tiny babies in incubators as we passed through the NICU and then we met again on the first day of school. He has discussed, thought, edited, critiqued, researched, and written parts of the book as well as shouldered domestic duties so I could write. His work as an orthopedic hand surgeon, his athleticism, and his desire to close his eyes and stretch out in clean grass has had an influence on our philosophy of treatment. He averages only five hours of sleep per night but lets me get closer to eight and is willing to have many conversations.

I have been thinking about, reading about, talking about, asking about, and studying creativity for thirty years, so this was the chance to put it all together. Over time it has become more and more clear to me that moving my body, using my hands, doing what interests me, telling myself the truth about my issues, and talking with my friends takes me to a better place.

—Carrie Barron, MD

I GREW UP IN THE country amid fields of cotton, field corn, and soybeans. Running around barefoot and lying hidden in the tall grass with my dog imbued me with the sense of calm that only nature can provide. There was plenty of hard work to be done by hand to help my parents maintain the vegetable garden, the barn and yard and fences. We did our own automobile and tractor maintenance, and when something broke, wooden or ı——ıhanical, we repaired it. Early on, I learned that my hands were my primary tools that could get me where I needed to go.

From engineering in college, a year in dental school, painting houses in Austin, to medical school and ultimately orthopedic surgery, my hands built and now sustain my life. They are the tools for my livelihood and my creativity. And nature is my fuel.

Carrie and I began medical school together twenty-six years ago and began new journeys, with each other and our patients. They told us their stories, and we listened and learned. They taught us lessons about pleasure, peak moments, rising up, perseverance, hope, and faith.

Over the years, we refined our respective techniques for helping those who came to see us. My efforts are founded on anatomy, physiology, exercise, conditioning, good nutrition, and becoming stronger and more flexible. Carrie's efforts are founded on the need for patients to gain psychological insight, to understand their past so as to improve their present, and to design a better future. We began to notice that with a certain change in lifestyle—with more physicality, handwork, and meditational practices—some patients felt better and were even able to give up medications.

Introduction

Scientific data began to emerge that questioned the efficacy of anti-depressant medications in patients with moderate anxiety and depression. Carrie began to discuss these ideas with me. We were concerned and curious. We were struck by how often these medications were prescribed, and yet how so many people still did not feel well, on them or off of them. We met people who had ideas about what they wanted to do, how they wanted to live, or even how they wanted to feel, but who couldn't make it happen. After Carrie's extensive research and both of our clinical observations, we began to devise a method of treatment that people could customize to make their day-to-day experience better and to feel happier and more effective.

Our mission is to demonstrate that it is possible to improve your sense of well-being through creative endeavors. However, to uncover your true creativity, it is necessary to develop certain healthy habits. We believe that some form of creativity is not only possible but necessary for all people.

—Alton Barron, MD

W E BOTH HAVE THE privilege to work with many amazing artists and they are some of the people who have helped us clarify our ideas about the connection between creativity and health. We had a conversation with Bruce Springsteen about *The Creativity Cure,* and he wrote this for the book:

We are creatures of the mind, the body, and the heart. Few of us have jobs that engage these three spheres simultaneously. Even in my line, songwriting is primarily mental and emotional; recording, the same. But I'm lucky, for in live performance, I need to call upon all of these elements and integrate them to get the job done. Pushing your body, mind, and heart to their limits creates a cathartic "clearing," a "centering" effect in your being, in your soul. It makes you sweat, feel, and think.

If you can find something that brings you there, use it. It will bring to your day a richness of experience and a fullness of self. When I come off stage, I feel a heightened "aliveness" communicating with my audience provides. It's what all the noise, dancing, and shouting is about. I work hard that they may feel it too. That raw feeling doesn't last for long, it's not supposed to, but its remnant angels provide guidance, focus, and energy for future adventures. Mind, body, heart.

Good luck, Bruce

THE
CREATIVITY
CURE

1

Creativity and Happiness

EVERYONE IS CAPABLE OF CREATIVITY AND HAPPINESS

Over the past fifteen years, Alton and I have met so many people with fantasies that do not take form, ideas that never become books, mental creations that never make it to canvas, or wishes that begin as wisps and float away before they can be realized. This book is designed to help you find a way, because creative action is essential to mental health and happiness. Without some form of creative action, it is hard to feel content. If inherent talents and passions lie fallow, self-esteem, wellness, and joy slip away. Many people suffer from this. A lack of self-expression can make you feel incomplete. When you are able to create, follow your instincts, and turn dreaming into doing, euphoric moments follow.

For many years, Alton, an orthopedic upper limb surgeon, and I, a psychiatrist/psychoanalyst, have struggled to remain balanced in the midst of familial, professional, and social pressures and responsibilities. As I'm sure you have, we have experienced the deaths of friends and relatives, physical and mental illness in our families and our patients, fractures, breaches, disappointments, and unrequited effort. We have faltered at times with unfinished projects, physical setbacks, ailing parents, children in crisis, rejected manuscripts, loss of significant relationships and ideologies, feelings of doubt and inadequacy, and not enough time. But ultimately, we realized that by maintaining certain psychological and physical habits, we could manage stress, find answers, rise above, and move forward in a happier state. What we have learned is the foundation of *The Creativity Cure*. The first thing we want to share is that it *is* about you. It is about *your* creativity, *your* health, and *your* happiness. But it is also about others, because when you are well, generosity and compassion come easily. You are better able to nurture, contribute, and connect. If you understand your inner life and become productive, proactive, and creative, everyone wins.

We have met many "closet creatives" at parties, in school, on soccer field sidelines, and in our offices. We have been struck by passionate people with intriguing ideas who seem frustrated because they are not making it happen or cannot follow through. Creative expression through the proper form—the form that is organic for you—will make you feel well and sometimes even ecstatic. You need a method for discovering what you want to express, how you need to express it, and what might be getting in your way.

Creativity is important for happiness. Creativity is part of you, whether you are an artist, a bus driver, a stay-at-home mom, or a professional. No matter who you are, some degree of creativity is necessary for wellness and contentment. The goal of this book is to help you uncover your creative potential and use it for greater fulfillment, so that you can be happier. Creativity can make everyday life interesting, lead to great accomplishments, or both. Everyone is capable of happiness and creativity, but the path is unique for each of us.

If happiness were not possible, if you had not already known it, felt it, dreamt it, or been dissolved within it, you would not be seeking it now.

What is happiness? Happiness is being absorbed in something—a dream, a mission, a project, an idea—greater than yourself. Happiness is feeling free, able, hopeful, and inspired. It is a state you wish you could sustain forever, but happiness is usually fleeting.

Think back on your happiest times.

- What were you doing?
- Was it planned or did it occur by chance?
- Who were you with?
- How did you feel?
- Were you sad when it ended, or at peace and satisfied?

If you think about your happiest times, you will probably remember a series of moments rather than extended periods of time. The poet Robert Frost said happiness makes up in height what it lacks in length.

Our goal is to increase the number of happy moments in your life and heighten them or deepen them, as the case may be. Rather than pursue the state of happiness, we believe in pursuing habits that give rise to happiness, thereby creating more opportunities for experiencing moments of joy, inspiration, purpose, and meaning. This is a surer thing than trying to capture the mood itself, because happiness is the aftermath of certain kinds of engagements. Though you may not be able to sustain perfect pleasure, you most certainly can bolster contentment and have a greater number of happy moments if you follow the right steps. Teaching you those steps is our goal with this book.

Have you ever noticed that when you decide you want to have a good time, the good time might not show up? Has anyone ever told you to "be happy," as if you could just summon the mood? This book is designed to help you develop healthy, creative, proactive habits and build the mind-set and stamina to maintain them so you can find your focus, become a more satisfied person, and have more happy moments.

Perhaps you have struggled with these:

- Sadness
- Dissatisfaction
- Mild to moderate depression
- Mild to moderate anxiety
- Rumination
- Overstimulation

Have you pursued happiness but still feel burdened, blue, fraught, overstimulated, or dissatisfied? Do therapy, self-help books, engaging conversations, pills, yoga, sojourns, intellectual gains, artistic achievements, or spiritual retreats provide some succor, but not enough? Are you able to work, to love, to socialize and function, but you want to feel better in your private moments?

Are you a member of the worried well, an active or able person with hidden angst?

If you are, you may need this book. *The Creativity Cure* is about true, lasting internal change, not tacked-on solutions. See if these descriptions of sadness, dissatisfaction, mild to moderate depression or anxiety, rumination, and overstimulation sound like you.

Sadness Symptoms

- Sleeplessness
- Listlessness
- Lack of energy
- Lack of interest
- Tearfulness

Sadness can be a healthy response to a traumatic or tragic situation such as loss, as long as it does not persist, dominate, and do you in. But maybe you have felt one or more of these symptoms for too long, for several months or over a year.

Perhaps you fought with a friend, left a lover, lost a loved one, missed a promotion, were mistreated, or departed a treasured place, and you just cannot get over it. Are you having trouble picking up the pieces and moving on?

Perhaps it is not quite sadness you feel, but rather nameless dissatisfaction.

Dissatisfaction Symptoms

- Pessimism
- Resignation
- Fatigue

- Low energy
- Feeling out of sorts
- Feeling unsatisfied

With dissatisfaction, the basics are in place—work, love, leisure—but you rarely feel happy. Maybe you feel a chronic blueness or a low-grade rumbling terror that never leaves. Things that are supposed to be fun are not, but you cannot pinpoint a particular problem. Whatever joie de vivre you once had has slipped away. You grew up, and it was gone.

Perhaps you think, "It's too late, and I don't want to bother anymore." Maybe you feel your peak has passed, opportunities are over, and you should accept your fate. Is not life supposed to be full of "quiet desperation," in the words of Thoreau, or "ordinary unhappiness," as Freud professed? Maybe you have achieved success, but inside you feel exhausted or as if you are only repeating what you have already done. Do you feel stuck, uninspired, or resigned?

Perhaps what you feel is more pressing or troubling.

Mild to Moderate Depression Symptoms

- Despair
- Depressed mood, flat feeling
- Hopelessness
- Fatigue
- Indifference
- Guilt
- Low self-esteem
- Poor concentration
- Lack of motivation or energy

Do you secretly suffer but hide it masterfully? Would friends, relatives, colleagues, or neighbors be shocked if they knew what festers behind your warm, friendly smile? Many good, kind, loving people are experts at hiding depression. Maybe you can banter at a party or be a great host, cooperate with colleagues, get your kids to school, and muster a meal for the potluck, but inside you are in a pit and you just cannot find a way out and up. You do not even feel like trying. Are you afraid of burdening others?

Maybe it is not so much that you feel deflated or flat, but rather racked with worry.

Mild to Moderate Anxiety Symptoms

- Overworry
- Fatigue
- Irritability
- Tension
- Agitation
- Insomnia
- Poor concentration
- Dread

Are you an overly anxious person? Do you worry about the email you just sent, the way you spoke to a colleague, what others think? Do you fret about whether you will be asked, included, valued, or invited, and what it means if you are not? Do you wake up in the wee hours and worry about the little things?

Excessive anxiety occurs when you move from worry to worry and cannot let any of them go. Your mind turns round and round, your pulse revs up—everything in you races. Yet you feel fatigued. Your head spins with negative possibilities and you fear that minor mistakes will lead to major consequences. You say to yourself, "Oh, no, what did I do?" way too often. You cannot let yourself off the hook. Even if you try to tell yourself, "It's no big deal," you are not reassured. You can be pretty irritable, and it may be hard to control it.

A little anxiety is good for motivation, but excessive anxiety can be paralyzing. Having no anxiety whatsoever can be equally destructive, because lack of any anxiety compromises motivation and risk assessment. If your anxiety cripples you, you might need psychotherapy or possibly medication. But do not rush to the pills. Some forms of anxiety are well served by medication, but many are not.

One form of anxiety that is very common is rumination.

Rumination Symptoms

- Overthinking
- Rehashing
- Inability to let go of a thought or problem
- Obsessive worrying
- Trying to master a gnawing problem through repetitive thoughts, but being unsuccessful
- Repeatedly trying to "get to the bottom of it," but only becoming more twisted up

You might be familiar with the pain and agony of rumination. Rumination consumes energy, feels like a psychological paralysis, and is similar to an addiction or an obsession. You cannot stop doing it even though you know it is not getting you anywhere. Rumination is like treading or thrashing in water instead of swimming straight and reaching the other side. Trying to fathom the unfathomable or obsessing over something that cannot be changed will exhaust and depress you. We have the fantasy that repeated evaluation will master the problem, but in actuality it does not help us solve or evolve.

Does rumination wake you up at 3:00 a.m. or not let you fall asleep in the first place?

Rumination is a racing hysterically round and round, but there are other kinds of mind racing.

Overstimulation Symptoms

- Feeling overwhelmed
- Feeling overstretched
- Numbness
- Feeling frazzled and grumpy
- Resentment
- Inability to focus
- Feeling as if you are "all over the place"
- Feeling desperate and hopeless because of a chronic can't-catch-up feeling

Do you feel overwhelmed much of the time? Do you have too much to do, too many contacts, too much responsibility, and so many messages to respond to that you feel as if you are on the verge of collapse? You, who take pride in your timely responses, are so swamped that days go by before you answer? Overstimulation is not a formal diagnosis, but in our technological age it is ubiquitous.

Overstimulation—too much coming at you from the outside, such that you lose touch with inner energies and inclinations—can cause depression and anxiety. It can make you feel out of control. Even for easygoing people, a life of loose ends is no fun. Even if you have the stamina to handle all the duties, dinners, requests, emails, and contacts, you might feel that you would rather be applying your energy to something that makes you feel more excited and alive.

But what?

WHAT CAN HELP?

Awareness begets change.

Like many people, you may have searched for satisfaction and asked yourself, "Why don't I feel it? How do I get it? What is wrong?" You may have resorted to shopping sprees, therapies, late-night TV, and massive self-probing and still found yourself plagued by anguish, uncertainty, or a feeling that there must be something better.

While two-thirds of people in psychotherapy find that it helps, that leaves one-third who feel that it does *not*, according to Jonathan Engel in *American Psychotherapy: The Rise of Psychotherapy in the United States*. Studies by Irving Kirsch, PhD, author of *The Emperor's New Drugs: Exploding the Antidepressant Myth*, and Mark Zimmerman, MD, of Brown University School of Medicine, have shown that about 75 percent of people on antidepressants may not need to be taking that medication. For many, pills have the same effect as a placebo—they are "expensive Tic Tacs," in the words of writer Sharon Begley in her article for *Newsweek*, "The Depressing News About Antidepressants." One in ten Americans, 30 million people, takes antidepressant medication every day. According to a Rand Corporation study in 2002, only 20 percent of people who are prescribed these medications actually tested positive when screened for depression. Doctors Ramin Mojtabai and Mark Olfson of Johns Hopkins, who studied antidepressant use, say that there has been a "substantial increase in antidepressant prescriptions by non-psychiatrist providers without an accompanying psychiatric diagnosis." The rate of antidepressant use has doubled in the last decade, and yet we are still not happy.

People who suffer from what are often called human condition ailments—mild forms of depression such as loneliness, low energy, dissatisfaction, excessive worry, or overstimulation—need a different approach. Dr. Jay C. Fournier and Dr. Robert J. DeRubeis, of the University of Pennsylvania, published a study in the *Journal of the American Medical Association* that showed that antidepressants may not do as much for mild to moderate depression as we hoped. In a 2010 article by *New York Times* reporter Benedict Carey, DeRubeis is quoted as saying, "Look, medications are always an option, but there's little evidence that they add to other efforts to shake the depression—whether it's exercise, seeing the doctor, reading about the disorder or going for psychotherapy." Medication or psychotherapy, though comforting, may not be addressing the actual need or the full picture.

My client Francesca had had years of psychotherapy but still felt dissatisfied with herself and her life. She felt she had become addicted to talking about her problems and feelings. While she treasured the support of her former therapists, she needed something more. She needed to develop the mind-set and habits that would allow her to experience the creative, joy-producing parts of herself.

In our fast-fix, achievement-oriented, psychologically minded culture, it is easy to cling to a diagnosis, swallow a pill, feel like a victim, or panic over sad, angry, or anxious feelings. It is easy to feel that you should have more or be more, or that you have not been given what you deserve. (Feelings of persecution may be justified, but when taken too far they can undermine rather than serve.) It is easy to forget that there are answers in the palm of your hand.

If you feel that you do not know where else to turn because you have tried every pill and program to manage your unhappiness, dissatisfaction, or lack of contentment, there is another way.

Many people for whom medications or psychotherapy do not work well enough, or do not work at all, can benefit from self-initiated change: small shifts in mental and physical habits, and tailor-made self-care. Many people need a lifestyle change, a mini cultural makeover in their personal lives. Deepak Chopra, physician, writer, and wellness expert, writes that "75% of people who improve their psychological state do so not with a therapist's help, but by themselves."

Do-it-yourself techniques are effective for happiness. If you look within, you will be able to find ways to help yourself. We have known about, used, and respected the concept of self-help for a long time. The idea that self-reliance leads to happiness is not new. *Self-Help; with Illustrations of Character, Conduct and Perseverance* by Samuel Smiles, a book that champions self-reliance as a source of wellness, was written in 1859.

What is the Creativity Cure, and what does it have to do with self-help?

The Creativity Cure is a do-it-yourself prescription for happiness and overcoming mild to moderate depression, anxiety, and discontent. It will help you understand yourself in a deeper way and give you tools for inner satisfaction. The Creativity Cure can help you have a greater number of happy moments and a more satisfying existence by teaching you how to develop Creative Capacity. Creative Capacity involves accessing your unconscious mind.

Why is access to the deeper mind (the unconscious) important? The unconscious reveals true feelings, desires, fears, and interests. When you know, own, and use what goes on in the depths of your being—your truth—life is richer and more livable. Your unconscious mind opens up possibilities. By honoring unconscious expressions—wisps, clues, clamor, random thoughts, or even conflicts that bubble up from the recesses of your mind—you can feel better and go far.

When you have self-awareness, you make better choices about

how to be most effective, what to get involved in, and whom to be with. Being open to thoughts that arise in random moments and being curious about them is useful. Rather than blocking them out, shutting them down, or judging them, seeing where they take you can help you understand yourself, others, and your world in a deeper way. When you allow for this flow through your mind, dreams, fantasies, ideas, and intuitions emerge. Acting on these, bringing them into form, and expressing them through prose, in product, or just in the way you live from day to day provides a valuable experience for you and for others. A scientific study by Dr. Charles Limb and Dr. Allen Braun of the National Institutes of Health has shown that when jazz musicians improvise, they feel more pleasure than they do when following printed notes because part of the prefrontal cortex is stimulated with this activity. Improvisation is a form of Creative Capacity or following an intuitive inclination.

Creative Capacity exists to differing degrees in all of us, because we all have an unconscious. Whether your Creative Capacity is highly honed, needs some polish, or is rough and untouched, developing it will be useful for your ongoing vitality. Even Freud said, "People who are receptive to the influence of art cannot set too high a value on it as a source of pleasure and consolation in life."

The Creativity Cure operates on this principle: development of Creative Capacity will lead to creativity, health, and happiness.

This book is different because it will help you develop Creative Capacity. It will foster internal change rather than just offering behavioral solutions or actions. True, lasting change is what happens when you alter your inner life—your mind and your emotional makeup—as well as your actions.

WHY THE CREATIVITY CURE?

Hephaestus, the Greek god of crafts, was a "bringer of peace and a maker of civilization."

The Creativity Cure is unique because of its emphasis on self-reliance and creating your own happiness. But it is the combination of meaningful creative activity (especially using your hands) and a deepened understanding of yourself that truly sets it apart. Research has shown that creating things by hand or tending things by hand is an important part of wellness. Dr. Kelly Lambert, a researcher and chair of the Psychology Department at Randolph-Macon College in Virginia, explored the relationship between using the hands, current cultural habits, and mood. She concluded that "hands-on work satisfies our primal craving to create solid objects; it could also be an antidote to our cultural malaise."

Clinicians and researchers have discovered that weaving, sewing, and even chopping vegetables can be useful for decreasing stress, relieving anxiety, and modifying depression. Consider how you felt the last time you made something by hand. Whether it was a cake, a home improvement project, a garden, an art piece, or a scrapbook, it was absorbing and satisfying, right?

Creating something with your hands fosters pride and satisfaction, but it also allows you to physically express the things that spring up in your mind, in the moment.

HOW CAN CREATIVITY HELP YOU?

Creativity is a powerful tool for changing inner states because constructing, inventing, and expressing ourselves makes us happy. According to Andrew Brink, of the Department of Psychiatry at McMaster University, in his book *Creativity as Repair: Bipolarity and Its Closure*, creativity is "the original anti-depressant." In the words of D. W. Winnicott, psychoanalyst, pediatrician, and creativity expert, "It is creative apperception more than anything else that makes the individual feel that life is worth living." In your body, in your own two hands, and within your nuanced, complex, rich, and wonderful mind are many possibilities for joy and meaning. Really.

The more you reshape something outside yourself, the more you reshape your inside. But the converse is also true: transforming what is *inside*—instincts, conflicts, feelings, aesthetics, and knowledge—into something *outside* can heal the self. Psychoanalysts Janine Chassegeut-Smirgel and Jean Sanville, who have studied creativity, have cited the role of creative acts in self-repair. Tending, repairing, making, and reshaping help us express and work through inner conflicts, though we may not even recognize or verbalize what is occurring.

Further, accessing your creativity makes you more self-reliant, and self-reliance is linked to health and well-being, as philosopher Ralph Waldo Emerson knew. When you are a self-reliant person, the world is a less scary place; even when events throw you, you can remain intact. It is not that you will eschew all dependencies—some dependencies are essential for health—but when you can rescue yourself, you have a greater sense of control, and this leads to more elevated feelings.

Using your hands, which you will do as part of the Creativity Cure, facilitates self-reliance, psychological movement, creative activity, and happiness.

WHAT IS CREATIVITY?

At this point, you might be wondering:

- What is creativity, exactly?
- What does it mean to be creative?
- Does it mean something different from what I thought it did?
- What am I getting into?

Creativity means different things to different people. There are many definitions. Here are a few:

"Creativity is allowing yourself to make mistakes. Art is
knowing which ones to keep." (Scott Adams, cartoonist
and writer)
"Painting is just another way of keeping a diary."
(Pablo Picasso, artist)
"Creativity is the process of bringing something new
into being." (Rollo May, psychologist)
"Whatever creativity is, it is in part a solution to a problem."
(Brian Aldiss, writer)
"Creativity is the doing that rises out of being." (Attributed to
D. W. Winnicott, pediatrician and psychoanalyst)

Creativity starts with how you think and then becomes about
what you do. Creativity is a capacity of mind that can lead to original expressions. You do not have to produce something to be creative;
you can simply find a creative approach to, for example, an interpersonal matter or a professional program, but if you develop Creative
Capacity, you might just end up bringing concrete items into being.
Creative products can include anything from ideas to paintings to
home-cooked meals.

What might you create? Where do you get ideas? When you have
Creative Capacity, possibilities appear on your doorstep, and in the
words of choreographer Twyla Tharp, "Ideas are everywhere." When
you are creative you can think of alternatives, be comfortable with
more than one solution, and find value in what others might throw
away. Combining old things in new ways is a great way to be creative.

You can be creative in the domestic sphere, where creativity can
involve anything from tulip gardens to grilled tuna, refurbished lamps
to appliquéd shades, repaired computers to finished basements, home
design to personal style. Or you might prefer writing, music, performing arts, or visual arts. Whatever you choose, when you commit,
immerse, and improvise, your chances for joy increase.

The psychologists and creativity researchers Drs. Mark A. Runco
and Ruth Richards identified two types of creativity: eminent and
everyday. Eminent creativity is creative greatness, the profound out-

put of writers, artists, and scientists. Everyday creativity is "original-ity brought to the tasks of everyday life." Eminent creativity may be more intense than everyday creativity and therefore involve moments of angst as well as periods of ecstasy. Research by creativity and mood disorder experts and authors Nancy Andreason, MD, and Kay Red-field Jamison, PhD, suggests that some famous artists may have suf-fered from depressive disorders, but depression is not a requirement for creative output or experience. Creative engagement can provide peak experience or serve as an antidote to despair for both eminent and everyday creators.

HOW DOES THE CREATIVITY CURE WORK?

The Creativity Cure leads you through a therapeutic, creative process that moves from exploring your mind, to employing your body, to interacting with yourself and others in a positive way. The Creativity Cure is unique in that it is a twofold approach: simultaneously devel-oping understanding of the inner self and building a practice of cre-ative activity.

In Chapter 2, you will be introduced to your do-it-yourself prescrip-tion, the cornerstone of the Creativity Cure, and then you will begin the process of change. This prescription involves exercises for mind, body, and hands that are designed to hone your Creative Capacity.

In Chapters 3 and 4, we address the psychological factors that inter-fere with happiness and creativity and reasons why you might resist, fear, avoid, deny, feel guilty about, or snuff out the creative processes that lead to happiness—and all without even knowing you are doing so. We are going to address unconscious phenomena and the ways in which you might protect yourself from knowing and facing inner truths. Facing truths frees us and ultimately makes us more fulfilled.

In Chapters 5, 6, and 7, we will cover mental and physical activities that lead to creativity and happiness. For example, we will build healthy coping mechanisms such as resilience and sublimation (turning raw feelings into refined outcomes). In general, from a mental health per-spective, what you do with what happened is far more important than what actually happened. Then, after looking at how the mind can help or hinder you in your quest for happiness, we will turn our attention to our bodies and hands. As we will demonstrate, engaging your body will help you be happier and more creative.

In Chapters 8 and 9, we will explore positive ways of interacting with ourselves and others, as these internal and external connections are integral to creativity and well-being.

In Chapter 10, we will review what we have covered for solid implementation and future growth.

All of the exercises in the book are designed to help you develop Creative Capacity. Our responsibility is to give you tools and techniques. Your responsibility is to engage in life-enhancing activities.

THE RELATIONSHIP BETWEEN CREATIVITY AND MENTAL HEALTH

In the book *Eminent Creativity, Everyday Creativity and Health*, Dr. Arthur Cropley, former professor of psychology at the University of Hamburg, established the characteristics of a mentally healthy personality. What is remarkable is how these characteristics overlap with those of a creative personality, as defined by Dr. Cropley and other prominent researchers including Silvano Arieti, MD, author of *Creativity: The Magic Synthesis* and Mihaly Csikszentmihalyi, PhD, author of *Creativity: Flow and the Psychology of Discovery and Invention*. You may already have some of these characteristics, or you may not. Either way, working through the Creativity Cure and your do-it-yourself prescription will help you develop these characteristics for greater contentment.

Characteristics of Both Creative and Mentally Healthy Personalities

- Autonomy
- Openness
- Flexibility
- Humor

- Playfulness
- Willingness to try things
- Ability to elaborate ideas
- Realistic self-assessment
- Ability to express drives (inner passions) or feelings
  in a productive way
- Ability to cope with or adapt to change or catastrophe
- Freedom from dependence on outside circumstances
  for happiness
- Ability to acknowledge and use unconscious material
  (impulses and instincts)

One of the most creative and well-respected psychoanalytic thinkers, D. W. Winnicott, said, "It is only in being creative that the individual discovers the self." Winnicott, who practiced in the mid-twentieth century, wrote prodigiously about play and creativity. He was concerned with the concept of authenticity. He coined the terms "True Self" and "False Self" to describe children's responses to caregivers. An attuned and empathic caregiver who allows the child to express real feelings and impulses fosters the True Self. The True Self is healthy and has happy moments. The False Self arises when the child feels he or she must be overly compliant to extract love, thus suppressing spontaneous energies. The False Self suffers.

In this book, you are going to hear the terms "True Self" and "Creative Self" very often. You will hear "False Self" occasionally.

The True Self represents being, mind-set, or Who You Are, and the Creative Self represents doing, action, or What You Do with who you are. The True Self is authentic, and the Creative Self is effective. The Creative Self is the happiest, healthiest, and most productive form of the True Self. When you uncover your True Self, you are then able to realize your Creative Self. If you are not already fully living in your True Self, you might be in the grip of the False Self, and that is exactly what we are going to work on.

Creative Capacity, a mind-set, will lead you to your True Self while minimizing your False Self. You can develop Creative Capacity by following the steps in this book.

Remember the adages "To thine own self be true" and "The truth will set you free"? These adages do not tell you *how* to be true to yourself or how the truth will set you free. Creative Capacity leads to the True Self and then the Creative Self and contented experience, because Creative Capacity gives you access to your unconscious mind, wherein the truth and the road to freedom and happiness reside.

My client Karen was a successful stockbroker and had pushed to achieve professional excellence all her life. She succeeded but was not happy. When she developed Creative Capacity and uncovered her True Self, she realized that she needed more, that something was missing. At one time she had been quite proficient in music. She moved into a Creative Self by reincorporating music into her life. She said that listening to favorite pieces from the past exhilarated her and shifted her mind and mood. This had a positive impact on how she approached her business pursuits.

Characteristics of the True Self

- Authenticity
- Organicity
- Spontaneity
- Feeling

Characteristics of the Creative Self

- Effectiveness
- Productivity
- Resourcefulness
- Improvisation

Characteristics of Creative Capacity

- Receptivity
- Autonomy
- Fluid state of mind
- Access to the unconscious

When you take full advantage of your Creative Capacity, you allow your mind to go where it will and your True Self to feel what it feels, without judgment. When you identify and act on true inclinations, you feel relief. When you know who you are and use what you have, you are free. Self-knowledge leads to happiness because it cultivates an organic existence. Naturalness is lovely to live and to behold.

This is what it means to be your True Self, and why your mother, Shakespeare, and the Bible recommend that you simply be yourself. Do note that being your True Self does not mean you should act upon every instinct or do whatever you feel in the moment, for that could violate others. The key is to understand your feelings and to employ considered action. Self-knowledge also helps you distinguish between self-enhancing desires and self-destructive ones. You can teach yourself to recoil at impulses or behaviors that could hurt you as well as others.

To develop Creative Capacity, you will go where your mind goes even if it seems illogical. Developing your Creative Capacity will help you dig down to discover and inhabit your True Self. Chances are you will be happiest being your True Self, because when you live in accordance with your nature, you are more at ease. Even if you have avoided your True Self until now—you may have had some understandable reasons, but we will work through them—if you allow it to emerge and let yourself make the most of it, you will feel better. Knowing your deeper self can also clear up symptoms of anxiety, depression, dissatisfaction, and free-floating unhappiness. You can stop getting in your own way.

Though depression and anxiety can be biologically based, these ailments can also stem from unconscious conflict, the lingering effects of past experience or current difficulties. Freud did write about "ordinary unhappiness," but he also said that artistic, intellectual, and psychical work can heighten pleasure and create joy. By working creatively with your mind and body, you can burrow down to the source of conflicts and conundrums, uncover resilience and gifts, make better choices, and untangle yourself. You cannot remove all obstacles, but you can be better prepared and approach them with equanimity. You can be much happier.

WHY IS CREATIVITY MORE IMPORTANT NOW THAN EVER?

Technology has made many aspects of our lives easy, efficient, and fast. We are inundated with external forms of stimulation that require directed thinking, as opposed to undirected thinking. Directed thinking mandates deliberate focus, whereas undirected thinking involves letting the mind wander. We have far less time for a free-floating mind, yet undirected thinking is crucial for creativity, health, and satisfaction. With too little down time and so much stimulation from the world around us, we lose the connection with our deeper selves, our unconscious inclinations, and our daydreaming minds, which are great sources of pleasure.

Maybe you feel you do not have time for an active inner life or a dreamy mind. Maybe cultivating them feels impossible, backward, and even undesirable. You do not have time, and even if you did, you would be bored. Or so you fear. Do not fear a wandering mind. Boredom can be a path to creativity, happiness, and even cerebral prowess. It allows us time and space for mental puttering, just as sleep allows us time and space to dream.

With our senses stilled by flat screens, our bodies atrophied from sitting, and fingers tapping keys rather than making or doing, we lose our vitality. An absence of five-sense experience, full body movement, and active hands can cause malaise—a sense that something essential is missing. When your natural abilities and inclinations atrophy, all parts of you wither.

In spite of our technological overload—*because* of our technological overload—we must sometimes make the effort to pause, to take the long road, to make things ourselves, to do things slowly and imperfectly. In other words, we must make the effort to create. Creativity is more necessary for health and happiness now than it was in decades past because it puts us back into our bodies.

Though creative pursuits have always been linked with contentment, we never had to pay much attention to this truth because in one way or another our daily lives demanded creative engagement. Now they do not. We need creativity now more than ever to be well, happy, and natural.

Because it is so easy to purchase, hire, replace, and stay in place, we have stopped making things, repairing things, and using our hands. We are losing "process," but process is gratifying. Process, not product, is what we need to feel alive and well.

We are starving for it.

In the past, objects were created for livelihood and subsistence, whereas when we do make things now, we often make them for pleasure rather than necessity. So why does that matter? Is not the overall need being met? Only partially. Ironically, there is sometimes more pleasure in doing for necessity than in doing for pleasure, because the former involves stakes, commitment, effort, and thus exultation when a goal is achieved. When you overcome as well as produce, you get a double boost.

But who would choose the long road in this day and age? Now that we have become accustomed to immediate gratification and inured to constant stimulation, it is hard to imagine life without it. Who would choose hours of silence when we could be checking up, chatting, buying, viewing, posting, and comparing? Someone texting us or checking our status even as we sleep (if we sleep at all) suggests that we are central. We are wanted! In the thick of things! Important! Even if it is just spam, it keeps us occupied. It provides purpose, but in many cases, this is purpose without meaning.

Meaning is what we want and need. Meaning makes us happy.

CREATIVE CAPACITY AND HAPPINESS

You may have observed or experienced that people in deep states of concentration experience great pleasure. The psychologist Mihaly Csikszentmihalyi dubbed this state "flow," a state of joy born out of engagement in a task in which ability and required effort are well matched. Flow is bliss, and you can experience it by immersing yourself in a creative process. Csikszentmihalyi says that optimal experience is when we "make something happen."

My client Jim talks about being in the zone when he plays soccer. My friend Wendy, a singer, feels solace when she sings. Betsy, an anesthesiologist, feels most at peace when she gardens. Alton exults in washing the cars, but the world really falls away when he reconstructs a shattered hand. He often has his patients choose the music that plays during their surgery, which helps him connect to them and keeps him in the proper zone. When you develop Creative Capacity through engagement with do-it-yourself tasks, you are more likely to experience blissful flow.

> The first few songs are like running the first mile. You're breathing hard; you feel heavy. After that it's easy. You're carried along. It's the greatest feeling in the world.
>
> —BRUCE SPRINGSTEEN, musician

"I AM NOT THE CREATIVE TYPE."

But you may secretly worry whether you're the creative type:

"None of this applies to me. I am not creative."
"I haven't made anything since kindergarten."
"I'm obsessive. I make lists and check things off."
"I haven't a single creative bone in my entire body."
"I am a good accountant, mother, shopper, student, lawn
    mower, mathematician, or friend, but I am not creative. I
    don't have time."
"I make things—dinner, the bed, and Lincoln Log cabins with
    my kids—but I don't enjoy them. They're not especially
    creative and they're not fulfilling."
"I'm only good at coloring between the lines. I'm no creator."

Not true, not true!

If you were never artistic, that is fine. The Creativity Cure does not require that you be an artist; it requires only a willingness to explore your Creative Capacity and put it to use. Painting, singing, sewing, woodworking, or making pots is not the point. I once tried to make a pot, and there was more clay on me than on the pottery wheel.

We can learn from artists, and you might end up enjoying some artistic activities, but you do not have to be able to draw a straight line or fashion a clever trinket. The Creativity Cure will not ask you to make pottery, draw still-lifes, or compose songs. The cultivation of Creative Capacity does not mean you need to pick up a mound of clay and become the next Rodin. You might, but that is beside the point.

To be an artist, you must have Creative Capacity, but you can have Creative Capacity and not be an artist, at least not as that term is usually defined by the world. You can be a lawyer, data enterer, father, teacher, stylist, student, business owner, plumber, or executive assistant. When you have Creative Capacity you will be open to all parts of yourself—your inner logic, leanings, and longings. And you will find a way to harness and cultivate them so you can get more enjoyment out of your life—and have an impact.

Even if your Creative Capacity is currently in peak form and you are open with yourself, you still might resist using your Creative Capacity. Many people are afraid to step into action. Resisting completion or production is common.

You may have resisted because you do not want to have your work sent back to you in a self-addressed, stamped envelope. Or you may not want to open yourself up to criticism or ridicule or be the one who is torn apart by important others. (Important others are past or present figures that hover inside your mind: a reviewer, a boss, a teacher, a parent.) You might be afraid, unsure, insecure, doubtful, or pessimistic. You may be blocking all your true desires with your well-honed defenses.

Even though you are restless, ready for change, and imagining something different, you do not start, maintain, or complete the transition. Maybe you have excellent rationalizations such as:

"I don't have time."
"I'm not sure if I can."
"Why should I bother?"

"I feel guilty when I attend to my own needs when there are others who need my time."
"Why should I put in the effort?"
"Isn't it selfish?"
"Does it really matter?"

It matters.
Indeed, there are five reasons why creativity is essential.

FIVE REASONS CREATIVITY IS ESSENTIAL

Reason #1: Soul Satisfaction

Cultivating Creative Capacity fills you in a way that superficial activities and material things cannot. Journeys within the imaginative mind can be more gratifying than journeys outside. Being a spectator does not provide the same thrill as being your own choreographer. When you are energized, your loved ones benefit too.

Reason #2: Self-Possession

Things are given, things are taken away, and outcomes are often not within your control. You can fall from a social or professional pinnacle. You can make an unwise investment and see almost all of your savings disappear. You can receive a bad review or a bad grade, or lose a friend or a loved one. Fate is fickle, and the best defense against challenging times is self-possession—inner resources for solace. Self-possession is a form of psychological self-reliance. When you are less dependent on institutions or outside forces for your identity, self-esteem, and satisfaction—less *other*-directed and more *self*-directed—you are more empowered. Further, practicing what we know and do well—self-generated habits—keeps us stable in difficult circumstances.

My former professor Dr. Richard Druss once told me that people with severe illnesses get through the day by concentrating on habitual tasks.

Reason #3: Engagement and Peak Moments

When you are deeply engaged in a project that interests you, you feel satisfied. The process often provides more gratification than the product. You do not have to divorce yourself from the desire to succeed, to finish, or to achieve, but if flow and peak moments arise via the ongoing engagement, it is worth it, whatever the outcome.

Creative Capacity and the habits that cultivate and maintain it deliver value because the ongoing engagement can often provide more than result.

> It's like discovering that while you thought you needed the tea ceremony for the caffeine, what you really needed was the tea ceremony.
>
> —ANNE LAMOTT, writer

Reason #4: Professional Prowess

Creativity, according to some, is the future. Innovation will trump applied knowledge and test-taking ability. In *A Whole New Mind: Why Right-Brainers Will Rule the Future*, Daniel Pink, author, speaker, and business analyst, says, "The right-brain qualities of inventiveness, empathy, joyfulness, and meaning increasingly will determine who flourishes and who flounders. For individuals, families, and organizations, professional success and personal fulfillment now require a whole new mind." We need to be more right-brained, with time devoted to undirected thinking. In doing so, we will develop the twenty-first-century skills that can help us contribute to our economy and community, and help us succeed professionally. In their recent book *That Used to Be Us*, columnist Thomas L. Friedman and Johns Hopkins professor Michael Mandelbaum concur that creativity is essential for our economic health and future success. There is more than one upside to Creative Capacity.

Reason #5: Improved Personal and Community Relations

So often in my practice and other places I hear people bemoan the state of their bodies. While Alton and I are great believers in fitness, it is really the inside—the loving, receptive, energized inside—that engages another person and makes him or her want to be around you.

With Creative Capacity, productivity and generosity come naturally. Actions range from a favor for a friend to a community contribution to having a larger impact on society as a whole. It is easier to give when you feel nurtured, whole, and free.

PEOPLE LIKE YOU

In *The Creativity Cure*, you will meet people who moved out of dissatisfied or troubled selves and into authentic, creative, effective ones. You will see that in some cases their lives changed in dramatic ways, such as a change in career, while others experienced a slight but critical shift. Either way, creativity and concrete steps helped them and will help you.

- Kevin was riddled with anxiety until he was able to let go of the family expectation of becoming a doctor or a lawyer. His Creative Capacity set him free. He maintained his day job as a lab technician, yet made time for cooking, friends, running, and drawing at night.

- Erica's feelings of inferiority and defeat were apparent the first time I heard her voice. She left a message on my voice mail that said, "I was hoping you would take me as a patient," in a tone that suggested she expected otherwise. "I'm creative, but I can't create," she said the first day she came in. Erica eventually transformed what she described as the "green blob" of malaise into a high-paying job as a designer. She overcame her unhappiness and uncertainty and found her Creative Self.

- Walter was so frazzled when I first met him that he did not finish his sentences. Raised in the South by a hardworking single mother, he sometimes went without dinner so as not to disturb his mom's sleep when she collapsed on the couch. When he began to move his body and calm his mind, his unique sensitivity led him to write nuanced screen plays. He could focus rather than being pulled in all directions. His True Self kept him grounded.

Creativity may once have been the province of a select few artists, writers, performers, or inventors who, driven by passionate interest, simply could do nothing else. Now, however, creativity is necessary for all.

If you can "jump over the chasm," in the words of choreographer Merce Cunningham, and into the unknown, you start to get some beautiful dancing—and some real happiness.

GETTING READY FOR TRUE CHANGE

Okay, so how do you put the Creativity Cure into practice? What are you going to do? You are going to turn to Chapter 2!

> Whatever you can do, or dream you can do, begin it.
> Boldness has genius, power, and magic to it.
> Begin it now.
>
> —GOETHE, poet

2

How Can I Cultivate a Creative Self?
The Five-Part Prescription (5PP)

Find a happy person and you will find a project.

—SONJA LYUBOMIRSKY, psychologist and writer

MATTERS AT HAND

In this chapter you will be introduced to the Five-Part Prescription (5PP), a do-it-yourself treatment for mind, body, and hands based on self-awareness and physical engagement and designed to help you feel happier, healthier, and more creative. At the end of each chapter, you will receive a 5PP with five actions you will take: Insight, Movement, Mind Rest, Your Own Two Hands, and Mind Shift.

Insight = self-knowledge
Movement = physicality and exercise
Mind Rest = relaxation
Your Own Two Hands = using your hands in a purposeful way
Mind Shift = positive thoughts

In this chapter we will go over each part of the 5PP in detail so that you know what these terms mean, the different ways of practicing them, and why following this prescription will help you reach creativity and contentment. The components of this prescription are based on scientific research.

What Are You Going to Do?

You will be given your 5PP in Chapters 3–9. You will probably discover that you are already doing some of it, and the rest you will easily learn. Because the 5PP is a custom-made program, it is designed to fit naturally into your life and to suit your personal makeup. By deepening self-knowledge and increasing physicality, guided by the 5PP, you can alter your inner being, habits, body, and actions. You will train yourself to link thought to action, dreaming to doing, and mind to body.

The 5PP will help you develop Creative Capacity.

Discomfort for the Sake of Comfort

There is effort involved in the 5PP, but the process is stimulating, fulfilling, and often fun. Measured effort and engaging tasks, even if they include a bit of discomfort, are excellent paths to health, creativity, and happiness. Remember, the goal is to build habits and Creative Capacity for a greater number of happy moments. It will take some effort to begin, but then the habits will become second nature.

Engaging in an absorbing effort can make people ecstatically happy, even if they retain the notion that nirvana involves endless days of idleness. A modicum of leisure, vacation, rest, boredom, nothingness, and play is also important for a relaxed mind. Such unbound mind time can lead to intriguing thoughts and ultimately a passionate engagement.

How Much Time Will It Take?

To start your 5PP, you need to commit about an hour a day for the prescription.

- 10 minutes for Insight
- 15 minutes for Movement
- 5 minutes for Mind Rest
- 20 minutes for Your Own Two Hands
- 10 Minutes for Mind Shift

Over the next seven weeks, you will gradually increase the time to two hours. You can double the time for each part or maintain ten minutes for Insight and Mind Rest while increasing Movement and Your Own Two Hands to forty-five minutes. Learn what makes you feel most alive—contemplation or physical action. After a forty-nine-day (seven days for seven weeks) deep immersion, you will have developed some great new habits.

It is important to remember that all five components of the 5PP are crucial—the curative agent is in the chemistry. So making time for every step is important. Ideally, you will follow the order of actions laid out above, because each step prepares you for the next. After Insight you will practice Movement, Mind Rest, and Your Own Two Hands. These prepare you for the psychological change involved in Mind Shift. You can do the 5PP all in one hour, or you can break it up and fit the steps into your day as needed.

However, in the interest of Creative Capacity—that is, fluid thinking, receptivity, and autonomy—you can mix up the order and switch steps around to fit into the corners of a packed day. You can be open-minded and do it your way, which is the overall point of the Creativity Cure: to access your original spontaneous, vibrant self. You can also combine the steps.

You can combine:

- Movement and Mind Rest
- Your Own Two Hands and Movement
- Your Own Two Hands and Mind Rest

Combine if it feels right to you. You can decide if you need or want to do more with any one part. If you have to squeeze parts into patches of time and do less, that's fine. Being benevolent and flexible with yourself is essential, as is being truthful. But even if you combine or switch some steps, we recommend that you always conclude with Mind Shift.

You might consider closing your day with Mind Shift to remind you of positives before you go to sleep. It packages up the day and allows you to descend to the depths of slumber on a pleasant note.

How and Why Does the 5PP Work?

The 5PP involves immersing yourself in the Creativity Cure for seven weeks, and then integrating the 5PP into your everyday life forever. Immersion is the best way to initiate change. A large initial dose of a new mode of action or treatment gives you a solid start and makes it easier to continue. Think of language immersion programs in which one studies a language intensively for a period of time. Immersion makes the behavior part of you. Seven weeks, one hour per day minimum, is your initial immersion.

When you practice the 5PP—Insight, Movement, Mind Rest, Your Own Two Hands, and Mind Shift—long enough, it becomes part of your life, part of you, and not just a temporary treatment. In *The Creativity Cure,* we are after true change, which means unconscious shifts and altered habits.

You have to be willing to stay the course and do some things poorly or with discomfort. Ineptitude is good because it means that you are letting yourself learn and experience the process. Process is more important for happiness than product.

An Out

Action is critical, but if you want to read *The Creativity Cure* now and follow the 5PP at a later time, that is okay. You may be the kind of person who needs a gentle introduction, to hang back and scope it out for a while. Sometimes letting ideas wash over you and filter in by osmosis is a great way to initiate change. Just don't let yourself put it off forever.

Working Through: A Process of Healing and Change

The 5PP involves a process of "working through" (a term coined by Freud), which is a creative process (the application of Creative Capacity or unconscious material) and a therapeutic process (psychological development) combined. Both lead to greater happiness.

Working through means that by repeated handling of your inner life—memories, feelings, issues, concerns—you wring out toxicities and craft a more hopeful and truthful narrative for yourself. By building upon what was good in your past and breaking down and relinquishing what was not, you reconstruct a more empowered self. Working through allows you to manage and draw energy from forces that once undermined you.

You reconcile the past so that you can have a better future. The 5PP uses the process of working through to turn inner conflicts into usable energies.

Dark feelings are inevitable, but you can learn to use them instead of running from them. Inner tumults can be sublimated—turned into refined prose, actions, projects, or better outcomes in your personal and professional life—by working through. Learning these strategies will give you the skills to live a happier life, as they promote the development of the True Self and the Creative Self.

With the process of working through, you will discover that you do not have to be afraid, that you can enjoy your life, that you can handle what comes your way, and that even if you are hurt, you are not going to be destroyed.

Results

So, what is the 5PP going to give you?

- Self-knowledge
- Physicality
- A calmer mind
- Renewed and meaningful hand use
- Increased ability to quell negative thoughts
- Kindness to self and thus to others
- Decreased avoidance and inhibition
- Decreased mind clutter
- Increased resilience
- Authentic connections with self and others
- Self-mastery and refinement
- Happiness
- A psychological and physical makeover

THE FIVE-PART PRESCRIPTION

Insight

If we are to achieve the upper reaches of creativity, our talent must be animated by energy from deep within . . . the broader unconscious encompasses problem-solving and creativity.

—ETHEL PERSON, psychoanalyst

REQUIRED ACTION

Insight frees. What exactly is insight? Insight is truth about your inner life, about your unconscious, about you. So we will ask you to keep a journal. At the end of each chapter you will find prompts—suggestions for what to write about—to deepen your understanding of yourself, even the side you keep hidden from yourself or others. If you can learn to dialogue with yourself effectively and use your insights well, you can achieve greater satisfaction because your choices about what to do and with whom you should do it will be better informed. As you move through the book, you will become more introspective and get to know yourself better. Such exposure, even to yourself, can feel uncomfortable, but it will be worth it.

Insight is important because when we understand our own truth, the deeper self—who we are and why we do what we do—it is easier to change and to make the right choices for ourselves, our loved ones, and even our not-so-loved ones. Insight helps us clarify and even validate our intuitions.

You will develop insight by beginning a process of self-analysis with your Insight writings. You can buy a journal and write by hand, or you can set one up on your computer. Research has linked penmanship to increased cerebral capacity and shown that cerebral capacity is enhanced by five-sense experience, so a journal that you can hold, smell, and write in has some advantages. But your brain may be freer if you are used to typing as a way to express yourself. It is up to you.

Whether you type or write by hand, use the proper ergonomics so that you do not have to visit Alton or another orthopedic surgeon for treatment of a repetitive stress injury. (If you're writing by hand, use a gel, rollerball, or fountain pen. If you're using a keyboard, keep your wrists in a neutral position, neither extended nor flexed, as you type.)

For 5PP Insight writings you will be given specific prompts and you will write whatever occurs to you in response. Writing whatever comes to mind in whatever order, even if it is illogical, grammatically incorrect, repetitive, or full of disturbing complaint is okay; you are freeing your mind, and that is our goal. If you can make writing a habit, your deeper desires, conflicts, fears, and fantasies will emerge on the page. We do not want it in polished form. Loose ends, rough edges, errors, and embarrassments can lead you to the truth, which will emerge one way or another. Your true, idiosyncratic, unique, and interesting self will have a chance to come out.

Do not edit. If you feel oppressed by your inner grammar teacher, tell her you will get back to punctuation later. You can write in the context of the past, the present, or both. Detouring and deviating may lead to spontaneous bursts of inspiration or insight, so do not try to be linear or sensible.

You might want to avoid painful feelings, but know that if you work through them, they become weaker and hold less power over you. Allow those feelings to find expression on the page.

To reiterate:

Do Not

- Polish
- Edit
- Punctuate
- Correct
- Judge
- Be dismayed by flaws and ramblings (they are inevitable)

Do

- Embrace loose ends
- Tolerate rough edges
- Be curious about errors
- Weather embarrassments
- Be interested in your own mind
- Live with some pain

> I have forced myself to begin writing when I've been utterly exhausted, when I've felt my soul as thin as a playing card; when nothing has seemed worth enduring for another five minutes . . . and somehow the activity of writing changes everything.
>
> —JOYCE CAROL OATES, writer

A recent *Harvard Mental Health Letter* outlined the therapeutic benefits of writing. Writing helps you understand and manage what feels irrational, troubling, or even terrible. It helps you heal. According to research by psychologist James Pennebaker, author of *Opening Up: The Healing Power of Expressing Emotions,* and recent advances in the field of narrative medicine, pioneered by Dr. Rita Charon, the physical act of writing is important for healing. Charon says, "Without narrative acts of some kind—talking, writing, or enacting—the patient cannot convey to anyone else what he or she is going through. More radically and perhaps equally true, without narrative acts, the patient cannot himself or herself grasp what the events of the illness mean."

Writing helps you know what is going on inside you. When you write, you catch delicate, fleeting thoughts that you might otherwise dismiss. All of it is important for your development, even what appears random, silly, or superfluous. Nothing is random. Everything is linked to something deeper and more telling.

You chose this detail instead of that one, this memory instead of that one, for a reason. Recognizing these choices is how you get to know your unconscious. The unconscious has its own strange logic, order, and authority, and when you decide to listen to it, you can learn much.

When you are done with your Insight writings, put them aside. Save the prose on your laptop, or write on yellow legal pads, tear out the pages, and store them in a secret place. For now, it is only about the process.

Writing every day may seem burdensome or even tedious, but remember that it is only ten minutes and that when you commit to making it a habit—when you commit to happiness practices—it will become less so. Besides, the exploration of your inner workings (in moderation) is overall an uplifting endeavor because it frees you. So much of the burden and stress we experience is because of psychological tangles lodged in our unconscious. Insight writings expose them. If you are in psychotherapy, this process can be integrated into your treatment.

Insight is healing because it can relieve suppressed conflict that drains you. "I got a hit!" my client Kelly used to say when we came upon important revelations. He would clap his hands or throw a punch in the air. When your unconscious becomes conscious, things inside loosen up and start flowing. The burden lifts. You feel better.

Ideally, insight enables a patient to reconsider life patterns that once
seemed inevitable or uncontrollable, and leads to the identification
of new choices and options.

—HARVARD MENTAL HEALTH LETTER, September 2010

INSIGHT SUGGESTIONS

We will give you plenty of prompts to stimulate your Insight writings
in Chapters 3–9, but remember, don't edit, don't judge, and don't aim
for eloquence or excellence. Let your mind go where it wants to go and
do what it wants to do. Honor imperfections. If you try to correct too
soon, you might miss something interesting and useful.

Movement

Only when I'm given an actual physical burden and my muscles start to
groan (and sometimes scream) does my comprehension meter shoot
upward and I'm finally able to grasp something.

—HARUKI MURAKAMI, writer

REQUIRED ACTION

Choose a form of Movement. We will provide many suggestions. We
offer a walking plan throughout the book as a sample, and you may
choose that. If you are used to more, do more.

How is Movement important for Creative Capacity, the True Self,
and the Creative Self? When you were a toddler and first discovering
the joy of moving independently, you were fearless, free, and impassioned. Your love affair with the world began. Recapturing this feeling
is the physical basis of Creative Capacity. If you can do it with your
body, you are more likely to be able to do it with your mind. If you can
do it with both your mind and your body, you have a greater chance
of happiness.

Attunement to the physical self fosters creativity. If you want to
develop Creative Capacity, you have to involve your body. So much
of creativity and happiness is based on physicality: writing is about

sound, singing is about breath, minds become free in running, sculpting is about shape, swimming is about immersion.

Furthermore, exercise is a scientifically proven form of treatment for both anxiety and depression. Studies show that exercise, either combined with cognitive-behavioral therapy or alone, provides the same benefits as antidepressant medication for mild to moderate depression. John Ratey, MD, a psychiatrist at Harvard Medical School, says, "Working up a sweat could very well be one of the most potent, underused prescriptions we have today." There is solid evidence that exercise elevates mood, and we will cover this in detail in Chapter 7.

In brief:

- Movement boosts serotonin, dopamine, and norepinephrine, neurotransmitters that are also the chemical basis of many antidepressants.
- Movement releases endocannabinoids and endorphins, which can stimulate euphoria.
- Movement makes you smarter because it increases a hormone that boosts brain function.

Very likely you already know the benefits of exercise, but you may struggle with starting or maintaining it. We can tell you to run a lap, swim a length, bike a mile, or walk to the river, and to do this at least three days per week, but you may no more listen to us than you have to others or to yourself. You know you should exercise, but it is tough to start it, maintain it, and make it feel organic to you. We are going to combat that.

Alton points out, "The truth about motivation is that if you can teach yourself to love what you do, you can keep doing it. If you can keep at it long enough, you will engender a physiologic need, a healthy little addiction for the exertion."

Sometimes you cannot maintain commitment or achieve mastery because you are pursuing the wrong form of movement. You want to find a "goodness of fit" with exercise as much as with other people and environments. You need to find the right exercise, one that you can maintain, one that does not bore, and one that works with your anatomy. There are many great options.

The goal is to make movement part of who you are. You are going to start slow, take small steps, and be positive about the fact that you are showing up for something you have been resisting. In medical school, the professor on our general surgery rotation asked my psychiatry colleague Bella what her strength was. She replied, "My strength is that I show up." Let this be your strength too.

It is better to exercise for five minutes every day than to wait six weeks, then go on an exercise binge and risk injury and burnout. You are trying to develop an identity as someone who is physical for yourself, not to outdo your peers or show someone from the past how great you look. This initial movement is not about fitness; that comes later. For now, you are forming a habit, making movement part of your everyday life and part of you.

MOVEMENT SUGGESTIONS

All of these movements can enhance our posture, our breathing, and our awareness of our bodies.

- Walking
- Running
- Swimming
- Lifting weights
- Biking
- Skating
- Rowing
- Dancing
- Yoga
- Spinning
- Mowing the grass
- Building a fence
- Raking leaves
- Shoveling snow

(The last four options overlap with the activities we'll discuss in connection with Your Own Two Hands.)

VARIETY

You may not be able to play football anymore, if you ever could, but you might be able to lift some weights or do some sit-ups and pushups while you watch football. Do floor exercises or stretches during your favorite movie. Research indicates that flexibility and variety can help with sustained interest.

MUSIC

Music that you like has been shown to increase the speed and distance of your effort.

Mind Rest

Sometimes too much focus can backfire. . . . [R]esearchers have found a surprising link between daydreaming and creativity—people who daydream more are also better at generating new ideas.

—JONAH LEHRER, writer

REQUIRED ACTION

Choose a form of Mind Rest. We will offer suggestions. You can switch as you wish; increasing your self-knowledge may alter your tastes, needs, and relaxation requirements.

Mind Rest is a time for you to relax your brain. It is a chance to ponder, putter, and be still. Mind Rest rejuvenates you. Your ordinary life keeps you busy, constantly on, and you need time to disengage and refresh. Mind Rest is about letting, not doing. Like meditation, it is undirected rather than directed mind time.

Your mind needs rest periods in order to flourish. Mind Rest makes you smarter. According to Sonja Lyubomirsky, psychology researcher and author of *The How of Happiness,* "A number of intriguing studies have even revealed benefits of meditation for . . . intelligence, creativity, and cognitive flexibility."

As much as our technologically oriented culture and Ivy League–obsessed parents promote it, round-the-clock achieving, striving, and accomplishing backfires at any age. Ideas have to simmer, and information needs to be digested in order for it to be truly integrated or to lead to creative applications. Brain studies have shown that rest periods are key for the brain to synthesize and connect pieces of information. Daydreams and reveries are fruitful, grounding, and pleasurable for many people.

Stuffing your mind can snuff out your mind. Letting it float is good for your physiology and your mental health as well as your cognitive prowess.

Herbert Benson, Harvard cardiologist and author of *The Relaxation Response,* discovered that a meditation technique could provide the same benefits as medication. A quiet place, a relaxed position, a repeated phrase, and a passive inner stance led to:

- Lowered blood pressure
- Decreased nervousness
- Decreased anxiety
- Decreased depression
- Decreased pain
- Increased inner harmony
- Increased quiet mind and happiness

Even though it might feel almost impossible to stop, slow down, sit still, or even to sit at all, that is the very reason that you need to do it. The best time is when you have no time.

Why is that? If you have no time, you are probably running hither and thither at the behest of your external commitments. These obligations may once have represented power and choice, but they no longer create a feeling of inner freedom. If you take five minutes for Mind

Rest, you are allowing yourself to say no to the idea that others are in control and yes to the idea that you are in control. Five minutes is a tiny step toward your identity as a person who has taken charge of your mind and ultimately your life.

MIND REST SUGGESTIONS

What was the most peaceful time for you as a child? Try to reproduce some special quietude from years ago.

- Do nothing
- Lie on your bed
- Putter around
- Sit in a chair
- Sit on a stump, boulder, or dune
- Lie in soft grass
- Meditate
- Say a mantra (a repeated phrase, borrowed or invented)
- Sing a song you already know
- Sing "Ah" if you do not know the words

You may be surprised to hear this, but singing is all about controlled, conscious breathing, so it provides some of the same Mind Rest benefits as meditation, as long as you breathe properly and do not care about the sound. Actually, you don't even need to make much of a sound. You can take a really deep breath and hum a song low on the subway. This facilitates rhythmic, controlled breathing. Or you can hum underwater while you're swimming.

Your Own Two Hands

When I saw and realized that all this was a creation of my own hands, my whole nature began to change.

—BOOKER T. WASHINGTON, *educator and reformer*

REQUIRED ACTION

Choose a meaningful activity. Engaging your hands will help you with the process of working through. We will give you several suggestions. Picking one project and exploring it completely and deeply over a period of time is best for producing happy moments.

What do your hands mean to you? Have you ever thought about it? Alton's patients frequently comment that they did not realize how much they needed their hands until they were injured. But hands are about more than manual capacity. As we will cover in Chapter 6, research indicates that hand use enhances cerebral capacity, elevates mood, and elicits creative thought.

Your hands are excellent tools for Creative Capacity and for freeing your mind as well as making things. For the duration of the Creativity Cure, you will engage in a creative process with a concrete outcome. If you commit to meaningful hand use in a creative endeavor, it will enhance your health and happiness.

Each week Alton sees dozens of people whose hands are their lives, livelihoods, and means of self-expression: musicians, conductors, carpenters, painters, stagehands, sculptors. For them, their hands are everything.

Many of my clients are surprised when they note that using their hands in *meaningful* ways, from crafting to carpentry to cleaning, relieves anxiety. What do we mean by meaningful hand use? That the activity is both something you enjoy and something that is purposeful or linked to someone you care about. Whether it is mundane or routine, whether it involves concentration and construction or rote movement and free thought, hand use has meaning if it nurtures your family or others, improves the aesthetics of your surroundings, awakens your inner life or makes you feel calm because it creates order.

Once I asked Gary Schneider, an artist and professor at Mason Gross School of the Arts at Rutgers University, if art had to be beautiful. He said, "It is not about beauty; it is about order and disorder."

When she studied the effects of hand use on the psyche, Dr. Kelly

Lambert, chair of the Psychology Department at Randolph-Macon College in Virginia, discovered many benefits of hand use, including:

- Decreased depression
- Decreased anxiety
- Decreased stress
- Increased positive emotions
- Enhanced cognition
- Decreased loneliness by increasing human touch and social contacts
- Increased concentration
- Increased self-esteem

Remember when you said as a child, "I made it with my own two hands"? As you work your way through the Creativity Cure you will rediscover that feeling of fulfillment.

The Creativity Cure will help you take your imaginings outside the mind, through the body, and into the world. When we turn abstract thought into concrete action we feel joy. You may start with domestic activities and move on to craft or artistic creation. You might be surprised at what interests you uncover or what you can do.

No artistic talent or previous experience is required. Remember, this is about process, not proficiency. From the very start you will train yourself to keep your hands moving, to keep engaging, no matter how insignificant your creations may seem. Embarrassment? Shame? Frustration? You may experience them. We will help you move through them as you progress through the Creativity Cure. Live with those feelings for now and congratulate yourself on using Your Own Two Hands.

When you make things, even small gains are good. The small physical step can be a large mental step. It takes psychological strength to tolerate one's smallness in the present. Learning can feel humiliating. But do it anyway. Humans possess a biological urge toward growth, so you are bound to improve if you persist.

If you learn new activities in small steps, you will find them much less overwhelming. A large leap may feel powerful in the moment, but without technique, skill, and preparation, you may do a belly flop instead of a knife-sharp dive. Try not to discharge your energies all at once. The small step is the start of a long, slow, invigorating life. Remember how you were told to dip just one toe first in the water to start swimming? You can do it.

Some meaningful hand use suggestions:

Art
- Write by hand
- Paint
- Draw
- Cut out and paste
- Photograph
- Design
- Play an instrument

Craft
- Sew
- Knit
- Sculpt
- Weld
- Whittle
- Disassemble and rebuild
- Decoupage

Domestic
- Repair
- Prune
- Mend
- Wash and hang
- Fold
- Sweep
- Cook
- Set the table
- Weed or till the garden

Other

• Sign up for a class you always wanted to take

If you do not have a good spot in your home to work with Your Own Two Hands, then find a space somewhere else, perhaps a community center.

Mind Shift

People who learn to control their inner experience will be able to determine the quality of their lives.

—MIHALY CSIKSZENTMIHALYI, psychologist and writer

REQUIRED ACTION

Set up a journal for Mind Shift. If you are writing in a notebook for your Insight writings, you can use the same journal if you want. Or you can open a new document on your computer.

Mind Shift is a shift in your state of mind from a negative, hopeless, injured stance to a positive, hopeful, able stance. Mind Shift is a dynamic process, a purposeful technique that moves you out of a pit and into possibilities. We all have a tendency to slip, but when you practice Mind Shift enough, you can integrate optimal thoughts into your core thinking and recover faster from missteps and assaults.

When you are approaching the concept of Mind Shift, first respect the idea that a positive outlook is useful and can be deeply felt, not just pasted on. What is positive? Positive means able, open, rationally optimistic, and at peace with your limitations as you come to know them through this process. Positive means recognizing and developing your strengths, your good traits.

How do you stay positive in a deeply authentic way as opposed to wearing an "I'm Content" T-shirt? How do you create true, real, and lasting psychological change? If you know and accept the fact that you cannot completely erase pain, you can develop a way to channel it and make it work for you.

In Insight, you will write about painful experiences. In Mind Shift, you will write again, this time with a different perspective that allows you to feel less victimized, more empowered, and grateful. The field of positive psychology has established a substantial amount of research showing that a grateful person is a happy person. When you can focus on what you gained instead of what you lost, what you have instead of what you lack, and how your lot is not so bad in comparison to that of many others, you feel better. The purpose of Mind Shift is to teach you not to wallow but rather to look for a crack of light and turn toward it. Research in the field of cognitive-behavioral therapy shows that you can shift your mood by shifting the perspective.

It is true that tragic, wrenching, terrible events occur that might change you or your life forever. And it can be hard to overcome, let go, or stop wishing that they had never happened. It can be hard to not feel resentful, bitter, angry, and unforgiving, to cease the "Why me?" thoughts and the hand-wringing. The point of Mind Shift is to let you know that in spite of what happened, you are not excluded from elevated moments and satisfying interactions. They are still possible. Benson has shown that by managing our thoughts in a masterful way, we can combat physical and psychological pain to a great extent. In the words of philosopher and psychologist William James, "The greatest weapon against stress is the ability to choose one thought over another."

For Insight, you will write about challenging times or painful states. For Mind Shift, you will consider what you wrote in Insight and alter your perspective on those experiences by writing about them from a different angle. The goal is to shift from the first state of mind to the second: from lonely to connected, injured to resilient, and so on.

Experts in positive psychology and cognitive-behavioral therapy have found that when you train your mind to think differently, to approach difficult or troubling experiences with an assured, positive mental framework, you can:

- Decrease depression
- Decrease anxiety
- Decrease rumination
- Increase pleasure
- Increase peace

In the 5PP, we employ Mind Shift to train ourselves to move to a mental position that is adaptive, useful, and positive. Mind Shift is a version of cognitive-behavioral therapy, which has been shown to be equal to medication in its effectiveness for certain kinds of depression or anxiety. Cognitive-behavioral therapy holds that by changing the thoughts, we change the feeling. It is a psychological treatment that trains you to think differently about yourself and your circumstances, so that you feel more resilient and less pessimistic. It seems simple, but we have to remind ourselves to do it, that it works, and that it's okay to stop ruminating. Instead, we can distract ourselves, substitute different thoughts, fashion new patterns of response, and move on.

The intention of Mind Shift is not to help you become a more virtuous person, although that might happen. Rather, Mind Shift helps you become a freer person. Sometimes we need a forceful inner voice that will not let us wallow, that makes us get up and go.

You do not need to wipe out negative, hurtful thoughts completely. That would be impossible and unnatural. But you do not want to overemphasize the negatives, either, since they can lead to rumination, which feels like psychological action but is actually a form of paralysis. You want to be positive yet also truthful and realistic.

The point of Mind Shift is to force yourself to honor the good things about yourself, others, your life, your past, and your circumstances, in spite of any negatives that may have happened. You do not have to pretend that things are better than they are, but you can still identify the good in your present circumstances or future prospects. In psychiatry, we use the phrase "the good enough mother" (coined by D. W. Winnicott) to refer to parenting that is acceptable and growth-producing. When you can appreciate and respect that you and your life are good enough, you open yourself up to contentment and change.

Sometimes positive perspectives can seem light or superficial, while negative perspectives seem more truthful and substantive—more "realistic." In fact, our negative perspectives are often irrational or misguided and sometimes just plain wrong. The positive way of perceiving a situation or yourself may be more accurate. Some people overinflate their positive qualities, but many underestimate them. The key is to find what you can truly value in yourself, your real strengths, and develop them further. Then the positive mind-set will be genuine and easier to maintain.

As William James said, "Man can alter his life by altering his thinking."

MIND SHIFT SUGGESTIONS

Mind Shift prompts will be provided in Chapters 3–9. Remember, write freely, but keep in mind that you are allowed to let go of the injury, the complaint, the powerful perpetrator, and your identity as a victim. Let your mind go as you write, but permit yourself to inhabit a part of your mind that is interested, able, excited, and alive.

Key Concepts

- You now know the steps of the Five-Part Prescription: Insight, Movement, Mind Rest, Your Own Two Hands, and Mind Shift. You are going to devote at least one hour per day, for seven weeks, to the 5PP: ten minutes for Insight, fifteen minutes for Movement, five minutes for Mind Rest, twenty minutes for Your Own Two Hands, and ten minutes for Mind Shift.

- You will keep a journal of Insight writings. You will be given prompts. You will write what you want to write and let your mind go where it will.

- You will begin to think of yourself as a Movement person. You will do what you can to make physicality part of your everyday life. Habit is power and small steps are everything. You do not have to do it with prowess; you just have to show up for your physical self. Therein is a form of psychological prowess.

- Mind Rest will renew, refresh, and calm you. Even if you think you cannot afford the time to do nothing, you probably can for five minutes.

- You may combine parts of the Five-Part Prescription, such as Movement and Mind Rest. Some people find it hard to sit still, so repeat a mantra while you walk.

- Your Own Two Hands are a resource for your happiness. You will tend, construct, or repair in the 5PP. Using your hands is therapeutic. Let what you do or create be imperfect or mundane, but *use* your hands.

- Mind Shift involves opening your mind. Making a conscious effort to shift the mind from negative to positive, from anguished to able, helps you feel better. We will give you prompts so you can start to train yourself to alter your thoughts.

> True happiness is a verb.
>
> —Attributed to EPICTETUS, philosopher

Throughout the chapters of *The Creativity Cure* you will repeat the steps of the Five-Part Prescription until they become second nature. Repetition of action is not boring if the thoughts, feelings, associations, and ideas in your mind change each time. Because you are about to delve deeper into your dynamic, exciting, fluctuating inner life, the process will be compelling.

The 5PP—Insight, Movement, Mind Rest, Your Own Two Hands, and Mind Shift—will help you uncover your True Self, bolster your Creative Capacity, develop your Creative Self, and increase contentment. But be patient. It takes time to develop new habits and to reconstruct the self.

Remember, if you make what you feel is a mistake, just reinvent from it. In this process there are no errors, no regrets. Everything is useful.

3

Creativity and Inhibition

MATTERS AT HAND

To change your core, your being, you must dig deep into your mind (psyche) and uncover fears or feelings that might be inhibiting your True Self. Inhibition is a form of defense, a behavioral style. Where there is fear, there is protection, or at least an attempt at it. If you can develop insight into what you might be afraid of, if you face those underlying feelings, you will find that your inhibitions fall away. You will realize you can handle fear or discomfort, live with it, even use it. Many a wonderful outcome has resulted from channeled fear. Sometimes you fear yourself, your dark feelings.

One of my clients said to me in our first session, "I don't love my father." Her father had abused the family, forced them to flee for protection, and created a lifetime of grief. When I heard her story, her declaration made sense to me, and I was impressed that she was not afraid to say it. It came from a strong True Self that acknowledged her feelings. Feelings are feelings, and the more truthful the better. Feelings cannot be wrong, only uncomfortable or comfortable. Sometimes we sequester primal, bitter feelings in the deeper mind, where they continue to exert power over us, but it is best to examine them and own up to them, so that they have less power.

If you try to change without understanding the forces that hold you back, you have a good chance of going nowhere. Trying to change behaviors without first altering the inner life is often futile because hidden unconscious conflict has great power to inhibit. When you recognize your demon fears, it will be easier to change. Change requires less effort when you have insight because you are not fighting against unknown forces. The moment you realize that you can spend more energy on living and less on defensive self-protection is a happy one. When you quell your conflicts, creative drives emerge and your energies move toward life-enhancing behaviors. Your inner resources no longer need to be wasted on misguided or obsolete forms of self-protection. Your intrinsic urge toward health carries you.

A child psychiatrist once told me that most therapy with children under the age of six involves naming. When you identify (name) your fears, feelings, inner bullies, and exhausting conflicts, solutions emerge.

Before we confront fears and begin our therapeutic process, let us review the concepts of True Self, False Self, Creative Self, and Creative Capacity.

TERMS TO GRASP

Creative Capacity

Creative Capacity is receptivity, autonomy, and fluid thinking fed by the unconscious. It means letting unconscious thoughts float into your mind without judging them. It means being open to your inner world.

True Self

Your True Self is an impassioned, vital, spontaneous, and authentic you. You are able to express yourself. You have a good sense of your identity and your real feelings. You may not always express them overtly—it is good to have some boundaries—but you know who you are and what you feel. Your True Self makes your everyday life enlivened, interesting, and meaningful.

Creative Self

The Creative Self turns *being* into *doing*; passion, vitality, spontaneity, and authenticity become action, thought, production, and creation. The Creative Self, fed by internal sensibilities, inclinations, and instincts, is effective and energized. The Creative Self is original. The Creative Self can make products, design programs, improve the surroundings, create positive interpersonal interactions, and feel great.

False Self

The False Self is the inauthentic self. A False Self is a guarded, manufactured, people-pleasing self. A False Self prioritizes acceptance by others at the expense of authenticity.

There are two kinds of False Selves, healthy and unhealthy, as established by D. W. Winnicott. The healthy False Self adapts and complies in order to create social harmony but never loses a sense of True Self. Poise, discretion, and smiling when you feel otherwise are good, healthy choices in certain professional and social situations. We all have to present a False Self at times in order to be tactful or socially appropriate.

The unhealthy False Self, on the other hand, goes too far in the direction of soft-pedaling and compliance. The unhealthy False Self annihilates the True Self in order to be accepted. This is a painful inner state and does not usually elicit adoration or true acceptance from others, although that is what it is designed to do. Ironically, people feel safer and more attracted to those who are more independent and less anxious about pleasing. Those displaying a False Self are permitted to hang around the periphery, but they never truly gain respect or admission to the fold. If you live too much in your False Self and inhibit the real feelings, ideas, and energies pulsing through you, you might feel depressed or anxious. You are more likely to be left out. However, you can get rid of your unhealthy False Self by developing your Creative Capacity and your True Self. When you discover how much more compelling that is, you will move toward it.

Sometimes survival depends upon developing and presenting an extremely compliant False Self in the early years. In childhood, it can be crucial to cultivate a False Self in order to survive home or school dynamics. In this case, excessive and ongoing compliance is not unhealthy. Being someone that you are not in order to survive a situation from which you cannot escape can represent good judgment on the part of a child or adolescent. You might have sequestered your True Self in order to free him or her later when you arrived at a safe place.

PEOPLE WHO CHANGED

Ginger

Ginger grew up in a small southern town with a violent stepfather and a religious, financially strapped family that "didn't know art existed." She was admonished for any negative feelings that pulsed through her and was told to keep her "nasty" feelings to herself. She was also told to "get along" with her stepfather even though he demeaned and insulted her. She never snapped back, but her anger made her feel aggressive and unfeminine. Though she worked hard to forgive, overlook, smile, and be soft-spoken, she could not maintain this internal state. It did not feel sincere. Her rages felt real, but she held them back.

Ginger manufactured a False Self because doing otherwise would have displeased her beleaguered mother. She set aside the painting she enjoyed and became a cheerleader in her sports-centered small country town. She was accommodating and able to forgo her own desires to make things easier for others. Though taking this route was adaptive—fitting in and adjusting the self can make things easier— she felt increasingly depressed, confused, insecure, and full of self- doubt as she grew up. She even felt physically ugly. Her inner tumult distorted her objective sense of her body. She felt ashamed of herself.

After Ginger married and had children and her own home, she decided to undergo psychotherapy. She felt ready to face her inner life and her True Self with its secret rages and shames. Confronting the past, reliving her feelings, and accepting the reality of a disappointing childhood was painful, but it freed her.

When negative emotional truths emerged, Ginger became interested in painting again. She reported to her studio regularly. If she had to miss a few days, she tried to make it up, and she forgave herself when she could not. She formed a habit of showing up for the canvas. Ginger felt most alive and energized with a paintbrush.

What Ginger hands us: Facing inner conflicts and past conundrums frees your True Self.

Thor

Thor is a rock musician and artist with waist-length hair. He grew up in a town where Ford pickups and Friday night football lights dominated and where his "bull-headed" stepfather, who entered his life when he was twelve, bellowed about Thor's long hair. Thor told me that he somehow knew not to engage in battles he knew he could not win. Thor developed an internal, self-preserving "Oh, whatever" mantra. In one ear and out the other was just the right solution.

In spite of seeing his biological father die after a long battle with cancer when Thor was ten, in spite of being depressed, in spite of being different, Thor survived. His Creative Capacity helped him live in his True Self—good and bad—and moved him forward. He somehow did not fight the pain of this loss, but rather channeled it.

Thor's biological father, an engineer and would-be artist, had hand-stitched his three children's Halloween costumes each year. Once Thor was the Mad Hatter. Once he was a Martian. His favorite was the genie. "He died in August," Thor told me, "and by October, I knew I had to take over making the costumes, or it wouldn't happen."

"At ten?" I said.

"It was up to me," Thor said.

Thor tolerated finger pricks, imperfect seams, and uneven stitches to produce costumes for himself and his two older siblings. By bringing his loving biological father to life within himself via this creative activity, he survived—that and the fact that "Mom drove me all across town and paid for expensive drum lessons on a teacher's salary." Appreciating, remembering, and holding on to her sacrifice for him also helped Thor keep his True Self in action. Maintaining an internal image of the mentor, teacher, or parent who supported you is a key survival mechanism.

Thor lived a hand-to-mouth existence for many years as a handyman and sometime chef. Now he is a well-respected, high-earning drummer in two bands that play all over the world. At the age of forty-six, he can finally support himself with his art. Through difficult periods, Thor's hands sustained him: he labored as a plumber and carpenter. He constructed drums and hammered dulcimers. He flipped tortillas and mixed chili, painted canvases and hung them in friends' coffee shops and beauty salons. Self-reliance and manual competence kept him psychologically, physically, and financially stable.

"Thor, how do think your dad would feel about who you've become?"

He smiled. "I'm probably not what he would have ordered, but he would definitely be proud."

What Thor hands us: True Self and Creative
Capacity help you survive.

HANDLING FAMILIES

Ideally, we would all have a good family that understands, nurtures, and mirrors our real selves with sincere enthusiasm. Such families are not as common as one would hope. Parents mean well when they tell you to study chemistry or write for the school paper instead of sing in the school musical, but they may be pushing you toward what they think is best rather than what is best for you. Thor's mom was able to support him, but often parents have too many fears and inhibitions of their own—both rational and irrational—to do so. And they may turn those fears and inhibitions into ill-fitting ambitions for you without being fully aware of this. They may push you to "do it right" for your own sake, but also because something inside them feels unlived, unfinished, or even inadequate.

The deeper mind, the unconscious, thinks that if the problem is externalized, taken from within and placed outside onto another person, it can be dealt with more easily. For some anxious parents, competing in conventional ways may seem to be the only road to success or solvency. Some children can comply, but others find it impossible to conform, even if they have to suffer badgering or battering.

My client Steven loved to sing as a child but was discouraged from doing so by his parents. They wanted him to study math instead so he could be an engineer and earn a good living. He gave up singing, but he thinks about it often.

Whatever your parents did or did not do, understood or missed, you can work with it and find your way. Some forms of neglect are actually good for self-reliance.

It takes strength to hold on to the True Self. Whatever your nature is and your parents' nurture was, you chose certain coping mechanisms, certain defenses, to get through your life. Some defenses that may have helped you early on, such as inhibition, could be interfering with your Creative Capacity and True Self now. If defenses do not serve a purpose anymore, dismantling them is a good idea. Once you work through your fears and defenses, you might end up returning to a former interest or developing a new one.

In the rest of this chapter, we will explore ten unconscious fears that might have led to inhibition or avoidance. When we make the unconscious conscious, confront deep-seated fears and give them a name, they become more manageable. Better options for being, doing, and living then present themselves. Creative Capacity opens up.

GETTING A GRIP ON TEN COMMON FEARS

1. Fear of Mental Freedom

Fear of your free mind may seem illogical. Why would we want to protect ourselves against pleasures such as mental freedom? What is there to fear about using your imagination? Wouldn't following your instincts and going your own way be the easy, natural path?

There are some good reasons for fearing imagination, freedom, and our own deeper truths. Freedom can be scary because we worry that if we move away from certain people, places, or ideologies, we may fall or fail and get hurt.

In order to embrace mental freedom and the joys and imaginings that can come from it, you have to develop the capacity to be alone. It is easier if you have a strong internal sense of a cherished being—a parent, a friend, a higher power, or a lover, for example, no matter whether the person is still living or is no longer with you—holding your hand as you move through unknown or tumultuous territory. If you had a strong, sure attachment to a loving person at an early age, even if life was difficult and even if your exposure to this person was minimal, you can foster the loving figure within. A fragment is enough to build upon if the attention was empathic or sensitive, meaning that you were understood as well as nourished.

When you have had adequate attention (and we don't mean *excessive* attention, since constant attention or hovering can shut down the development of inner resources), you develop an internal sense of safety, the sense that you are being held. Then you can let your mind go wherever it might. But if your sense of internal safety is fragile, you may well want to find a safe corner, sit tight, and rein in the impulses that pass through you. You might shut down or suppress your imagination, your unconscious inclinations, or your mental freedom.

Letting our minds go gives rise to unconscious phenomena—scary truths, unpleasant imaginings, or uncomfortable thoughts—as well as pleasures, fantasies, and interesting journeys. If you do not have a sense of a loving figure within, then you can develop one.

Ideas to Grapple With

• Can you recall a positive fragment or full-bodied memory of a loving person?
• What did this person—teacher, relative, friend, neighbor— do for you? Were they a caring listener?
• What did this person do for your psyche or self-esteem?

Hold this thought: Creative Capacity flourishes when you can rely upon loving figures within.

---

2. Fear of Your Own Aggression

If you let your mind go, you may discover feelings that make you worry that you are a bad person and thoughts about which you feel guilty. They may include:

• Hatred   • Dislike
• Vengeance   • Disdain
• Rage   • Contempt
• Retaliation   • Repulsion

You have to find a way to be tolerant of your own hatreds and dislikes.

Feeling hatred or dislike seems ill-advised, right? What good could come from welcoming the gnashing wild mind? Should you not err on the side of forgiveness, generosity, tolerance of transgressions, or being kind to those who hate you? Why honor the negative?

The reason is this: if you cannot identify the cruel figures, wild things, or vengeful bullies that inevitably lurk in the recesses of your mind, you cannot be in control of them; instead, you might be controlled *by* them. You cannot develop healthy assertion, the ability to speak up rather than slug it out.

If you deny hostility, it will manifest in other ways. Repressed hostility is far more destructive than direct assertion—expression of a wish or gripe—for both you and those with whom you interact. Have you heard of the term "passive-aggressive"? It refers to repressed hostility, wherein you express the animosity through unconscious behavior or action. When you are late to an event, do not hand work in on time, do not invite your neighbor to your evening get-together, or are a public figure who cheats, you might be expressing rages and drives in errant, unproductive ways, and you will likely arouse ire. Your actions may be due to deep-seated feelings of which you are unaware. (Or you may be overstressed, out of time, and too busy. It is true that sometimes a headache is just a headache.)

Either way, use self-awareness to figure out the truth of your matter. Protect yourself by knowing your unconscious and not letting your hostilities or intense emotions lead you into situations that hurt you or others. It is best to be aware so you are not surprised to find yourself in punishing situations.

Maybe you dislike yourself when you experience negative emotions. Maybe someone taught you to be ashamed of them. It can be hard to handle your inner rancor, but if you want to experience your best and most effective self, you must come to know and work with it. You can acknowledge dark feelings without losing your kindness, your conscience, your manners, or your restraint. You do not have to act upon your inclinations. You just have to know them and own them. What you want is a healthy level of assertion rather than uncontrolled aggression or ineffectual passivity.

Sometimes action and reaction are called for, and the best way to act is in a healthy, positive, assertive, non-aggressive way. In this mode, your aggression feeds the action, but it is tamed into an effective solution. This is another form of sublimation. For example, rather than shouting in despair at your neighbor about the lunging, barking dog, you might insist on an invisible fence. When you know your inner self and you can manage ire, you can have a strong and balanced response.

Here is an anecdote that captures aggressive feelings and assertive action. When Alton was twelve, a phys ed coach harshly paddled Alton for accidentally knocking over a steel chair during a dodgeball game and startling him. When Arlene, Alton's mom, heard about the injustice, she immediately drove to the school, marched into the principal's office, and said, never raising her voice but looking straight at the principal, "No one is ever to lay a hand on my son again. If he has done something wrong, I will discipline him." The coach apologized to Alton the next day.

This is an excellent example of aggressive feelings turning to assertive action. I know this, because she told me how shook up she was to hear about what had happened to her son. She spoke up rather than breaking down or running anyone over.

Ideas to Grapple With

- What experiences have you had with aggression?
- What experiences have you had with assertion?
- Which forms of action gave you a better sense of yourself, a better feeling inside?

Hold this thought: Turning aggressive feelings into assertive action will decrease fears and increase psychological resourcefulness, which is a form of Creative Capacity.

---

3. Fear of Hurting Others

Erica, a twenty-two-year-old from San Francisco with delicate features, a tiny frame, and tousled blond hair, conveyed apology from the moment I heard her message on my answering machine. "I was wondering if you would take me as a patient," she said, rather than asking, *I was wondering if I could make an appointment.* The first time I saw her walk from the waiting room into my office, her tentative glances, slow pace, and slight crouch all suggested, *I am not worthy.* Low self-esteem and an utter lack of confidence would emerge in our sessions.

Erica had shown creative talent in a number of areas—drawing, design, cooking—but she felt her younger brother, a photographer who was once hospitalized on a psychiatric ward, "had a monopoly on all the creative real estate." In the second session she said, "I'm creative, but I can't create." She was concerned about her brother, whom she described as fragile. She often worried about his feelings, self-esteem, and ego at the expense of her own. Erica also said that if she surpassed her colleagues at her job, she felt guilty. If she even thought about being promoted, she panicked. When we worked through her fears, her self-esteem increased, and she felt more deserving. She ultimately discovered she was a talented website designer and secured a high-paying job.

There are some good reasons why you, like Erica, might feel reluctant to develop your Creative Capacity, and one of them is that you fear your own prowess or power. If you work hard at something that interests you, if you become strong and able and surpass friends, siblings, or loved ones, you might feel guilty. You might worry that they interpret your success as their failure. They might retaliate. In order not to risk ruffling feathers, rocking boats, or disrupting long-standing relationship dynamics, you might hold yourself back. You might tell yourself:

- I am unworthy.
- I am undeserving.
- I should stay put.
- They need it more than I do.
- It's better to make sure they will always love me.

Ideas to Grapple With

- Have you often worried about hurting others?
- What do you imagine the consequences will be?
- How will it affect you inside if you do pursue your talents—or if you do not?

Hold this thought: Your accomplishments will not hurt others. If someone else has a fragile ego, he or she is the only one who can fix it; you cannot. Forward movement will help you contain your fears and exercise your Creative Capacity.

4. Fear of Independence

The idea of creativity usually summons positive connotations: beautiful paintings, fresh approaches, inventive recipes, inspired words, innovative technologies, freedom. Yet true self-expression and creative expression can be risky. You can fear having a mind of your own or being independent and on your own. If what you think or create is different or strange, contains an odd combination of elements, or is not what people around you are expecting, they may not welcome it or like it. Some people cannot value something they do not recognize. Unless they have good intuition or a very open mind, they may not get it. Try not to let lack of support stop you from thinking what you think.

Have you ever noticed how some people cannot tolerate different points of view? Or they feel so pleased when you agree with them that it is hard to resist doing so? Disagreeing can feel aggressive, combative, or even hurtful, as if you are rejecting them. It is so tempting to make other people happy by applauding their ideas.

If you sacrifice your own mind for the sake of pleasing others or being one with them, you can lose yourself and become depressed. You can go too far with empathy. Empathy, by the way, is not the same as sympathy. Sympathy is more about compassion and less about comprehension. Empathy is about compassion *and* comprehension—the ability to both care about and identify with another's plight. Empathize and think about the effects on your inner being before you comply or merge. This allows you to maintain your sense of independence, your creative mind, and your vitality.

My professor Dr. Richard Druss once said to me, "I want you to say, 'Fuck you, Druss!' I want you to go your own way!"

Ideas to Grapple With

- Try to distinguish between when have you felt empathy and when have you felt sympathy.
- When have you merged and when have you maintained an independent position?

Hold this thought: Empathize but do not merge, because merging can create self-annihilation. Your independence may alienate some, but it will attract others who can support your Creative Capacity.

---

5. Fear of Others' Envy

Envy and competitiveness can destroy relationships. You really cannot do anything about someone else's envy, but you can focus on empowering yourself, developing your own capacities, and minimizing your own envy. You can do this by developing Creative Capacity and your True Self.

If you spend an inordinate amount of time comparing yourself to others, your energies are wasted on what others are being and doing. They begin to define you. You have neglected, not been interested in, or not developed unique parts of yourself. Being swept away by envy of others can be a defense against your True Self. Observe and learn from others, but take the stimulus, transform it, and make it your own.

In college, I was in an acting class where participants were instructed to utter a sound and a movement and pass it to the next person. That person, in turn, had to repeat it and then modify it with something of their own. When I think about it now, I realize it was a way to teach observation, empathy, individuality, and going with your instincts. It revealed where you can connect with others and where you must remain separate. A dancer friend once explained partnering to me: "Even though the partners hold on to each other, they each have their own dance space."

Those who can feel envy without retaliating, withdrawing, or violating are psychologically evolved and good to have around. Overly competitive, envious people can undermine your Creative Capacity and your True Self. If you cannot find a way to resolve conflict with them—and some people are not capable of insight, self-examination, honest dialogue, or change—then exit gracefully and get on with your life.

Ideas to Grapple With

- When have you felt envy, and when have others envied you?
- When have you felt competitive? When have you felt that others were competing with you when you just wanted to get along?
- Is it hard to let go of people even if they make you feel wretched, despairing, or confused?

Hold this thought: Manage your own envy and avoid those who have pathological envy, and you will have less fear and more Creative Capacity.

---

6. Fear of Disappointing Others

If you are too responsive to someone else's needs, if you cannot say no, and if you jump when requested, you can become psychologically exhausted. Do as much as you will for others, but make sure you are actually *choosing* to respond as you are, and that it is not a knee-jerk reflex. It is good to give, but do it with consideration and thoughtfulness.

Some empathic, bighearted people cannot resist self-sacrifice. If you feel guilty when you do not do things for others, if you cannot let

THE CREATIVITY CURE

them cry or suffer, if you cannot bear to see them in pain, it may have more to do with your own displaced need for nurturing. If you want to be the vehicle for others' well-being, you have to remain strong and well-nourished yourself.

In order to live in the True Self, you have to weather the guilt of neglecting others at times and know that they become the beneficiaries of your better, stronger self. You have to get over the guilt. A child analyst once told me that in this entitled age, benign neglect of one's children can foster their humility and self-reliance—traits that are scarce today.

My client Susan is a writer and speaker. She travels all over the country to give talks and leaves her two young children in the care of a nanny. She is rife with guilt about this. "I have to get over the guilt," she told me. "Even though I know there is no correlation between the hours a mom spends in the home and the happiness of her kids, I still think that if I don't bake bread with them on Saturday mornings, I will really screw them up."

We can be too dutiful toward friends, parents, kids, neighbors, and family members. So many people tell me, "I just can't say no," even if they do not have time to say yes. Saying no is not part of their narrative, almost as if they do not know how, or as if it is not possible. Yes is an automatic reflex. Sometimes you have to practice saying no when you're by yourself so that you are prepared and your boundary is established. And yes, you may gather yourself and think about what you might be able to offer without resentment or excess self-sacrifice. Practice saying:

- "I would love to, but I can't this time. Will you ask me again?"
- "Thanks for asking. I'm currently swamped, but let's get together in two months."
- "So sorry, I wish I could, but I can't."
- "Sounds great, love the idea, but I am just not in a position to be part of this right now."

Hold this thought: You are allowed to say no. Before you offer yourself, remember to honor your inner needs. By doing so, you increase Creative Capacity and true generosity. Do not exaggerate guilt or others' disappointment. You will give when you really and truly can, and probably give more.

7. Fear of Pleasure

The blissful immersion of flow, whether in creative, athletic, or academic pursuits, is a peak human experience. There is nothing more delightful than letting go of all the particulars and entering that deep creative place in the self. However, leaving others behind in order to reach flow can cause internal conflict. You may feel so intoxicated by the pleasure and so disconnected from the "real" world that it makes you anxious.

Some people are also pleasure averse. Though they seek happiness, they actually fear it. Happiness can feel ungrounded or too fleeting. You might not want to experience something good because you are afraid to lose it. You'd rather avoid it than long for it. Also, without angst you might feel empty or idle. With nothing to sink your teeth into or solve, you may feel adrift. You may feel guilty about being happy.

If you let yourself go completely, with a full commitment to an absorbing endeavor, you might feel you are losing control, letting go of the reins, losing connections, letting go of responsibilities.

You might also avoid flow in order to avoid the torture of being interrupted. My friend Annika, an interior designer, has techniques for managing this. She has meditated for many years and explains that meditation allows her to weather her toddler's interruptions when she designs. Meditative capacity allows her to move in and out of a deep place without losing her momentum.

So often in life the issue is not falling off the track, as you inevitably will, but rather making sure you have a method for getting back on.

Expect to fall or even fail. Teaching yourself to go back to the activity can be lifesaving, psychologically speaking. You get credit for consistency, for getting back up.

Ideas to Grapple With

- Have you felt panicky or anxious right after feeling happy?
- Are you tempted to destroy the moment by drumming up some negative thoughts, comments, or complaints?
- What can you do to manage your inner life when you are interrupted?
- How can you reengage?

**Hold this thought: Grant yourself pleasure.
Honor your drives. And find a way to
deal with interruptions.**

---

8. Fear of Being Ordinary

It is extraordinary to live ordinary life well.
—Attributed to a FORMER HEADMASTER at the Masters School
in Dobbs Ferry, New York

Discovering you have given yourself completely to a goal and finding yourself surpassed can be demoralizing. The secret wish or belief you can make it to the top is often what helps you stay motivated.

But what if you cannot? How do you manage the realization that you are not as talented as you hoped or thought? You can fake it, hide it, project a grand self-image or an affected strut, but unless you have a fantastic capacity for denial and self-deception, you still have to own up to yourself. Accepting that you might fall smack dab in the middle in terms of talent, ability, or success is hard.

As Dr. Druss said, "The hardest thing in life is to accept being an ordinary person."

But why?

We want to think we are special, and in some ways we very well might be, but even if you accomplish great things, you still have ordinary needs and probably, like most people, famous or not, a few soft areas. And what is ordinary, anyway? I am sure you have encountered some astounding, selfless, generous, brilliant, astute, extraordinary people whom the world has never heard of—people who have a profound impact on the way you think, how you live your life, or what you believe in; people who are, in your opinion, smarter, more talented, or more able and aware than so-and-so on TV. In the words of Alton's high school football coach, "It doesn't matter how good you think that player is—he still has to get up in the morning and put his pants on one leg at a time."

If you want to be at the top in whatever way, go for it, enjoy, and be proud, but do not lose your grounding. Don't be restricted by the idea that it is beneath your dignity to "take out the garbage" (an illustrious rabbi performed this menial task for a reluctant congregation member by showing up at his door to teach him a lesson on humility), and don't forfeit true fulfillment for a ribbon around your neck.

The pursuit of "greatness" can turn a potentially pleasant existence into a tortured one. There are enormous pleasures to be found in ordinary things, not to mention that there is decreased pressure to achieve the ultimate. Try to cultivate ways of being happy that do not depend on external reinforcement.

My client Trina was a star actress in college and attended a prestigious graduate school for acting, but after four years of training she could not secure prime parts. Her dream to be an esteemed and recognized performer was shot. At first she felt devastated, because this sort of acting success was all she had envisioned for herself. She was not vain or grandiose; she had great talent, but fate, poor luck, and competitors squeezed her out of the top positions and opportunities. She saw others secure parts for which she thought she was better suited, and it was painful. But she found a way to live with this and to move on.

Depending on good fortune or external gratification for pleasure or self-esteem is a slippery slope. Even with extensive effort, you may not be rewarded. Teaching yourself to compose an existence in which pleasures come from things to which you have ready access—friendship, spirituality, culture, nature, animals, family—is a way of taking control of your fate and providing pleasure.

Ideas to Grapple With

- How does your wish to be extraordinary play out?
- Can you be extraordinary without being famous? (The answer is yes.)
- What are your ordinary pleasures?
- Did your childhood offer any ordinary pleasures that you can build upon now?

Hold this thought: Embracing and celebrating our ordinariness can be grounding and empowering. Finding possibilities within the ordinary is a way of enhancing Creative Capacity.

---

9. Fear of Criticism

Be discreet, understated, subtle, and modest. A refrain like this may be running through your head. Or you may tell yourself, *Whatever you do, do not say something foolish, speak out of turn, or act authoritative.* Is that how you think?

My client Alessandra, a highly respected researcher, has every right to be authoritative, because she *is* an expert. But she is not comfortable being the one in the know. Her father could not tolerate it when Alessandra bested him with a Rubik's Cube, and he stopped bringing home science games for her to play with. Now Alessandra inhibits herself. She does not want to upset others, risk rejection, or feel their criticism. In her mind, it is better not to show what she has. She describes herself as having a social phobia.

My new client Sam has written three novels but has published none. He once had an agent, and he has received positive feedback, but when a publisher rejected his first submission, he was crushed. He continues to write, but he is afraid to pursue representation for fear of being rejected again. I asked him about the nature of the comments; were they constructive or cruel? Some people are extremely sensitive and experience any sort of critique as injurious, while others can see it as a growth opportunity. Ideally, we want feedback that fosters growth and development, not inhibition.

Ideas to Grapple With

- What do you imagine you will be criticized for?
- Who is going to come after you, hurt you, leave you, or leave you out?
- How can you manage criticism from inside your own mind, or from others?
- What can you learn from critique, and how can you tell the difference between critique and criticism?
- Is it okay to learn from someone else, to have another person know more than you?

Hold this thought: The ability to use constructive critique enhances Creative Capacity.

---

10. Fear of Starting: The Five-Minute Rule

Starting is everything. You have to get over the hump of your inner resistance. Once you begin, you mobilize Creative Capacity and your liveliness. If you return to your task here and there during the week, for however short a time, you solidify a creative identity. The identity is far more important than any given project because it is a lifelong tool, not a momentary production. So how do you bring yourself to begin?

One way is to have low expectations. Your resistant, avoidant, and clenched-fist self will not have as much to fight if the bar is set low.

You can also face the fear of starting by adopting the Five-Minute Rule. Five minutes of action, higher thought, writing, or handwork can alter what you think about and how you feel for the rest of the day. Five minutes counts. Important ideas can come in a flash, and your five minutes can be valuable and productive if you let them. Creativity is less about time and more about mental space. The Five-Minute Rule facilitates starting. If you know that you have to do only five minutes, it is easier to start, and there is less reason to resist.

After two years of psychoanalysis, I knew my client Frank had progressed when he said, "The best thing is that now, if I am sitting at my desk and I only have ten minutes, or even five, I will begin a paper." He used to say, "I don't have time. I'm not going to start." The not starting, not using the five minutes, would lead to weeks of torturous procrastination, anxiety, and depression. Even a small action can shift mood in a big way.

Ideas to Grapple With

- What are you not starting?
- What do you do instead?
- What goes on inside your mind when you do not start, and what goes on when you do?
- If you delay starting, does it become harder and harder to do?

Hold this thought: Lower your expectations so you can start. Taking the first step awakens Creative Capacity and removes the dreadful feelings that accompany procrastination.

CONCLUSION

When people list the circumstances that they view as obstacles to their creative life, they usually sound convincing. But when you dig deeper, it often becomes clear that a large part of the problem is internal; their fears and inhibitions are what truly stand in their way.

Neurosis—an anxiety-producing, distorted perception of past or present events that results from sequestered fear or past injury—is common, but when you know your particular form of it, you can control it. If you have a distorted, anxious, or idiosyncratic (unusual) response to a situation—if, say, you just can't get in the water—you have your reasons. However, it could be interesting and useful for you to find out why, to understand it. Neurosis, distortion, and idiosyncratic reactions can emerge out of old, unresolved experience. Releasing the unconscious material can clear things up or help you feel more at peace with the decision to avoid whatever it is that upsets you.

Sometimes, even if you achieve understanding of your fear, taking action is still hard. You achieve the "being," the true flow of feelings through your self, but the "doing" eludes you. You stop short at action. Perhaps you do not feel confident enough to take what is inside to the outside, to act on your inner energies and realizations. "I think I can, I think I can" is not in your internal script.

But that can change if you do not think too rigidly about your situation. Creative Capacity is about making your mind more flexible and open, being less rigid, and being less of a perfectionist with yourself. Lowered expectations can ultimately lead to higher results because a loosened-up, more relaxed self is less anxious and more able.

SUMMARY

In this chapter, you learned about unconscious fears and self-protective behavior. You learned how Creative Capacity can first help you find the True Self and then help you develop Creative Self. The ten fears you grappled with are:

1. Fear of mental freedom
2. Fear of your own aggression
3. Fear of hurting others
4. Fear of independence
5. Fear of others' envy
6. Fear of disappointing others
7. Fear of pleasure
8. Fear of being ordinary
9. Fear of criticism
10. Fear of starting

WARM UP FOR THE FIRST FIVE-PART PRESCRIPTION

Now you will start your 5PP, which will relate to matters of inhibition.

Remember to do each part of the 5PP. You can skip a couple of days if you must, but the more time you spend on it, the better. Immersion in the 5PP facilitates core change and initiates strong, healthy habits. The 5PP will integrate being and doing, mind and body.

As a reminder, you can do the first four parts in any order, but Mind Shift should be the last thing you do on a given day. The Insight writings should always precede the Mind Shift writings, because the goal is to shift your mind from the worries in Insight to the salves in Mind Shift. Movement, Mind Rest, and Your Own Two Hands exercises will facilitate that shift.

Just do whatever works. Really, *whatever works* should be the mantra for the Creativity Cure, because there are no perfect answers, just personal solutions. Learning to act without waiting for the perfect opportunity and embracing a flawed situation will help you progress. Being creative, flexible, resourceful, and open-minded about imperfect situations and non-ideal pockets of time will empower you. *It is painful to be dependent on perfect outcomes.* If you deviate because that is right for you, you are following the prescription.

FIVE-PART PRESCRIPTION: WEEK ONE

Inhibition to Engagement

INSIGHT WRITINGS (10 MINUTES A DAY)

This week, write about when you might have avoided something that was important to you or inhibited a part of yourself. Pick one topic or more. Describe how you felt: what happened in your body and mind, how you reacted, how others reacted, how their reaction affected your reaction, what you hoped, how you were pleased or disappointed, what occurred, what did not occur.

Do not judge yourself or your writing. Rather, be open, curious, interested, and easygoing with yourself. You do not have to love everything that emerges.

Write about fear of:

- Envy
- Action
- Engagement
- Pain
- Body damage
- Exhaustion
- Effort
- Pleasure
- Truth
- Hurting others
- Independence
- Ordinariness
- Exhibitionism
- Starting
- Saying no

Write about how you avoided a situation or inhibited yourself. Examples: not trying out for a sport or a show, not studying for fear of failing, not reaching out to someone you liked.

Write about when you employed an unhealthy False Self, and how that made you feel inside.

MOVEMENT (15 MINUTES A DAY)

If Movement is already part of your life, great. If not, choose an activity that interests you.

We are going to ask you to start by walking. There are many routes to explore, and because you already know the basics you might be less inclined to avoid this form of movement. We also chose walking for the sake of simplicity and affordability, as this form of movement requires no dependence on anything but footwear. We like you to be as self-reliant and autonomous as possible.

As we progress through the book, we will make the movement section a bit more rigorous each time so that it becomes a more engaging experience. We will call this Movement Enhancement. If you choose something other than walking, you can apply the enhancement principles to it.

The point is to choose something that will make you keep moving. We are after consistency, not skill. Just try to establish yourself as a physical person if you are not already. Be curious about your physical likes and dislikes as you move. Be aware of your body and what it is telling you. Think back to a time when you derived pleasure from physical exertion. Determine the conditions that make it easier for you to comply and to continue, such as rewarding yourself. *Sometimes you have to introduce an indulgence or combine pleasure with purpose in order to proceed.*

Consider:

- What makes it more appealing to move?
- What makes you want to stop?
- Do other moving bodies distract or motivate you?
- Would you rather have solitude or clamor?
- Do you require a reward?

- Does music help you move? Should you acquire headphones or create a playlist?
- Do you have a physical "ego ideal," an image of a body or a person that reminds you of yourself in some way, someone you could *realistically* be like? Hold this in mind.

Take a walk outside: around a pond, down an avenue, along your street, on a track, in the woods, along the boardwalk.

If outside options are not inspiring, take a walk inside: on a treadmill or on an elliptical machine. If you are on a treadmill and watching TV, choose a program that conveys a process of change: something involving cooking, renovating, building, crafting. Or your favorite show.

Outside or inside, use an iPod to listen to music, a podcast, interviews with inspiring figures, or a book on tape.

If you do not wish to walk, then try these suggestions from Chapter 2: swimming, rowing, skating, skiing, spinning, dancing, yoga, weight lifting, running, mowing grass, raking leaves, or shoveling snow.

MIND REST (5 MINUTES A DAY)

Here is your chance to avoid everything. Go ahead and give in to nonproductivity. But breathe consciously as you avoid. It helps to relax the mind. Let your mind go where it will.

Try these options from Chapter 2 as suggestions: lie on your bed, do nothing, sit in your favorite spot, putter around, listen to music that you enjoy, sing anything (or sing "Ah" if you don't know the words).

Or meditate, picking a mantra (a repeated phrase—anything that feels right, from prayer to a rhyme). Avoid all but your own thoughts and let them wander.

YOUR OWN TWO HANDS (20 MINUTES A DAY)

This week you are going to use your hands to write lists with a pen on paper. You can type them afterward if you want, but the feel and smell of paper and ink might be useful for memories and sensations. Each day you will write a different list.

For now, you are purposely *not* going to use your hands to make anything. Rather, you'll use them to help yourself contemplate how you used your hands in the past, how you might use them in the future, and the inner feelings your hand use elicited. You're going to do this by making lists:

List #1: Made-by-hand projects you started in your life but avoided finishing. Why did you not finish them?

List #2: Handwork you are drawn to: knitted items, crocheted sculptures, wooden bowls, well-shaped pies, carved boxes. Why do they attract you?

List #3: Things you made as a child that you were proud of or that gave you pleasure, from forts to mud pies to paintings, and how you felt about them. Things you engaged in without any resistance, inhibition, or avoidance. What were they?

List #4: Things you imagine doing with your hands but thought you never could; things that you think you do not have time for (such as welding, gardening, or woodworking) and why they appeal to you.

List #5: Mundane tasks that you do with your hands (for example, dishes, laundry, car washing) and what happens in your mind when you do them. Do you daydream, sing, recall, mull over resentments?

List #6: Chores you abhor and avoid, and ways you can out-source or combine them with pleasure. In this case it might be good to inhibit the overly dutiful self, if you have one.

On Day 7, you will pick a project from your lists or from the list below that you can perform daily for seven weeks. You can change projects as many times as you want until you find something that fits. It can be an art project, a craft, an instrument or a series of chores that calm you and clear your mind. This week try to acquire the materials you will need or sign up for the class, if that is what you want to do. The ultimate goal is to follow through so you can feel the pleasure of engagement and have peak moments.

> Art projects: write by hand, paint, draw, cut and paste, photo-graph, design, decorate, rearrange, play an instrument
> Craft projects: Sew, knit, sculpt, weld, whittle, carve
> Home focus: Repair, fix, mend, wash, fold, sweep, cook, deco-rate, set the table, garden

MIND SHIFT (10 MINUTES A DAY)

Look at your Insight writings. Let us try to reconstruct your inner story by bringing forth positive figures from your inner life. Write about people who loved you, nurtured you, understood you, and helped you face something that you feared or avoided, people who helped you overcome inhibition. Pick at least one situation where you were able to act, engage, or speak up, and write about it. Keep the loving figure within as you write. Do not avoid intimacy or affection for the other.

Here are some prompts:

- Did you feel protected by someone in an unsettling or scary situation?
- Was this person present in the flesh or in your mind or memory when you faced a fear?
- By what means did they help you? A touch, a nod, a glance, a word, a gesture? A push?
- If you were physically alone, what strengths or inner resources did you draw upon?
- What is it about you, what traits do you have, that allowed you to withstand or make the best of the situation?
- What True Self experiences have you had in which you felt alive, engaged, authentic, spontaneous, or happy?

Some of the things you can write about include:

- Letting go
- Feeling pleasure
- The burden lifted
- The sense of independence
- Starting and feeling motivated
- Saying yes
- Employing a healthy False Self

Okay. We are done with fears. Let's move on.

4

Creativity, Psychological Clutter, and the Well-Lighted Mind

MATTERS AT HAND

Perhaps you start a project enthused and committed, feeling you have found your calling, but then suddenly one day your mind clogs up and you stop. You check out. You avoid the project, having decided that it is urgent to run an errand. You no longer feel connected to this important endeavor, this outer expression of your inner self. It feels suddenly as if it isn't you. Shoulds, can'ts, and the irrational critic (soon to be defined) flood your mind.

Why the sudden disavowal and disinterest? You justify withdrawing for a couple of days with a sweep of the hand, saying:

- "I'll get back to it."
- "I just need a break."
- "I really need to run these errands."
- "My mother called."

But more time passes and your Creative Capacity goes missing. Your True Self has slipped away. You may feel restless, bored, and irritable.

Your feelings could be the result of your mental jam. Rather than focus on a project or skill, you've added trivial matters in order to distract yourself. While you feel compelled to do them, energy is seeping out of you. Minutiae fill your day. Perhaps you did need to address some details, but you have not returned to your project. Your Creative Self has shut down.

What happened? In the last chapter, we worked through inhibition and underlying fears. Inhibitions, as you know, often have unconscious origins, and fears can rule you without your full awareness. Psychological clutter works the same way. Once you identify and examine it, it loses clout. Uncovering its antecedents and impacts can even be illuminating.

However, while the unexamined life is not worth living, the overly examined life is not worth living, either. Though it is important to achieve insight, it is also possible to be paralyzed by overcontemplation. If your thought process frees you or invigorates you, keep thinking. If you feel mired or stuck, relinquish the thoughts and use some of the 5PP actions. Combining thought and action in attuned, considered ways can change your inner stance. The 5PP has five parts because you need different approaches at different times and it is good to have several tools from which to choose. Examine your inhibitions, fears, and your psychological clutter, and then move on to actions that enliven.

The point of this chapter is to tame harsh, moralistic, overpowering voices within—the psychological cutter that clogs up Creative Capacity. Move them out, quiet them down, put them in their place, or refocus them so that their raucous bellow boosts you up instead of dragging you down. Then you can make sound choices on behalf of yourself and ultimately others.

Psychological clutter passes itself off as rational, ethical thought. The shoulds, the can'ts, and the irrational critic are manifestations of a stringent inner authority that can lead you to disregard crucial inclinations—personal leanings—that are important for proper development and natural identity.

Sometimes you should go against your inclinations. We need an inner monitor so that we do not develop narcissistic (unhealthy) self-love and assume we are superior specimens when in fact we could use an overhaul. A monitor that counters unhealthy impulses is crucial for mental health. It is essential to have a means of self-control, a method of choosing right over wrong, and a way to minimize harmful involvements. However, balancing indulgence and restraint, pleasure and discipline, benevolence and strictness is key for health. If you are too harsh with yourself over the wrong matters, if you exercise misguided morality, you can get depressed. Knowing when to honor and when to resist impulses, when to act and when to suppress will serve you.

In this chapter, we will try to identify your brand of psychological clutter and diminish it. This will help to release your Creative Capacity and build up a healthy inner monitor.

TERMS TO GRASP

Psychological Clutter

Psychological clutter silences the True Self, Creative Self, and Creative Capacity with unnecessary strictness. Once identified and examined, psychological clutter diminishes.

Psychological clutter consists of the shoulds, the can'ts, and the irrational critic.

THE SHOULDS: "I HAVE TO, BUT I REALLY DON'T WANT TO"

The shoulds make you feel obligated to do something that may not be necessary or even as useful as you imagine. The shoulds tell you to do this and not that. The voice telling you that you should take certain actions may arise from avoidance of other actions. If you are polishing silver or buying extra presents rather than engaging in your project, you may be letting the shoulds derail you. The shoulds may also be the result of an excessive sense of duty or obligation. You want to be responsible, to step up, but doing so because of rigid inner control may interfere with your Creative Capacity. You can become overextended and lose your inner vibrancy. It helps to be aware of when you're distracting yourself or taking on too much at the expense of vitality. *You do not want to be living a life wherein you do not feel alive.*

Virginia Woolf named her should, an inner being who called her away from her writing, the "Angel in the House." The only way to keep her creativity alive was to abolish this inner detractor. She wrote, "I turned upon her and caught her by the throat. I did my best to kill her. My excuse, if I were to be held up in a court of law, would be that I acted in self-defense. Had I not killed her, she would have killed me. She would have plucked the heart out of my writing."

THE CAN'TS: "I AM INCAPABLE. I AM INCOMPETENT"

The can'ts make you feel as if you cannot when actually, with flexibility and ingenuity, you can. The can'ts are a defeatist, pessimistic mental position and can be a sign of depression or a long-entrenched psychological style. Sometimes, overcoming negativity is a matter of reeducation. *Can't* people can become *can* people with a cognitive shift, such as substituting positive thoughts for negative ones when the can't trigger is pressed. They can learn to distract themselves rather than fixate on self-recrimination. They can focus on motivating figures rather than defeating ones. It takes practice to de-energize the can't and adopt a can, but it's entirely possible. *You must be intolerant of your self-destructive thought processes.*

THE IRRATIONAL CRITIC: "YOU ARE NOT GOOD ENOUGH"

The irrational critic convinces you that you are not cut out for things and should not try them, or it tells you that you are deficient, with no hope for development. It looks and sounds level-headed, but it makes you feel dreadful. While some pursuits may not be suited to you and it might be best to steer clear of them, others are worth a few clumsy attempts for ultimate success. You are permitted your wobbly Bambi moment on feeble legs. Having an inner monitor that analyzes, critiques, and measures your actions, converses with you, and guides you well is useful. If you can gauge your weaknesses, look objectively at your strengths, understand how you have erred, forgive yourself, and correct what can be corrected, you are well poised for growth. We call this helpful monitor the rational critic. In contrast, the irrational critic judges you harshly, puts you down, sets you back, and punctures your hope. It has a lowering, demoralizing influence. The irrational critic can misconstrue and be cruel.

The irrational critic deflates or cripples you, whereas the rational critic feeds your growth and gives you a hand. The rational critic promotes development, while the irrational critic prevents it.

Know the difference between the rational critic and the irrational critic.

PEOPLE WHO CHANGED

Louisa

Louisa, a talented composer from the lower east side of Manhattan, received positive feedback on a piece she had written, but before she could expand it, she was stopped dead in her tracks by psychological clutter:

The shoulds: "I should spend more time with my boyfriend instead of finishing the work. He feels neglected. (Even though he is not taking the initiative to find things to do when I am busy.)"

The can'ts: "I don't know what I was thinking. I will never be able to finish this or sell anything."

The irrational critic (a finger-wagging pseudo-pro): "This work is awful. Give up. You're not good enough."

Eventually Louisa had three hundred pages of musical notes, thirteen restarts, and a plethora of unfinished movements.

When I first met her, Louisa wore bold framed glasses, a bulky sweater, and a coat with a torn pocket. As we shook hands, her easy, bright smile, shiny black hair, and notable height seemed to say, *There is more to me than it would appear.*

The colleague who referred Louisa told me, "She's not showing up at her day job, oversleeping, and avoiding her creative work." Louisa told me that she was withdrawing from friends and spending more time alone. She was depressed.

Though Louisa had graduated from a fine music school, had won awards for her performances, and was competent at many things, she was floundering. A similar depression had occurred when she cut most of her classes during junior year at a performing arts high school.

She described her childhood as "a basic nightmare, a shit show." While her mom asserted that the family was all about "unconditional love," negative comments and yelling were common.

One holiday, Louisa's sister announced that she was leaving to sleep with a boy she had met earlier that day. Louisa recalls the injured, helpless look on her father's face as her sister sashayed out the door. It was rare for him to display any vulnerability; he found some solace in his fourth scotch. The guests came late and left the dinner early, the empty seat of the sister seeming to hasten their exit.

"Family is a myth," says Louisa. "It never works, but my mom keeps trying. Then she goes up to her room and cries and catches a cold." Louisa described herself as having a headache for the first eighteen years of her life. She recalls best friends dropping her and periods when she had no friends at all. She spent hours at the piano, which helped her "forget."

We focused on helping Louisa master psychological self-reliance, regain her confidence, and overcome past pitfalls and trauma. She could not do anything about her disharmonious family history, but she could remove her psychological clutter:

- "I should love my sister."
- "I should visit my parents even though they torture me."
- "I've become such a loser."
- "I will never be a motivated person."

Then she could identify her personal abilities and see her options, psychological and otherwise.

Eventually she was able to access a kinder, saner inner voice and a conscience that considered her needs as well as those of others. Once Louisa felt less like a servant to a browbeating inner figure and more the master of herself, her Creative Capacity unfolded.

After about a year, Louisa discovered that although she loved composing, she preferred arranging and was better at it than she realized. It was easier to play with what was already there than to invent something new. Creating structure, changing things around, and reshaping came easily to her. (Remember, when we shape or fix a product, we have an opportunity to reshape or repair ourselves.)

One day while looking for some CDs in an old suitcase, she found some colored pencils she had used in middle school for her art projects. She spent the afternoon drawing with the pencils as she listened to the music. She felt completely absorbed in the task.

What Louisa hands us: You do not have to do what hurts you; you can do what makes you feel alive. What you do with what happened is far more important than what actually happened.

Walter

My client Walter has a knack for transforming negatives into positives. His character, his flexibility of mind, and his tolerance draw people to him. When he was stopped by the police for riding his bike outside the bike lane, he was so gracious and non-argumentative that the cop apologized to him. I often forget to collect the co-pay from my clients, yet Walter always pulls the money out of his pocket immediately.

When I first met Walter, I could not understand his sentences. Though he was a student in a competitive film program, his mind was so full of can'ts, shoulds, and the irrational critic that he could not find his way to the end of his own verbalizations. He was self-conscious and stumbling. He worried that he couldn't keep up, that he shouldn't neglect his family for his work, and that his productions were not up to par.

Walter, thin yet fit and usually dressed in a tight hoodie and crisp jeans, grew up in the South. His dad disappeared when he was five and he never saw him again. At times he went without dinner so he would not disturb his overworked single mother, who often fell asleep on the couch after work. When he was in college, he volunteered in a homeless shelter and served soup.

Walter had intrinsic strengths that were stymied by a lifetime of taxing situations. After we established a safe and predictable treatment setting and his self-awareness increased, Walter felt less self-conscious. His natural confidence, intellectual curiosity, and passion for aesthetics surged. When he feels the clutter coming on, the voice that says, "You don't know what you're doing," Walter has learned to shift his mind to the positives. He says he is tempted to keep wrangling with the irrational critic, but when he does, it "takes over my mind." He switches to a better set of thoughts, a new trigger, by looking at his fourth-year birthday card from his grandpa that says, "I love you."

When we worked through Walter's self-criticism and psychological clutter, he was better able to focus on writing his film treatments and forming lucid, beautiful sentences. His mind was clear.

What Walter hands us: Shift the focus,
find the grace.

FOUR CAUSES OF PSYCHOLOGICAL CLUTTER

1. The Difficult Family

As a child, you may have spent time and energy fending off familial discord. You tried to stop it, but you could not. You retreated. Maybe you slammed your fist through a wall or kicked in a door to make it stop, but the chaos continued. Not much changed when you tried to call attention to the problem. This can make you feel as if you failed or that you are a loser, even though you have been known to win races and awards and make many friends. Somehow you feel that this heart-wrenching mess is *your* fault. It is not, but you still think it is.

Maybe you harbor the notion that you were an impossible child early on and you upset your parents. Maybe they fought with each other and collapsed after work because you stressed them with your tantrums, detentions, refusal to learn the multiplication table, and escapades involving calls from the principal. Maybe you did such things, but so do most children. This was one of your jobs as a child: to annoy. That is the manner of growing beings who are finding their way. They frustrate and fail to do what they are bid. (Sometimes I think that one of the great challenges of parenting is to be able to tolerate our helplessness in the face of our children's self-defeating decisions.)

The overt discord, lack of restraint, unleashed panics, unruly passions, and overall intensity of this sort of family life can stultify a growing self. Raw emotion in large doses is hard for a child to digest and can lead to feeling overburdened, or as if the weight of familial angst rests upon your narrow frame or within you. Maybe you felt you had to do something—you had to act or you had to shut down.

This clamor and stimulation within and outside the self allows the irrational critic, the shoulds, the can'ts, and the ruminating self to reside in your higher mind, where better things could be happening. *Excess morality imposed upon the self after years of turmoil is an attempt to control the outer chaos and inner despair.* In her inner life, the child becomes a drill sergeant with herself.

Before we continue, let me just say that blaming parents and identifying yourself as an injured victim rarely transports you to the psychological destination you seek. It is useful to accept what happened in your family and ultimately to forgive, which really means relinquishing the past and making it less powerful and important than the future. Forgiveness increases your freedom and decreases the power of the perpetrator. When you diminish the perpetrator and your injury, energizing thoughts and activities move front and center. Forgiveness can be a true challenge and can require new ways of working through if it is to be maintained. Injuries can resurface as we move through life, and new provocations may occur. If you have a method for managing difficulties, for feeling the pain and then moving into forgiveness, it becomes easier to forge ahead or separate.

Psychological self-reliance saves us. If you are self-reliant, you will know upon whom you can depend and upon whom you cannot. The courage to break old bonds and forge new ones is part of it. If you cannot mend the old, then you can replace it.

Really.

2. Not Being Understood

Not being or feeling understood over a long period of time can be a form of trauma. It affects your sense of identity and the decisions you make. To make good choices, you have to know your True Self and be in loving, rich relationships with people who understand you.

As we said, it helps to be raised by someone who understands you and is actually happy about who you are. If you were not understood early on, you may repeat the experience by choosing friends, schools, and work environments wherein you are misunderstood, are devalued, are treated unkindly, or just do not mesh. Often it was a caregiver who did not understand you, but it may also have been teachers, coaches, colleagues, neighbors, siblings, or even friends.

My client Julie drew a precise geometric drawing in second grade, and it was so good that the teacher accused her of copying it. The teacher could not be convinced otherwise and whacked her palm with a ruler for lying. She grew up to be a mathematician with an even hand and an artistic eye. Did something like this happen to you? Your job is to figure out what happened, why it happened, and how to put it behind you, so you can follow your natural trajectory.

The best way to be understood by others is to understand yourself. By building your identity upon your self-knowledge and changing long-standing behavioral styles that no longer suit you, you will feel better. Adopt behaviors and attitudes that fit you now, and move through life with greater equanimity.

3. Low Self-Esteem from Not Developing Good Habits

Habits are everything. Good habits—thoughtfully chosen, well practiced, and based on your organic capacities—are a major power source,
right up there with insight. They are a crucial part of building, healing, maintaining, and reinventing the self. So much of success is about
embracing the concept of small steps.

Maybe you rebelled against athletic, academic, artistic, or even
grooming standards when you were young. Instead of integrating a disciplined self into your developing character, you resisted. Rather than
practice, organize, study, or persist, you goofed off and did things that
did not solidify your identity or ground you. You also may have yet to
acquire some habits that are useful for concentration and commitment.

Perhaps you avoided making the effort at activities you were drawn
to because you doubted your talent, worried you would fall short, or
assumed it would be for naught. You could have smothered your natural inclination by such thoughts as:

- "My work isn't worth an A." If you have an all-or-nothing
  attitude, a though such as "I cannot do it perfectly, so why do
  it at all?" might have passed through your mind.

- "I don't really like this that much." Maybe you did not per-
  severe long enough and master your activity well enough to
  make it interesting to you.

- "I'll never be as good as my classmate, who started last year."
  Maybe you are more competitive than you realize, which can
  be harnessed and put to good use if you focus on your own
  initiatives.

- "James isn't joining, so I won't, either." Maybe you were very
  sensitive to peer pressure and did not want to apply yourself
  if others were not.

Your irrational critic and the can'ts can rear their heads with this
psychological history. If you did not learn something early on, you

may think you cannot now, but you can. Remember, though, that you cannot discover you can sing first soprano instead of alto until you practice your scales and proper technique for a good long time. You have to incorporate:

- A capacity for delayed gratification
- Points for small victories
- Using and honoring what you have
- Compliance with instruction
- The belief that results are about incremental steps
- Patience and a belief in process

Habit will deliver you from can't to can. How do you acquire good habits? Good role models and the right environment help. Being around energetic people is useful, as action breeds action. In the words of William James, "there is no happiness without action."

It is *never* too late to learn new habits. Being engaged in something is far better than being idle, no matter what age or stage of life you are in. Learning something new can give you confidence, but you need to be willing to be stumped, scoffed at, or frustrated at times during the process. Trying on new ideas, exploring new activities, or returning to past interests can be rejuvenating. If you are more interested in the process than your image, if you aim for mastery but are pleased with solid development, then you can have a good time.

Good habits can be hard to maintain. Maybe you cannot stick to them or think you cannot. Let's think of ways you can.

The key is to start and commit. Taking action creates a psychological boost. Don't think about starting, just do it. You might try saying, "Don't think. Don't think. Don't think." (Alton says this to himself when he has to get up and go after three hours of sleep.) Then take your action step.

- The first step is monumental and catapults you. Transcend anxiety with your initial push. If you then latch on to the routine, you will rise.

- Believe in, trust, and be humble before the power of habit. Habit is about mastering yourself, making yourself a tool and creating an effective self at a realistic pace. Tolerance for slowness is an excellent trait.

- Sticking with it when you just do not want to becomes easier when you have a track record of resisting your resistances.

- Know that immersion and consistency deliver results. Keep this in your mind. When you put in the time, you get somewhere.

- Embrace and celebrate small steps. Small steps are everything. They are your building blocks and the greatest form of personal empowerment.

- Accept and be comfortable with discomfort. Adopt the idea that some discomfort and effort will lead to an improved situation.

- Hold the goal in your mind. Do not let it go. Holding it in mind keeps you a little bit tense, anxious, and revved up, in a good way.

- Get it into your head that much of the time it is easier to do than not to do.

4. Reaction Formation, or Being the Opposite of Your Organic Self

Reaction Formation is doing the opposite of what you are naturally inclined to do because underneath you believe that who you are, what you want, or how you feel is somehow wrong. This defense mechanism is a form of self-betrayal that feels like self-protection, but it is actually a form of self-oppression.

If you feel that your deep-seated feelings, your nature, or your impulses are unacceptable, then you may compensate for them by doing or trying to feel the opposite and going against your instincts. This reaction creates a strident, conflicted, tension-filled inner state.

It can manifest as moralism, discrimination, or intolerance, in the sense that one deems another person or a group inferior instead of grappling with one's own feeling of lowliness. There is a rebellion against your organic self. This is related to the shoulds problem, because some voice inside tells you that who you are is not okay and should be altered. This is a wearing, undermining False Self predicament. If you can accept who you are and not fight it, if you honor and value the True Self and its natural leanings rather than turning against the self, you are less at risk for turning away from others.

Better to just be in your True Self as is and see what it can offer you. This is far less draining than trying to fight it. Besides, whatever you are, have, or can do by nature is worthy in and of itself.

Know your own mind and all that is in it. Ask yourself some questions:

- In what ways might you feel that you don't measure up?
- What behaviors or actions might you have adopted to compensate for these feelings of inadequacy?
- Is there something that you feel very moralistic about?
- How might you be able to have a different attitude about yourself and who you are?

FIVE WAYS TO GET A GRIP ON PSYCHOLOGICAL CLUTTER

1. Build Up Positive Figures, Tear Down Negative Figures

First you have to know both your positive figures and your negative figures inside and out. What and who are they? We all carry inside us parts of the people we have known, those who shared, taught, influenced, and directed us. They persist in comments they uttered to us, objects they gave us, or experiences we shared with them. These figures can offer positive or negative commentary, and we tend to have dialogues with them inside our minds. It is okay to conduct inner banter; in fact, it's healthy, especially when inner negative figures arise and they are critical. You might have to talk with them, correct their thinking, and take charge in order to go in a different direction.

Sometimes you should heed the can't or should, or even a harsh inner critic, if it causes you to give up destructive habits. The rational critic offers caring strictness if you are slacking off or messing up. Sometimes you need tough love from your rational critic. Early on in my psychoanalytic training, Dr. Druss supervised me as I worked with my traumatized but stalwart client Hannah. "Enough with the empathy! She needs a football coach!" he told me. He saw how strong she was. "No pain, no gain" was the most useful attitude to help her to foster resilience within, so that she could reach her goals.

"No pain, no gain" can be applied to psychological phenomena as well as physical ones. Sometimes linking your behaviors to critical thoughts leads you away from self-destructive actions. When the behavior becomes wretchedly distasteful to you because you have objectified it and made yourself see it for what it really is, it is easier to relinquish it. You now have the mental space for positive pursuits. But you might need some support or an encouraging inner voice to act.

How do you build up positive, supportive figures in your psyche? You can do it with just a sliver or a fragment of a good, caring person who said something kind and astute to or about you. Some people have a bevy of loving figures within, others have to build them up from a tiny drop of affection. Some people were not nurtured as much as others. Think of:

- Your kindergarten teacher who said you were special
- Your friend who said she respected your taste
- Your grandfather who said you were a beautiful person, inside and out
- Your neighbor who said you helped her by touching her hand after her son died of AIDS
- Your child who said, "Thanks for getting me through that, Dad"

It helps to think of someone who supported you, believed in you, or told you that you could master a problem or that you had a special trait—someone for whom you made a difference and who told you so.

- Did you heed this person?
- Did you believe him or her?
- Did you think this person erred in his or her perception?
- How did you feel receiving this compliment?
- Was this person rational worthy of your respect?
- Is there truth in what he or she said?
- Do you actually possess this talent or quality?

You might have this quality, and others can see it, but you cannot. Or maybe you did not or do not yet have this quality, but you can fake it a little until something shifts and you truly develop it. Take the good figures—even if they are just tiny peeps from the past—and build upon them.

Recently, my client Kevin told me he wished he had a life coach who lived in his apartment. This person would secure a new job for him by sending out his résumé, renovate his kitchen, and make him act on his own behalf. Kevin procrastinates and becomes depressed. We discovered that he was much more able to be motivated when he focused on an art career rather than one of the "professions." His grandmother had encouraged him to "follow your desire." Part of the work in the Creativity Cure is to re-create your inner narrative so that it serves you, to bolster internal positive figures that you can call upon to move you up, out, and forward. The goal is to have a life coach inside you and to rely on yourself.

Ideas to Grapple With

- What positive fragments or memories can you build upon?
- To whom are the negative voices linked? Do they deserve space in your mind? Do they really know what they are talking about?

- What can you say to negative critics? Practice that response a few times so you are ready.
- Can you just commit to the first step?

Hold this thought: Build up positive figures and reject negative, undermining figures. Find your inner coach.

---

2. Get to the Bottom of the "I Am Defective" Issue and Turn Flaws into Strengths

How are you defective? The feeling that you are defective or "less than" is usually self-created, a distortion that arises out of suppressed inner conflict. For example, you might malign yourself rather than malign a hurtful past figure lodged in your psyche. It can be easier unconsciously to find fault with yourself than to face the fact that someone else failed you or slipped up. Such realizations can involve wrenching disappointment, a loss of idealization, painful separations, and grief. In order to bypass the pain of the truth, you knock yourself around rather than someone else. This pain seems preferable (in the unconscious) because somehow you can tolerate the idea of your badness, even if it isn't true, more easily than you can admit their badness. Instead of being critical of them (which means having to live with the truth of who they are and what they did), you might focus on your personal flaws instead and lock yourself into a painful self-consciousness. You might assume these flaws are glaring or obvious and experience them as major defects when in fact they are just minor human imperfections. They are probably a whole lot less relevant than you imagine. Maybe you obsessively think:

- "My thighs are horrible."
- "I'm not smart."
- "I'm not sophisticated."

- "My hairline makes me look twenty years older."
- "I am boring. I have no ideas. I hate parties because I have nothing to say."
- "I know nothing about the continents, or all of geography, for that matter."
- "I don't deserve to have that."
- "I can't do math."

Or perhaps you were traumatized by something someone said to you in seventh grade or what your ex-boyfriend said when you broke up, such as:

- "If anyone else really knew you, they wouldn't love you."
- "Your dress is ugly."
- "You can't play handball with us."
- "You have no friends."
- "You are *soooo* dumb."

Let us stop listing these cutting comments and supposed defects. You may have recognized some things you've said to yourself or been tempted to add others, but resist the allure of the negative. The bottom line: so what? Are these really defining defects or just minor blips or distortions? Will you really let them hold you back, define you, or deflate you? Is it possible that you are exaggerating your undesirability?

Have you noticed that when someone has a great personality, when she is engaging and compassionate, you do not notice the size of her thighs or what her hair is like, and even if you do, it does not matter? Eventually, the so-called flaw becomes a part of her identity, her uniqueness, and part of what makes her interesting. My mother used to say, "Make friends with your flaws."

Our outsides are certainly noticeable. Even Freud said that we worship external beauty. People, landscapes, paintings, icicles, architecture, outsider art, homemade pies, hand-knit mittens, tightly woven rugs, and fine leather shoes compel us. But in a deep, abiding, and perhaps more gratifying way, we also respond powerfully to inner beauty.

Let's look more closely at why you inflate or focus on your supposed shortcomings. Some personal drawbacks or imperfections are inevitable, so why do you feel you have to make them the whole story, rather than an interesting yet less significant part? Just as you might displace your wrath from another to yourself, it is possible that you dislike your inner self and that you are scapegoating your outer self instead.

Hatred, greed, envy, resentment, or excessive competitiveness often can make you feel that you are a bad, undeserving, unattractive, and unworthy person. You may feel guilty, angry, or beaten down, and you may displace all internal trouble onto an external scapegoat or body feature.

So what can you do to combat this response?

- Identify your supposed defects.
- Ask yourself if you really have these defects or if you just think you have them.
- See if they are a major or minor matter.
- If you feel these defects or differences are real, figure out how to:
  - Use them
  - Live with them
  - Minimize them
  - Get rid of them
  - Turn them into an advantage or opportunity—
    "Use the disadvantage," in the words of actor
    Michael Caine

If you learn to confront your flaws and accept them, you can tolerate the idea that in some areas you are weaker than others. This is freeing. People with very sensitive self-esteem can find it hard to admit any weakness, flaw, or imperfection to themselves or to others. These are the same people who find learning difficult because they cannot tolerate *not* being an expert from the get-go. This can make life very painful and panicky. A deep acceptance of the self as it is and as it can be is necessary for wellness.

Try to make an honest appraisal of yourself. Take a rigorous inventory. *There is enormous strength in knowing your limitations.* Here are some ways to think about them:

- What are your limitations?
- How do you feel about them?
- Is there something you wish to change?
- Is it possible to change it?
- What do you imagine that would be like?
- Will changing it accomplish what you hope to accomplish?

How can you turn your weakness to advantage? Through attitude and inner authority. "If you make a mistake, make it with authority," one of my acting teachers once said. You can also do it through having a flexible mind and allowing yourself to find possibilities and opportunities in what you have. To do this successfully, you have to be willing to be different. One client told me she was made fun of for wearing pants that were too short—"high-water pants"—and from then on she wore them daily. She stood her ground and became master of the situation. This is a useful attitude to develop.

Chasing after something that is not within your grasp can create depression, whereas reshaping what you have can bring surprising pleasure. My client Sasha was born with curly hair and her siblings had straight hair. This tortured her. She ironed it, blew it dry, Scotch-taped it, braided it, and wore scarves and wool hats to press it down. One day she began to look in magazines for models with curly hair whom she found attractive. She studied the photos and tried to figure out the anatomy of the curls: how to make them look best, how to highlight them, how to tame them. Shame transformed into pride, and Sasha created a hairstyle magazine.

Idea to Grapple With

- What flaws might you turn to strengths?

Hold this thought: Use your disadvantage to your advantage, and be authoritative about it.

---

3. Channel Your Neurosis

A neurosis is a distorted or hypersensitive response to a situation or person based on past experience. You were hurt, and now you find it hard to respond to the situation with aplomb, distance, faith, and confidence. Instead you panic. Maybe you were bitten by a dog and now you fear dogs. Perhaps when you fly you imagine damage to the plane's wings because your brother smashed the model B-52 bomber that you built and treasured. Whatever the subject matter of the neurosis, you experience fear, clinginess, a tendency to shrink back, or a wish to avoid.

You can teach yourself to get over the fear, your neurosis, by learning to control the anxiety with graded exposure or desensitization. These are behavioral approaches that involve incrementally increasing doses of the feared object with the support of a therapist. Medication is also useful for severe symptoms.

Or you can accept the fact that you are not comfortable with a certain stimulus and simply avoid it. This latter solution is perfectly acceptable as long as you find rich alternatives. You do not have to conquer all. In fact, limiting yourself in one area might lead to expansion in another. People who lose one of their senses often find that their other senses become more acute and capable. Sometimes it is fine to practice avoidance, to accept this limitation in yourself, to have a phobia. It is okay to have some problems.

Our dear friend Marshall did not like to fly. He lived in New Orleans, bought a lake house in the Texas Hill Country, and needed a way to get there. He bought a Lincoln Town Car with a red leather interior that we fondly called his "land barge," country-and-western CDs, and cowboy boots. He made the most of his limitation and found a way to live it up.

Why do you have to have a perfect psychological makeup? You do not. You can have idiosyncrasies. You can have neuroses, survive them, and even use them to your advantage.

Idea to Grapple With

- Are you allowed to have some problems? (The answer is yes.)

Hold this thought: You can have some neuroses, some limitations, and still be a normal, well-functioning, and satisfied person. In fact, you might be more content if you let yourself have limitations and see where they lead you. You could be pleasantly surprised.

---

4. Decrease the Pressure to Achieve

More than a couple of my clients have told me that their parents expected them to grow up and do something grand such as win a Nobel Prize or become secretary of state. When they told their stories, they seemed daunted, sad, or slightly peeved but not vain. When the goal is too lofty, the self can get lost. It can be hard to feel that anything else is great or even good enough. It can confuse your development and obscure true desire.

If you can tell yourself that you are not on this earth to move mountains but rather to be in awe of them, you put much less pressure on yourself. You might move a mountain, or hammer through one like John Henry, but in the meantime, you can enjoy the honest practice of the task. When you can be immersed in what you are doing, rather than burdened by the need for what you are doing to be important or impressive, then you are free.

Sometimes what absorbs someone can be surprising. I once heard about a man who lost his job and turned to spending his days skipping rocks across the water. He became so good at it that he was interviewed about it on the radio. There is something fascinating about witnessing someone else in deep concentration. It is more about the capacity and less about the particular task. Tune up your insides and good things happen.

Our son Nicholas, now nine, has always loved vacuum cleaners. When he vacuums he appears to be experiencing flow. For the record, we don't *make* him vacuum. He used to follow his former babysitter around as she zoomed the vacuum cleaner over the Cheerios and beg for a turn. I do not know if it is the hose, the hand use, the noise, the big powerful machine, or the vibrations, but last week he asked to vacuum the whole house, so Alton handed over the vacuum. Nicholas feels powerful when he can crash around in this way. Although we would prefer he study his math facts, how can we deprive him of the true satisfaction he gets from vacuuming? This appears to be important for him.

I have treated young people so riddled with anxiety about achieving that they cannot function. They feel they are not allowed to be average in any way. Because of the goals they have set or that have been set for them, they break down under unconscionable loads of performance pressure. They feel and act so competitive with their peers that true friendships suffer, they feel shame if they do not measure up, and they panic about the consequences of not being among the elite. Because they are so goal-oriented, overscheduled, and tired, creative life is nonexistent.

A colleague who is a child psychiatrist told me that a boy came to her after being accepted at Yale because he was depressed. He said, "I lost my whole childhood." She says she is continually stunned by this cultural phenomenon of kids whose entire lives are spent preparing for college admission. "What about the ones who do not get the reward?" she said.

This is not a moral issue but a mental health issue. Rigid ideas of success can be very painful and limiting. There are many ways both to achieve and to achieve happiness if one has an open mind.

My friend's son, who has been building furniture since he was ten, might become a woodworker rather than get a job in academia now that he has completed his doctorate. She says, "He is brilliant, but he has no tolerance for BS. He can't stand alpha-male academics." For her birthday, he made her a bookshelf. He has made tables and mirrors by hand from carefully selected wood.

Idea to Grapple With

- Are you practicing shoulds that push you to achieve in ways that do not give you pleasure?

Hold this thought: Allow yourself to develop a nuanced, complex, and evolved definition of achievement.

---

5. Stop Ruminating

I wrote a paper about rumination once, called "I Think Therefore I'm Not," and presented it at a meeting of the American Psychoanalytic Association. The journal I sent it to contemplated, considered, and reflected for three and a half *years* before deciding to publish it with a different title. This might be an academic form of rumination, or perhaps the editor has too many papers to read and believes one has to give deeply of time and thought in the critique. I actually started to feel sorry for the editor.

Should I or should I not . . . ? What if . . . ? Why . . . ? How can those people do . . . ? et cetera, et cetera. Call it what you will—navel gazing, overthinking, obsessiveness—but let me tell you right now, you are never going to get to the bottom of it. There will never be a clean slate or a clean, well-lighted place of understanding, because people who violate boundaries, are insensitive, display irrational behavior, or exhibit mental distortions will never make sense to you. And they will (almost) never do the right thing. They terrorize intimate relations and present themselves as victims to kindhearted others, who get swept up in their drama. It's a nightmare, but one you can wake up from and not repeat.

Does rumination have you lying awake at 3:00 a.m.? Rumination is a prison, a trap, a paralysis. It offers a feeling that you are in action, moving, and making progress, but you are not getting anywhere. So why do you do this? What purpose does it serve? Why can't you just let go of it?

It is so annoying when people say, "Just let it go," or "Smile," or "Get over it," or "Be happy," as if it is just a decision. The truth, which is actually rather simple and even freeing but hard to implement, is that letting the thought go is just a decision, though one that requires follow-up.

You can make the decision. But how do you stick to it, feel it as real change, and employ the mind effort necessary for self-preservation and rumination removal? Nike has a point with the "Just Do It" motto. Physicality can help you tame rumination. If you can discipline your body, you can elevate your mind above the rumination.

Do not wait until the snow has melted, until you have the right shoes, until you have had enough sleep so you can wake up without the alarm. Get out and go. Ruminate on your walk, if you must. Decide that during your walk or run or weight-lifting session, your thinking about the problem will have a beginning, a middle, and an end, and then it will be over. Even if you do not have an answer, it will be over. Your well-being is more important than making sense of a senseless situation or an insensitive person who will not change. Cease and desist with the thought process and plant another one in your head. Choose a stopping time for your rumination, and when that time arrives, focus on the first thing you see and make up a rhyme or mantra about it. Repeat that instead.

Decide to do it. Then do it.

Ideas to Grapple With

- Can you live with not resolving every dilemma?
- Can you let go after thinking gets you nowhere?

Hold this thought: You can.

CONCLUSION

Psychological clutter clogs up Creative Capacity and blocks the True Self and the Creative Self. Negative voices stir up negative internal energy and thwart your natural flow. When you challenge the harsh moral voice, redirect it, shut it down, or use it for a good purpose, you will have control and feel better.

SUMMARY

In this chapter we covered psychological clutter, the can'ts, the shoulds, the irrational critic, and the rumination. We elucidated four reasons for clutter, including:

1. A difficult family
2. Low self-esteem
3. Not being understood
4. Reaction formation, or being the opposite of your organic self

We also looked at five ways to combat it, including:

1. Build up positive figures and tear down negative figures
2. Get to the bottom of the "I am defective" issue and turn flaws to strengths
3. Channel your neurosis
4. Decrease the pressure to achieve
5. Stop ruminating

In the next chapter you will start to build a benevolent inner voice and resilience, so that you can move on to more positive experiences.

FIVE-PART PRESCRIPTION: WEEK TWO

Cluttered Mind to Clear Mind

INSIGHT (10 MINUTES A DAY)

Write about when you experienced the can'ts, shoulds, the irrational critic, and the ruminating self. Pick one prompt or more. Consider the subjects that arose when you addressed your psychological clutter. What might have caused you to defer to these voices, inhibit Creative Capacity, and quell your True Self? Describe how you felt: what happened in your body and mind, how you reacted, how others reacted, how their reaction affected your reaction, what you hoped for, how you were pleased or disappointed, what happened, what did not happen.

Another goal of the journal prompts is to separate you from your inner critic, the scathing, sequestered voice that holds power over you. Your inner critic can inhibit you and make you feel unworthy or incompetent. Go ahead and be unworthy or incompetent on the page at first. Go ahead and fall apart, be angry, be ugly, whatever. Regress. We will pull the pieces together later and make something of them. This portion of the writing might feel as unpleasant as stepping on a tack, but you must work through this to get to the other side.

Things to write about:

- Feeling overburdened
- Being misunderstood by important others
- Habits that have been hard to maintain
- The inner feelings that accompany self-betraying behaviors
- Supposed defects
- Imagined flaws
- Limitations that worry you
- Neuroses or idiosyncrasies you feel you shouldn't have or of which you feel ashamed

MOVEMENT (15 MINUTES A DAY)

As we go along, we will suggest Movement Enhancements—ways to add depth and layers to walking. If you have chosen another form of exercise, try to apply the enhancement plan to that. Change your movement choice if you do not like it, if you do not want to follow the walking plan, or if you are bored, but do not use constant change as a form of resistance—or at least be aware if this resistance arises. Remember, some discomfort and boredom are good. Not committing might feel like freedom, but *happiness is more likely to follow deeper engagement.*

- Increase the distance, quicken the pace, or both.
- Remember a time when you walked, ran, jumped, felt vigorous, clear, uncluttered, light, and free. How was that for you? Think about those good memories as you move.

Or, as before, try swimming, rowing, skating, skiing, spinning, dancing, yoga, weight lifting, running, mowing grass, raking leaves, or shoveling snow.

MIND REST (5 MINUTES A DAY)

Let's move on to Mind Rest and a clear, well-lighted mind. Thoughts from what you've read in this chapter, from Insight writings, from past experiences, or from daily events may bubble up and feel troubling, but you can let them float around without immediate action or response. Let them be. You will survive and even feel better when you realize these thoughts can hang around without doing you in. "Be in the be," as my friend Ann used to say. I always liked the sound of that.

A new suggestion: find a place to sit still that feels particularly sacred, pure, and peaceful to you, such as a place of worship, a natural setting, a yoga or dance studio, your car, or near a pier, a bridge, or a body of water, and just "be in the be."

Or, as before, lie on your bed, do nothing, sit in your favorite spot, putter around, listen to music that you enjoy, or sing anything (sing "Ah" if you don't know the words).

Or meditate. Say a mantra (a repeated phrase—whatever feels right, from a prayer to a rhyme). Avoid all but your own thoughts and let them go where they will.

YOUR OWN TWO HANDS (20 MINUTES A DAY)
New suggestions here include:

- Find some old, previously used pieces of wood and make a sculpture or frame out of them.
- Clean out a closet, cut up an old blanket, and sew a small pillow from pieces of your past to recreate it.
- Throw out clutter and redecorate your space, or use junk and clutter to create something new.

Or do something you did last week:

Art projects: write by hand, paint, draw, cut and paste, photograph, design, decorate, rearrange, play an instrument
Craft projects: sew, knit, sculpt, weld, whittle, carve
Home focus: repair, fix, mend, wash, fold, sweep, collapse and recycle boxes, cook, decorate, set the table, garden

Perhaps you already chose a project, made a commitment, and are moving along with it. Let's check in with how that's going:

- Whatever the project—domestic, artistic, a craft, or something else—how are you doing with it?
- Do you feel like you need more time to engage fully?
- What is it like to use your hands?
- Can you think of other ways to employ a hands-on, do-it-yourself approach throughout your day?

MIND SHIFT (10 MINUTES A DAY)

Look at your Insight Writings. Let us try to reconstruct your inner story by bringing forth another perspective. Here are some prompts to write about:

- When something was absolutely clear to you: a message in a poem, a song, a book, a class, a glance
- Feeling understood by a teacher, friend, or family member
- Habits that you want to maintain or did maintain, or that make you feel good about yourself
- The inner feelings that accompany healthy behaviors
- Traits of which you are proud
- Useful limitations
- Acceptable neuroses
- When the truth was not great but still not that bad, and somehow freeing
- When you felt bountiful, as if you had enough
- How you feel when you clear out and clean up clutter
- What the idea of a clean, well-lighted space or a clear mind suggests to you

How is it going?

We are through the fears and harsh voices. Let's move on to resilience, and a softer, gentler, clearer, stronger inner voice. In the next chapter, we cover creativity and resilience.

5

Creativity and Resilience

MATTERS AT HAND

Everyone has a different psychological tolerance level, but you can increase yours by cultivating healthy and creative responses to challenges. You can become more resilient. By increasing resourcefulness, both psychologically and practically, you can tolerate tempests and endure. Resourcefulness is the essence of both Creative Capacity and resilience. It will help you to remain whole.

The relationship between creativity and resilience is reciprocal. If you hold yourself steady, you can create. If you create, you can contain (gather, bind, and hold) yourself, keep yourself steady. As you know from previous chapters, creative acts can reconstruct and redefine the self. What does not kill you *does* make you stronger, and when you are stronger, you are better able to access your innate talents and abilities. Creative Capacity, True Self, and Creative Self can build resilience, and in turn, resilience can protect them.

In the last two chapters, you confronted inhibitions, identified fears, and examined harsh inner voices. In this chapter your goal is to build inner strength. When you can withstand barbs and abrasions, let them pass, or respond with confidence, you get into less trouble. Preoccupations diminish. This opens you up for more happy moments.

TERMS TO GRASP

Mental Health

Mental health is the capacity to work, to love, and to play. When you are mentally healthy, you feel alive, interested, and able.

Resilient

If you're resilient, you can withstand and bounce back from adversity.

Healing

Healing is the process of reclaiming your wellness and returning to your authentic, vital self.

PEOPLE WHO CHANGED

Lee

Lee Woodruff, writer and wife of ABC correspondent Bob Woodruff, managed a situation that one can barely imagine or fathom. Bob suffered a devastating head injury from a roadside bomb while covering the Iraq war for ABC. His recovery involved more than twenty surgeries. Lee and Bob wrote their bestseller, *In An Instant,* about the experience and how they survived it. Where did she find the resilience to endure this trauma?

Some people develop post-traumatic stress disorder (which includes debilitating anxiety) after a devastating event, and some do not. Two people can be exposed to the same trauma and one will fall apart while the other can maintain equanimity, move on, regroup, and reinvent his life or himself.

I wanted to understand something about Lee's resilience. She told me that writing during the time that Bob was in a coma, when she was not sure if he would ever awaken, kept her going. Recording the experience as she lived through it gave her a sense of order and hope.

What Lee hands us: Writing through trauma is one way to remain resilient.

Lily

Lily, a lithe, petite lawyer from Rhode Island, lost her dad to cancer when she was twenty. She left her high-pressure college to sit by his bedside for two months, and at the end he died while holding her hand. When she was two, her parents had divorced; her mom moved to Europe to marry an old boyfriend, and Lily rarely saw or spoke to her.

Though Lily's dad had nurtured her and guided most of her activities—tennis, violin, and concerts—for much of her life, after he died Lily and her brother, one year younger, were left on their own. They had to get to and from college, clean, shop, buy their clothes, and figure out how to spend vacations. Lily recalls going into a daze at the grocery store, not really knowing what to do.

When I saw Lily, she was moving from boyfriend to boyfriend. She had trouble finding work that she enjoyed. She was haunted, restless, and sometimes listless. We had to figure out how to manage a loss that happened long ago but was still very present in her psyche.

How did Lily build resilience? We rehashed her history, examined her inhibitions and childhood fears, tamed her irrational critic, explored her guilt about not being a good enough daughter (a distortion), and zeroed in on her internalized "inner gleam," a version of self-esteem. I worked with Lily to conjure up the gleam in her dad's eye when he looked down at his young girl. Identifying that gleam, seeing yourself the way a loving parent saw you, and making it a permanent part of the way you experience yourself gives you strength. An internalized sense of the parent's pride fosters the True Self and the Creative Self. Though Lily lost her adoring father, she felt his presence within. He was part of her. He was elegant, smart, and able, and she was proud of that. These were usable truths that ultimately allowed her to regain confidence, to feel more grounded and to make commitments, in work and in love. These commitments, in turn, grounded her and increased her resilience.

What Lily hands us: The loving figure within can help you withstand difficulty and continue to grow.

Kit

Kit, a tall, wavy-haired owner of a health spa, tearfully told me about her childhood. She recalls enduring tense dinners, episodes in which dishes were thrown, and faces that were "red with fury for weeks." Her mom became, as Kit put it, a "religious freak" and attended church daily in their Southern city while Kit spent many hours alone. She did not want to play with other girls.

"Why don't you have any friends?" her dad asked.

Kit knew she did not have friends, but she did not know why. The question hurt. Kit worked with me for a year before she was able to tell me the details of an event in fifth grade that she felt had scarred her. During an art class, she spilled a bottle of red paint on the designer bag of a popular, pretty girl. It was not washable paint. Even if the bag could have been replaced, Kit was not sure her parents could have or would have helped her pay for another.

All the girls in the fifth grade stopped speaking to her, including her only friend. There was nowhere to sit in the lunchroom. She eventually ate alone in the school library for a month straight. This cemented a long-standing sense of alienation.

Kit and I used our treatment sessions to talk about friendships, family, breaches, and betrayals. She developed a sense of her own appeal as a companion and came to understand that past isolation did not mean that she was socially undesirable. After early injurious experience, she had become avoidant, but she actually had natural warmth and the organic ability to relate to others in a meaningful way. Difficult circumstances and the wrong school with some callous kids caused her to put relationships on the back burner for a few years. However, her sensitivity, humor, creative talent, and style make her an appealing person to be around. Her conversation is engaging and interesting. When she was able to expose her True Self with a sense of security, friendships and affection came more easily.

Survival in the early, lonely years depended upon Kit's deep engagement in projects such as tending a garden, picking and using the fresh vegetables she had grown, and playing the guitar. This kept her well and bred concentration and creative skills for later. The experience of feeling like an outsider cuts deep, but it can be used later for creative innovation.

What Kit hands us: Wounds can make you stronger, and being alone or having to go your own way at a young age can foster originality and resilience.

HANDLING FAMILIES

Often we attribute people's lack of resilience or their psychological vulnerabilities to early experience or parental neglect. Sometimes people ask, "Aren't all families dysfunctional?" Many families are dysfunctional in the sense that they spar and fracture at times, and everyone is neglected to some extent because misunderstandings, missed cues, and insensitivities are inevitable.

But a *dysfunctional* family is not the same as a *destructive* family. In a dysfunctional family, members have the capacity to be empathic, kind, and loyal. While quirky actions or thoughtless mistakes disrupt familial harmony, the overall feeling is one of love and caring. In a destructive family, vitriol, envy, competitiveness, and cruelty overshadow any good. The bottom line is that in a family, the good should outweigh the bad.

People who have been traumatized, who do not have natural resilience, and who could most benefit from the use of creative acts to repair the self may, paradoxically, be the most blocked. It is important for them to remove psychological obstacles so that they can be who they need to be. Others are naturally resilient, protect their True Self, and allow their Creative Self to emerge.

When Alton was seven, he was encouraged by older relatives to mount a horse. They then swatted the horse to get it moving, but it bolted and raced toward a barbed-wire fence. The horse stopped abruptly at the fence, and Alton was hurled to the ground. He picked himself up and became determined to become physically stronger and a better rider so that he could never be thrown again.

Turning straw to gold, trauma to triumph, and pain to productivity requires entwining resilience and creativity. The goal of this chapter is to give you some tools to do just that.

> No one has ever written, painted, sculpted, modeled, built, or invented
> except literally to get out of hell.
>
> —ANTONIN ARTAUD, playwright and poet

TEN WAYS TO GET A GRIP ON RESILIENCY

1. Manage Bitterness, Find a Blessing

Some people are given a raw deal. Some are given a great deal but feel as if they have been given a raw deal. If you have been treated in an unfair, unethical, or hurtful manner, you still have to find a way to work around it and rise above it. Once I attended a service for a friend and the speaker said, "Some people are brought into this world to build, others to tear down." You cannot alter the fact that certain people feel whole only if they are destroying something or someone, but you *can* alter your response to them.

Alton has these thoughts on resilience: "I met Sonny two years ago volunteering in the Southwest. Sonny, fifty-five and a severe diabetic, was late for his clinic appointment, and when he finally arrived, his clothes were covered with dust. His pickup had broken down two hours into the six-hour drive to the clinic, and he had hobbled and hitchhiked the rest of the way. I was struck by his friendliness and kind demeanor. He stood up to shake my hand with his left; his right hand was missing, along with his left leg. He had a prosthesis for his arm, but it was dilapidated.

"When I stepped out of the exam room to assist with another patient, Sonny talked to my daughter Chloe, fifteen at the time, and told her of his great life: how he left the reservation at sixteen to go work in Vancouver and spent much of the sixties living in California. He loved Berkeley and the beaches. He lost his arm years ago in a terrible train accident and his leg to diabetes, but that had not kept him from working or driving his truck. When Sonny left, Chloe choked up. 'Dad,' she said, 'he seemed so happy, and he never complained. Can you get him a new leg and arm?'"

What Sonny hands us: If you can rise above what has happened to you, push through the pain, transcend bitterness, work with your disability, and remain engaged, you can find pleasure and contribute to the world.

HOW DOES ONE MAINTAIN RESILIENCE AND CONFIDENCE IN SPITE OF INJURY?

Stephen King, in an interview with Terry Gross on the National Public Radio show *Fresh Air*, was asked how he dealt with being hit by a vehicle driven by, as King put it, a "character out of one of my own novels."

He said he was not bitter; rather, he was "glad to be anywhere." He was able to shift his focus to what he considered his blessings.

A cognitive shift to gratefulness is a great way to manage bitterness and build resiliency. Another way is to distract yourself by looking around you and then gaining perspective. Your difficulties may not feel as bad and you may be less bitter or resentful if you have a deep sense of what others have endured. This also makes you feel less alone, more connected, and more empathic.

Ideas to Grapple With
- Was there a difficult incident that made you feel bitter? Were you justified in feeling so?
- What happened?
- Do you feel as if the other person defeated you? Can you alter your view?
- If you reach out and learn about traumas others have endured, how might that change you or your perspective?

Hold this thought: Finding gladness releases you from victim status and restores some sense of control.

---

2. Use Limitations

Limitations are a blessing. Bounty can be a curse.

—TWYLA THARP, choreographer

Limitations can refer to personal traits, current obstacles, or past injuries. Working with one's limitations makes one more effective at living, more resourceful, and more resilient. Honesty about personal challenges and thinking about what you can do with what you have elevates you. Limitations are useful for creativity.

A client told me about taking a class in which students were given eight paper squares and instructed to make a design. The finite possibilities created surprising and varied results. Her classmates were forced to use the inner life, to invent using limited resources and self-expression, and as a result original thought emerged.

One of my clients who teaches art explained to me that limitation, rules, and discipline are important. It is about what you can't do as much as what you can do. When you have restrictions you focus. The inner self spills into forms and then evolves. It's not about having expectations or preconceived visions but about engaging in the activity and seeing what happens.

Ideas to Grapple With

- Have you ever been resourceful with what you were given?
- When have you sought more but felt better with less?
- Was there ever a task that was utterly absorbing and made you feel invigorated?

Hold this thought: Embracing your limitations can elevate you.

---

3. Go After the Right Things

People covet money, status, and fame, or so they think. Many people consider outpacing their peers a goal. However, trying to compete can be confusing. We might lose the True Self in the process of trying to acquire status. We might mistake an emotional need for a material need. We might sacrifice good conversations for a convertible.

We also covet the capacity to love and to create, but we might not know this consciously. We envy those with these traits and abilities. We think we want a Rolex, but what we really want are intangibles—close relationships, understanding, fun. Those who possess the capacity to love and create can have a good time in spite of the circumstances; they are not caught in the rat race. They make good use of their situation—what they already possess, both tangible and intangible. They are truly more content, or they can find a way to get there. Unconsciously, people envy the goodness and the creativity of others because these qualities are linked with personal empowerment. You can sense it in a person.

Ideas to Grapple With

- What gives you a feeling of empowerment?
- After you acquire items, for how long do you feel satisfied?
- Think of someone who embodies resilience, energy, creativity, inner power. What is he or she like? Does this person inspire you? Do you want to know how he or she manages this?

Hold this thought: Increase resilience by acquiring aptitudes rather than things.

---

4. Be Appropriate in Your Apologies

I knew a girl in college who said "I'm sorry" almost every time she spoke: "I'm sorry, may I have the water?" "I'm sorry, did you say that the Pledge was on top of the dresser?" A friend commented, "It's like she's saying, 'Hi, I'm Sadie, I'm sorry for just existing.'"

If you have this issue, this habit of thinking "I'm all wrong" or "Everything I do is wrong," it is important to understand it. You might want to reread Chapter 4, since this state is usually related to a harsh conscience, an irrational critic, or an overburdened or unaccepting self. Once you know why you feel this way, you can start to change it.

Many people throw out "I'm sorry" in a casual way that does not necessarily mean that they are overapologizing or devaluing the self. They say it out of politeness or habit. Concern arises when your inner self is so obsequious or degraded that you feel entitled to nothing or utterly undeserving, or when your complete lack of entitlement leads to masochistic choices. A little sense of entitlement is good; too much or none is bad. As with anxiety, the in-between is the best place to be.

Remember reaction formation, wherein behavior is the opposite of true feeling? If we look at overapologizing through the lens of reaction formation, we see that rages or disgruntlements can underlie the docility or the apologies. Reaction formation can foster False Self because you are overconcerned about compliance or correctness, and you are not allowing the true, real spontaneous feelings into your being. Were you to do so, you might cower less and stand up more, even if you do not outwardly or fully feel your zealous intensities. The point of reaction formation is to compensate for what feels unacceptable. Too much apologizing does not make you feel whole, does not make others respond to you with respect and enthusiasm (in fact, it can just make others treat you worse; as Dr. Druss once told me, "Masochism elicits sadism"), and does not make good use of your underlying anger. The deeper feelings need to be understood.

Ideas to Grapple With

- When have you overapologized? Why did you? Was it sensible? Might there be another feeling beneath the apologies?
- Did you ever not apologize and wish you had? (It happens.)

Hold this thought: Increase resilience by not being
too obsequious and thus degrading the self.
But never lose humility.

---

5. Rely on Routine

"You have to have a method," my former voice teacher Nancy Assaf used to say. She told me this after I had gone to see another instructor, one who sang beautifully but did not have a coherent teaching method. When you have a predictable routine—for example, a warm-up, scales, and then songs—you teach your body, yourself, to produce what it needs to, when it needs to. When you practice a song many times, it is "in your voice," Nancy said.

My friend Wendy injured her vocal cords from overuse and could not perform her gigs. She lost income and became depressed. She couldn't sing anymore. A laryngologist gave her a series of exercises that both healed her vocal cords and helped her regain her voice, her identity. Once she could resume her old practices and warm-ups, she felt safe, grounded, and comforted. She had not previously been aware of how the routine "held" her.

Clients have spoken about how having a structured schedule in their busy lives—consistency with mealtimes, exercise, nights out—offers a sense of containment and centers them. Method and routine help you muster fortitude, maintain identity, and eventually master your skill or situation. Routine leads to ability and empowerment. It helps you remain resilient in taxing situations.

Dr. Druss taught me that after people lose an arm or are diagnosed with cancer, one of the most stabilizing things they can do is to maintain a routine. Maybe it is a certain walk, a certain room, a piece of music, a crossword puzzle, or a set of tasks. Your routine can carry you.

Ideas to Grapple With

- Do you have a comforting routine?
- Do you have a method for accomplishing certain tasks?
- What does having an order in the way you perform your tasks or organization in your environment do for you?
- When you are forced to be haphazard, how does it affect you?
- Which circumstances tend to lead you into confounding disorganization, and how might you avoid them?

Hold this thought: Increase resilience by falling back on routine or an established method.

6. Express Yourself Nonverbally

Early on in my career I saw an eight-year-old boy named Cole twice a week for six months. He barely spoke. His biological parents had divorced when he was two, his mom had remarried when he was four, and now she had a baby with the new husband. Cole was doing poorly in school, did not get on with his stepfather, and was depressed.

We drew pictures with crayons, and he produced many sharks with sharp, bloodstained teeth chasing after little fish. He liked to play Candy Land. Little by little, he opened up. After Christmas, he told me that he had gone to his stepgrandparents' house and all the children were given a stocking except for him. He told me that it had happened the previous year, too.

How could he survive the sharks? Sometimes there is little we can do to change someone's situation, but we can try to understand their experience and communicate our understanding to them. At the time, I had a supervisor who helped me manage my own upset feelings and the wish to wrest Cole from the jaws of the uncaring. He said that even though giving gifts to patients is not done, giving him the Candy Land game at the end of our time together would be a therapeutic intervention. Cole smiled when I handed it to him.

We did what we could for him by creating a situation where he could communicate his experience through words and pictures. By breaking the rules to address a specific need, by giving him the game, we were able to communicate that he was worthy of a stocking, even if the family did not provide one.

There are times when verbal communication is premature or falls short. Much can be said without saying anything. Through nonverbal interaction, communication occurs and a bond and trust can be created. As with words, nonverbal communication can help you build resilience.

Ideas to Grapple With

- How do you best express yourself nonverbally? Have you ever thought about the way you express, communicate, reveal, or hide?
- Have you ever worried about revealing too much?
- Has a simple object ever had a healing effect on you?

Hold this thought: Expressing your feelings about
your situation, in whatever way, makes it
easier to live with.

---

7. Find the Right Form of Communication

Sometimes we have to search for the proper medium. Cole expressed himself through pictures. If you did not communicate in a form that could be received by the other person, you might feel ineffectual, impotent, weak, or helpless. Being savvy about how to connect or communicate with different kinds of people, having a skill set, gives you a sense of empowerment. If you can relate to and communicate with different people in different ways, you can handle unpredictable interpersonal situations or move through challenging conditions with resilience.

Wendy, my singer friend, told me a folktale about a king who decides to sacrifice children. The people object, but he is not moved. Only when they sing their plea is he able to hear it. As Wendy put it, "The music went straight to the heart, and the heart enlightened the mind." Finding the right form of communication is essential for feeling effective, and the search for the right form both breeds and reflects resilience. One singer told me that she "thinks in songs."

Resilience is bolstered by a layered inner process that links logic and feeling. If your ideas are not fed by emotion or empathy, you might make poor decisions that can weaken your position. Logical thinking that is detached from emotion is excellent for solving some problems, but hunches, instincts, and human feeling are essential for others. If you have many tools to draw upon when you want to communicate, connect to others, or understand a problem, you can proceed with confidence and resilience.

My mother used to say, "It is not about what you have to offer, but what the other can receive." I have found that I can apply this to many situations.

Ideas to Grapple With

- Have you ever felt that song lyrics conveyed your feelings or experience?
- What about music without lyrics—classical or jazz, for example?
- Have you seen a painting or a work of art that transfixed you and moved you to a new place emotionally, aesthetically, or even intellectually?
- Have you ever switched your mode of communication or style of relating and found that it worked—that you could get something good to happen?
- If you are flexible in the way you operate with others, does this give you a sense of resilience as well as effectiveness?

Hold this thought: Increase resilience by trying
different modes of communication to find
the most effective one.

---

8. Build an Assertiveness Track Record

There is a certain kind of depression that comes from passivity. I have noticed this mostly in people who have suffered abuse or neglect. People who have been abused psychologically do not feel that they can have an impact on their surroundings, so they do not even try. Their passivity is automatic and reflexive—not even a conscious choice. It is as if they are numbed or hypnotized in the face of an aggressor.

My client Drew came from a financially stressed, psychologically abusive family in Connecticut. His father was a plumber and his mother saved dollar bills in a dresser drawer with mothballs. Once someone told him that his money "smelled." He had vowed to never have to worry about money again, and ended up working for a bank. Drew had funds but was discriminating in how he spent. One day he went to work in a designer jacket that he had purchased at an outlet store. A coworker, bedecked in a well-fitting suit, somehow saw the receipt and made fun of him. The day of the comment, Drew left work early, downed four beers, and went to bed at seven. This was not an unusual occurrence—he was frequently chided at work, about everything from his vacation choices to his physique.

Finally he stood up for himself. Then he built up a track record of retorts and teasing jests that he initiated. This made him feel less vulnerable. If you teach yourself to take the offensive position or you are prepared to respond when a verbal missile hits, you increase resilience.

Ideas to Grapple With

- Were you ever taunted? Why do you think it happened?
- What did you do about it?
- Did you fantasize later about what you wished you had said? If you did, that's good. Your fantasy readies you should it ever occur again.

Hold this thought: Increase resilience through assertiveness, fantasy, and creative retorts, and prepare to speak up in the moment.

---

9. Choose Wants Over Needs. Pleasure Is Important.

Our friend Marshall enjoyed lounging around in his pool on an inflatable float. Marshall had AIDS, and the disease modified his philosophy about how one should spend one's days. He decided to trump the reality principle with the pleasure principle, meaning that his days of practicality were over.

"There are needs and there are wants, and I choose wants," he said.

Marshall bought Art Deco chairs, antique dolls, bronze statuettes, wooden sculptures, and a painting with a figure that was half angel and half man. He traveled. He threw big catered birthday parties for himself and invited a hundred friends.

"Who is going to throw a better party for me than me?" he said.

Marshall's philosophy is another version of "Life is short, eat dessert first," which is posted on a sign in our local bakery. Psychologically speaking, there is an important idea in the dessert. I once had a client tell me, "When I was young, I used to tell myself that first I have to get all my work done, and then I could play and do what I want. But after a while I realized that I was never going to get all the work done, that I could never catch up, and that it was making me depressed. So I taught myself to just stop and live a little. I was much happier that way, with the little gifts of pleasure."

Having a work ethic is essential for happiness. A work ethic fosters discipline and resilience because it focuses your mind and increases your stamina physically, cognitively, and psychologically. Getting the job done relieves anxiety. But you can take it too far, especially if the workload is monumental, which it is for many people. You want to do what stabilizes, sustains, fosters health, and keeps you safe, but without forays into freedom, risk, and fun, you can shrivel up, break down, or burn out. A little indulgence can go a long way in helping you feel nurtured, energized, worthy, and deserving—balanced. Some people who are too strict with themselves have to learn to live with the loose ends, the unfinished bits, or not getting it all done. While accountability is important, sometimes your mental health is more important than finishing the task on time or honoring an arbitrary, self-imposed, or unrealistic deadline.

Pleasures increase resilience by preserving your well-being.

Ideas to Grapple With

- Do you seek delights easily, or do you feel better when you deprive yourself?
- Are you pleasure averse?
- Do you have secret pleasures? Do you feel guilty about them? (It is good to have some as long as they are legal.)
- How might giving yourself moments of joy foster your resilience?
- Was there someone who enlivened you, whose friendship you enjoyed, or who made you think differently?

Hold this thought: Pleasure protects you
and preserves your resilience.

---

10. Consider Effort Because Leisure Is Overrated

Effort is counterintuitive. Why walk, rake, bake, or study when lounging idly on the sunny dock is so much more enticing?

Because leisure is overrated.

It turns out that people are happier with effort than leisure. We think that what we want is to have nothing to do, no obligations, just days in the sun, but actually idleness can cause depression. Too much laziness or too much of a good thing is bad. Downtime is essential, which is why we advocate Mind Rest, but only action can deliver the satisfaction of hard work, a job completed, a beautiful creation, or an item checked off your list. Action creates energy.

In *Rasselas, Prince of Abissinia*, by Samuel Johnson, the prince is unhappy because all needs are gratified in his "Happy Valley." He feels no desire or motivation. He is bored with beauty and perfection. Observing some worldly problems makes him happier because he gains compassion and perspective.

I believe it was Freud who said, "Happiness depends on contrast."

My friends Sam and Courtney take effortful camping trips, where they have to string up pails of food, set up tents with stakes, fetch water from streams, and build fires. At first I found it hard to wrap my mind around their vacations. I just did not see the point of vacationing with bears and a sledgehammer, but there is something about cunning, risk, calculation, and making your way outdoors that brings a satisfaction a stay at the Four Seasons cannot.

Ideas to Grapple With

- When has pleasure from effort surprised you?
- Have you ever had a vacation that was strenuous but joyful?
- Can you tax yourself and create an excellent, peace-producing exhaustion?

Hold this thought: Increase resilience by choosing
the harder path, at least sometimes.

CONCLUSION

Both creativity and resilience are about being resourceful and adaptable under duress. True Self, Creative Self, and Creative Capacity are assisted by resilience. If you can teach yourself to be resilient, you will be less inclined to collapse and more able to create. You want to get your inner life in order so that when you take action, as you will in the next chapters, the actions lead to peak moments, to happiness.

SUMMARY

We reviewed ten ways to build resilience, including:

- Managing bitterness
- Using limitations
- Focusing on trait development instead of material acquisition
- Apologizing appropriately
- Maintaining routine
- Expressing feelings
- Communicating effectively
- Speaking up
- Prioritizing pleasure
- Embracing effort

While we can be deeply troubled by traumatic events, we do not have to be destroyed by them. We cannot control all events or how others respond but we can triumph within.

FIVE-PART PRESCRIPTION: WEEK THREE

Injured Self to Resilient Self

INSIGHT (10–20 MINUTES A DAY)

Let us explore some injurious experiences. Writing about trauma is hard but healing, so you might want to take some time with this. Once a client told me that when she writes, she feels she is wallowing, complaining, and getting stuck in the negative. It does not feel good. Explore the negatives, but know that you can work yourself out of the injured position. If the writing becomes ruminative or too full of complaint, thereby dragging you down, change topics or go to Movement.

Here are your prompts. Do not edit. Write freely with robust inner responses and with descriptive detail. Record physical sensations.

Write about when you experienced:

- Loss
- Trauma
- Unfairness or a raw deal
- Bitterness
- Humiliation
- Overapologizing
- Waiting for an answer
- A big mistake, poor judgment, or a bad decision, and your inner response
- Regret
- Not speaking up or poor communication
- Disappointment
- Unrequited love or wishes
- Friends who did not like you as much as you liked them
- Being left out

MOVEMENT (15–30 MINUTES A DAY)

Before we offer the Movement Enhancement, let us think about a way to express resilience with our bodies: our posture. Persons with good posture are appealing, right? A colleague worked with some dancers and said afterward, "The carriage, the carriage!" The erect spine is also a physical expression of self-reliance. You hold yourself up.

Alton has some comments on posture: "It would be ideal if we could all walk and stand like ballet dancers or marines, but mental and physical exhaustion take a toll on our spines. We slump, sag, and feel self-conscious about it. Good posture conveys self-confidence and self-confidence attracts. Posture is something you have to work at, because slouching is natural.

"My mother, Arlene, is constantly remonstrating my father: 'Stand up straight, dear.' Sometimes he listens.

"Good posture can be achieved through neck, shoulder, and back conditioning exercises. Strengthen your core, and self-esteem and confidence will follow. The mental spine and the physical spine reinforce each other. Research studies indicate that physical stamina augments psychological resilience."

Some suggestions for Movement Enhancement: Continue to walk with increased pace, distance, or both. Try to go a few blocks or several minutes farther (five, ten, whatever you can). Stand taller. Make sure that you are standing up straight, that your spine is erect and your shoulders are back. If you are doing some other form of Movement (e.g., a rowing machine, an elliptical trainer, sitting on your John Deere riding mower), try to do it with proper alignment and physical grace. Express your pride and self-esteem in the way you carry yourself. There is beauty in self-confidence and an upright spine.

Or, as before, try swimming, rowing, skating, skiing, spinning, dancing, yoga, weight lifting, running, mowing grass, raking leaves, or shoveling snow.

MIND REST (5–10 MINUTES A DAY)

The effect in sickness of beautiful objects, of variety of objects and especially of brilliancy of color is hardly at all appreciated. . . . [They are] actual means of recovery.

—FLORENCE NIGHTINGALE, nurse

An object with sentimental value can comfort, calm, hold you up, or hold you together. When you hold it, you might be able to conjure up a better time or a positive memory. My client Thomas found that looking at a certain photograph helped him regain some positive past memories and feel whole.

My client Serena has a little embossed silver makeup compact that came in a black velvet pouch. Every time she sees this silver disc sitting in the second drawer of her bathroom vanity, it makes her happy. She has had anxiety in her life about not feeling feminine enough, and she says that just having this compact makes her feel a little more feminine. For her, this very specific item selection has a healing capacity.

Our new suggestion this week is to find some objects that are important to you, objects that bring back memories of a loved one or a cherished time. Feel the comfort they bring you—or even the sadness they bring, because sadness from missing someone is okay. We need to grieve; although we might fear the feeling, letting it surface ultimately brings relief.

Reread a poem or a cherished childhood book. Sing an old song. Let a time when you were well cared for float through your mind.

Or, as before, lie on your bed, do nothing, putter around, sit in your favorite spot, listen to music that you enjoy, sing anything (sing "Ah" if you don't know the words).

Or meditate. Say a mantra (a repeated phrase—whatever feels right, from a prayer to a rhyme). Avoid all but your own thoughts and let them go where they will.

YOUR OWN TWO HANDS (20–40 MINUTES A DAY)

What can you build from fragments? How can you make a new whole? Find scraps, broken pieces, or discarded objects, and see what you can do to rebuild and fashion something new. Alton's dad, Jim, says, "I love to take something broken and see what I can do with it."

Or, as before:

Art projects: write by hand, paint, draw, cut and paste, photo-graph, design, decorate, rearrange, play an instrument
Craft projects: sew, knit, sculpt, weld, whittle, carve
Home focus: repair, fix, mend, wash, fold, sweep, collapse and recycle boxes, cook, decorate, set the table, garden

Check in:

- Are you continuing with your project?
- How is it going?
- Are you feeling inclined to maintain? To switch?
- What thoughts come to you with rote activity? With concentrated effort?

MIND SHIFT (10–20 MINUTES A DAY)

Look at your Insight writings. Let us try to reconstruct the inner story by bringing forth another perspective. In the therapy field, there are about one hundred articles written on the negative for every one on the positive. It is important not to lose sight of the positive, because the positive is the point. We work through the negative so that we can make things better.

Here are some prompts to write about:

- Synthesis or reconstruction, or something you made that made you happy
- People who were good to you
- Refreshing discoveries
- Survival techniques, resourcefulness
- Ways of triumphing or speaking up
- What is it about you that lets you know what to do or say or how to manage?
- Ways you communicate well or are flexible in your method
- Acceptance and faith
- Favorite things or places

- Comforting routines
- Useful experiences of verbal or nonverbal self-expression
- Wants over needs
- Secret pleasures
- Times you put play before work and it was a sound choice

Good job.
We are ready for some concrete action now.

6

Creativity, Community, and Your Own Two Hands

Man was given the hand because he was given spirit.

—Attributed to ARISTOTLE

MATTERS AT HAND

You live through your hands. You earn your living and your self-respect with your hands. With your hands you nurture, express, emote, tend, touch, clean, connect, construct, and create. You make contact with your community and your world with your hands.

While we cover your hands throughout this book as part of the 5PP, we are going to take a deeper, broader look in this chapter and link the complexities of hand use to the benefits of community involvement. Why? Because science has shown that *purposeful hand use is associated with elevated mood* and that community involvement makes people happier. Combine the two in a way that makes sense to you, and you have taken steps to protect against loneliness, malaise, and mild depression. You have found a do-it-yourself antidote.

In the first five chapters, we examined your private psychological life. You expressed feelings, recalled events, made links between your past and your present, explored different perspectives, and attempted an inner overhaul. Now you can start looking outward and interacting with the world, as that will be helpful for you. Your hands, because they are tools for the expression of your mind and a way to be in contact with others, are a great medium for doing so.

Your hands are the most fundamental source of your autonomy. Probably nothing is more familiar to you than the back of your hand. But it is easy to forget your hands—their elegance, utility, intricacy, and potential—until they are injured or begin to fail you. Many people embrace mind-body approaches for wellness but somehow forget about their hands.

Alton treats patients who lose shoulder, elbow, or hand function for a brief or longer time due to injury. Many patients are astonished at how difficult their daily lives become with only one good hand or arm, especially if their dominant hand is involved. Unable to work, create, lift weights, hoist a sail, or lift a baby, some patients become dejected. During the recovery period, they gain a whole new appreciation for their bimanual capacities. Alton often hears comments such as "I'm right-handed, and I never thought I could do so much with my left hand!" It is always gratifying and a relief when patients report later with a smile that they could open a can of soup with their nondominant hand, heat it, and serve it.

While we are not trying to scare you into newfound gratefulness for your hands, we do want you to look at them in a new way.

One of our missions with the Creativity Cure is to reintroduce you to your hands. The goals of this chapter are:

- To show how important your hands are for mental health and well-being
- To show how your hands can facilitate more fulfilling contact with your community
- To link your creativity, your hands, your community, and your happiness

HANDS, HISTORY, CREATIVITY, AND
ANATOMICAL INTENT

Two and a half million years ago, our forebears were overwhelmingly concerned with survival. Probably the last thing they thought about was their creative potential. As they began to make better tools, to innovate out of necessity, and to work together, their brains grew, they gained better control of their environment, and they strengthened their communities. Their priorities also shifted. Now safe, secure, and entwined with one another, they became concerned about design, aesthetics, and beauty in their objects and homes.

Part of what facilitated their creative development was mutual cooperation and the sharing of ideas, tools, space, and materials. According to Professor Richard Sennett, author of *The Craftsman*, the first artists were craft workers, and many craft workers today remain artists; their work is imbued with originality, self-expression, and even a statement about their culture, community, or period of history. Craft workers derive joy from a unique symbiosis between their minds and their hands. Their work also ties them to a like-minded community, which supports a solid identity and fulfills the need to belong.

According to Dr. Abraham Maslow—father of humanistic psychology, author of *A Theory of Human Motivation*, the originator of the concept of the hierarchy of needs, and a man who was interested in stressing the positives as we move through life—the need to belong is fundamental. Even those who seem dismissive of group involvement are actually thrilled when they find out that they are wanted and welcome. Finding a community that reflects your creative interests or shares your mission will help you solidify your identity and offer a sense of belonging. Your hands might lead you to a place that's just right, with people who make sense to you.

But while you may or may not have hobbies that employ your hands, most of us no longer directly make physical things out of necessity, and therein may lie a source of our unhappiness. As we said earlier, when you use your hands to overcome pressing or practical problems, there is a great sense of accomplishment and joy.

Let's address the matter of simple hand use first, and then consider the advantages of hand use in a community context. Both the conscious use of your hands and community contribution can provide meaning and therefore contentment, so the combination can be powerful.

It is by having hands that man is the most intelligent of animals.

—ANAXAGORAS, philosopher

With the rise of technology and the conversion of our workforce from makers to data enterers, we use our hands less for meaningful activities. This has thrown us out of alignment with our nature, our anatomical intent. Making and using tools defined the rise of humankind and its evolving, enlarging brain, according to neurophysiologist and Nobel Prize winner John Eccles, author of *Evolution of the Brain: Creation of the Self*. Invention of these implements was an important means of self-expression, creative engagement, and fulfillment.

We have arrived at a point in human society where manufacturing by hand is almost unnecessary from a *practical* point of view but necessary from a *psychological* perspective. Conveniences deprive us of processes that elevate mood and foster internal well-being. It no longer takes a village or a layered and absorbing experience that involves both brain and hand to satisfy a practical need—but you might need that village and that experience to fulfill your need for a sense of well-being, to feed your mind, and to feel truly connected.

If you are consistently using your hands in meaningful ways, you are stimulating one of the largest portions of the somatosensory and motor cortex of the brain, more than other parts of your body do. Using your hands to make things is a way of exercising your brain! Dr. Frank Wilson, a neurologist and hand expert, argues that any theory of human intelligence must account for the hand-brain interface. Thus using your hands is good for your mind as well as for your productivity.

Antigone Sharris, an electronics instructor at Triton College, a two-year public school, who came up with the idea for a Gadget Camp for girls, said in an interview with Mokoto Rich of the *New York*

Times, "Not letting your children learn the hands-on component of the theory of science is killing us as a nation. You have to stop giving kids books and start giving them tools." These girls are learning to be skilled workers to fill a need in manufacturing and thus be primed for a growing demand in the job market. But hand use is not just about employment or stimulating the brain in a mind-body interface.

There are physiological reasons for making instead of buying. An absence of manual effort can lead to weakened limbs and ailments such as overuse strain and repetitive stress injury. When you shovel, lift, scour, and scrub, you keep your arms and hands in shape, which is more important than you might think. In an article for the *New York Times,* Alton wrote that construction workers, house painters, furniture makers, or bakers rarely have hand overuse ailments because their work keeps their hands and arms conditioned.

The underused limb is vulnerable to injury. Repetitive stress injury often results from too much typing with poor position or ergonomics. (It's best to have your wrists in a neutral position, neither extended nor flexed, while tapping the keys.) In addition, mental stress is often expressed through the hands—you grip a pen, computer mouse, or steering wheel tightly when you are worried.

Use of the hands for heaving and lifting as well for creative pursuits can release psychological stress, prevent physical injury, and foster self-sufficiency. Alton suggests that patients (and anyone else who will listen—such as his family, maybe) carry groceries, sweep garages, build things, do pushups, pump gas, plant herbs, and dig weeds for a sound mind and fully exercised anatomy. Sometimes the technologies and services we employ to elevate us can compromise our conditioning, so we have to be mindful.

HANDS AND MOOD

If we stop using our hands in the way they were meant to be used—to construct, create, repair, stir, mix, and manipulate—we churn within and become depressed. Dr. Kelly Lambert, a neuroscientist and psychologist, discovered decreased hand use is linked to depression and that meaningful handwork boosts mood. What does "meaningful" mean in this context? It means that the activity is associated with a project or person that you care about, from building bookshelves to mending pajamas. Crafts, because they combine hand use, self-expression, creativity, and often community, are a common but underutilized antidote to malaise, according to Nancy Monson, author of *Craft to Heal: Soothing Your Soul with Sewing, Painting and Other Pastimes.*

Studies indicate that handwork such as sewing, knitting, or improvising on an instrument lowers stress, decreases anxiety, and elevates mood. Often these activities take place in the company of others, so the link between purposeful hands and the presence of others may be operating in a relevant way.

Depression is essentially nonexistent among two interesting groups, the Amish in the United States and the Kaluli people of New Guinea. The Amish enjoy a strong community feeling but also manufacture by hand most of what they need. The Kaluli are modern-day hunter-gatherers and gardeners and use their hands continually. What makes both of these groups distinctive is they do *not* suffer from depression, while data show that rates of depression throughout the industrialized world have increased tenfold over the last two generations alone. The decrease in meaningful hand use cannot be discounted as a cause.

Over the last few years especially, our clients, patients, and friends have reported, with a certain surprise and spontaneity, that craft work, repairs, folding, clearing, cleaning, gardening, and cooking provide solace. Small actions, even ten minutes spent in what might appear to be drudgery, often assuage a rattled self. My client Jason feels tranquil when he folds clothes. My client Calvin says it calms him to wipe the counters in his biology lab. My client Jessica was recently excited by a do-it-yourself repair she completed with a toolbox she had not touched in ten years; her girlfriend helped her hold parts in place. With or without company, your hands can offer you more than you might realize.

Many activities that involve the hands are utilitarian and rote, such as scrubbing an alloy wheel or washing dishes. Repetitive hand use relaxes or frees the mind, as random but rich thoughts surface when our hands are occupied thus. Walking or running in a rhythmic way leads us to a higher place as well, as this exertion loosens up thoughts. But hands are special because they facilitate the execution of all that happens—emotionally, psychologically, intellectually—within us.

In this chapter we will explore ways that handwork and community can intersect and provide you with some avenues for satisfaction. In a later chapter, we will discuss nurturing relationships with important individuals in your life. While a deep intimacy can be crucial for your contentment, community is less about soul mates and more about friends and being part of a group, which can fulfill you in a different way. Sometimes you might just want to gather with a number of pleasant, interesting, like-minded people and use your mind, hands, and passion to make something meaningful or creative happen together.

TERMS TO GRASP

Of course you're familiar with some of these terms already, but for the sake of focusing on them anew, we're highlighting them anyway.

Meaningful

Having meaning, function or purpose, sense, or significance

Mind

The element of a person that enables him or her to be aware of the world and his or her experiences

Direct Attention

Cognitive focus on a specific subject

Indirect Attention

Free-floating, unfocused awareness or attention

Self-Direction

Activity instigated from within

THE CREATIVITY CURE

PEOPLE WHO CHANGED

Jill

Jill is a sturdy, determined, doe-eyed, auburn-haired young woman from upstate New York with a truck driver father and a waitress mother. Her parents worked nights, slept days, and were not home for her after school. Jill ate out of cans, "never saw a vegetable," and spent weekends discarding piles of papers, magazines, and stained Tupperware to neaten the home. The blue shag wall-to-wall carpet would have accumulated crumbs and gum wrappers had she not vacuumed regularly. Order and cleanliness calmed her.

Knitting and baking cookies on weekends kept Jill grounded. When she kept her hands busy, her mind floated to a happier place. Doctoring recipes—adding toffee chips to chocolate chunk cookies, or jam to sugar cookies—was pleasurable and relaxing. She found solace in the feel of the dough and the aroma of freshly baked desserts. She looked forward to touching yarn, contemplating colors, and chatting with the other knitters at the local knitting store. The sense of community was comforting. Knitting required concentration, and the steady rhythm of engagement made her feel calm. A beloved art teacher once showed Jill how to knit a stocking hat with a pom-pom. Handcrafted vintage wool hats, carefully chosen, now hang as decorations on a wall in her living room.

Jill's fingernails are usually manicured, and she carries a shiny bag with a multicolored modern print design. Though she works long hours at a data entry job, she knits when she can, sometimes at a city store where she can find companions, and cooks on the weekends for her friends. She has moved from opening cans to steaming fresh vegetables.

What Jill hands us: A five-sense experience, led by handwork, creates an elevated mental state. Handwork is grounding and uplifting, especially in a communal setting.

144

Chris

Born into a wealthy, blue-blooded family, our friend Chris said, "I was supposed to be a 'literary scholar,' but I needed to work with my hands." Chris excelled in academia, but he felt restless and unsatisfied. He took a job at a newspaper and in the evenings pored over woodworking magazines. He had always been entranced by the warmth and grain of wood; it felt "alive" to him.

When Chris was twelve, his six-year-old sister died of leukemia. The sister liked to draw and their mother had allowed her to use a wall of her room for her crayon creations. Once she and Chris had spent a happy afternoon doing a whole section of their own handprints across the wall using finger paint. On the weekends, the children spent time with their grandfather. They built a tree house with him and Chris learned how to use drills and saws, make accurate measurements, and create right angles. Chris recalls his sister spilling a can of wood stain and how his grandfather took out the turpentine to clean it off of her hands with a soft rag. He wasn't mad.

After he grew up and had four boys of his own, Chris went out one day and purchased big rolls of white paper. He spread it across the floor and then had the boys make "wallpaper" out of it by using their handprints, as he had done with his sister. He had the boys help him refurbish the basement to make a playroom. He did the design and carpentry himself.

Though Chris sometimes has a paint-spattered hand, he has an easy smile and a hearty handshake.

What Chris hands us: Do-it-yourself projects can be a way of repairing the self, dealing with the past, and creating at the same time.

WHY SHOULD YOU DO IT YOURSELF?

Let's clarify the benefits of do-it-yourself endeavors. To optimize your feeling of wellness, you need to use your hands in meaningful ways. When things feel out of control, going back to the basics—whether it involves following a routine, tilling the earth, or hands-on activities—can create comfort. Do-it-yourselfers have always enjoyed a special satisfaction. Their work promotes self-sufficiency, independence, self-esteem, and an option for greater involvement in community, which brings its own rewards. You can get others to help you bring something into being.

Says Alton: "When I was a kid growing up in the country, my father was the working foreman, and my mother, sister, and I were the workers. We built our barn, our tool shed, our barbecue pit, and a grass tennis court; we did the framing and poured the concrete for our sidewalks; we dug the post holes and built a fence around a ten-acre section of land; we took apart and repaired our lawnmower engines, did our own car tune-ups, grew most of our own vegetables, and did all the repairs on our home. Often my friends who lived in subdivisions would come over and, rather than wanting to play ball or Monopoly or watch television, they would ask to help me mow the grass with the tractor or pick vegetables."

Do-it-yourself endeavors are liberating. Even if you are not inclined to build things from the ground up, you can still derive pleasure from tending to your personal setting with an imaginative, careful eye. There is pleasure in simple improvement and fine detail, such as reconditioning a leather purse, fixing a broken shelf, or adding the finishing touches to a dish for someone else or for yourself. Making something look shiny or newly presentable can be cheering and economical.

Perhaps you have the inclination to make little leaves out of pie crust to garnish your Thanksgiving pumpkin pie, like my friend Betsy, a hardworking anesthesiologist.

"What's that all about, Betsy? Making all those leaves—it takes so much time, and you don't have any," I said.

"I just love Thanksgiving," she said.

Mark Frauenfelder, editor in chief of *Make* magazine, is helping to make people more aware of the benefits of hand use, creativity, and do-it-yourself endeavors. In 2005, *Make* magazine organized the first Maker Faire do-it-yourself expo, and *twenty thousand* people came; the same event drew seventy-five thousand in 2009. Other Maker Faires are springing up around the country, just as knitting shops, sewing centers, and teaching workshops are, too. Doing handwork in the company of others satisfies a psychological and physical craving as well as serving a practical purpose, and our communities are responding to the need.

"With our strengths and our minds and spirit, we gather, we form, and we fashion: makers and shapers and put-it-togetherers," says a 1961 Chevrolet advertisement cited in an article by *New York Times* writer Anand Giridharadas. Columnist Thomas L. Friedman and Johns Hopkins professor Michael Mandelbaum suggest that our economic health depends on returning to being the creators and innovators we once were.

Ideas to Grapple With

- Did you ever make something with your hands and find the process rejuvenating?
- How much time do you spend on your computer or smartphone every day?
- What if you spent less time with these devices and did something else?
- What might you do with your hands? With others? With others present, but doing your own thing?

Hold this thought: Hand use balances our digital, technology-focused lives and gives our instincts an outlet.

HANDS IN THE DIRT: GARDENING, COMMUNITY, AND CONTENTMENT

Using your hands to tend to a landscape can benefit your community or help you become part of one. Research has indicated that gardening also enriches your physical, psychological, and spiritual health. Gardening enhances self-esteem, pride, confidence, personal satisfaction, and efficacy. If you garden, you may be more equipped to accomplish other things.

The simple, intuitive, achievable tasks involved in gardening bring your hands into intimate contact with the earth, a contact that has healing power. Professor Dianne Relf of Virginia Tech University, who has studied horticultural therapy, reports in a study on therapeutic gardening that "40% of Americans find that being around plants makes them feel more relaxed." Even caring for a plant can be a treatment for depression in the elderly. Recently my friend Cate told me that weeding makes her happy—and that she was tempted to yank some weeds from between the stone slabs of my patio.

The Edible Schoolyard, a program founded by chef Alice Waters, involves children growing their own food as part of their curriculum. This program has bolstered nutrition, boosted ability, and created hope in communities where some children had never touched a fresh pepper or orange.

The presence of hope in the psyche is a fundamental component of happiness. Gardening is a hopeful act: you plant a seed with the hope that it will grow into a full entity. Seeing the positive, tangible results of something we have done makes us feel that we are effective and that who we are and what we think and do matters. It makes us feel special.

My father, who loved to plant pansies, crocuses, and tomatoes, once said to me when I was tense, "Put your hands in the dirt; just put your hands in the dirt."

Ideas to Grapple With

• Have you put your hands in dirt to garden or for another reason?

- What happens to the flow of your thoughts when you till, hoe, or plant?
- Have you thought about having a garden or plants but not acted? Why? Can you?
- If you do garden now, why is it important to you? What do you get out of it?

Hold this thought: Gardening has therapeutic benefits.

LINKING HAND USE AND COMMUNITY FOR HAPPINESS

When my client Charles was a child, his family would visit his grandmother. One of her unused bedrooms had four twin beds, each with a large stack of quilts that his grandmother had made by hand. She explained to him that quilting was a leisure activity where several friends would sit around and talk and laugh while designing and sewing. Working with their hands in the presence of others facilitated intimacy among the crafters. They shared stories, patterns, problems, patches, thimbles, and threads. Research suggests that such groups are good for well-being. One study showed that diminished depression is a fringe benefit of this type of community and group involvement.

My client Clyde struggled with depression for decades. Clyde was an avid fly fisherman. He joined a local fly-fishing club that met weekly to hand-tie flies and talk trout. Clyde always became animated when speaking about his fly-fishing club; it seemed to relieve his sadness. He was especially excited when his nephew gave him a handmade bamboo fly rod and he was able to share it with his group.

Since 2000, fellows of the American Academy of Orthopedic Surgeons, Alton's colleagues, have come together each year to build a playground in a needy area in the city in which they hold their annual meeting. Habitat for Humanity is a community-focused organization of volunteers who work together to build homes for families in need. These hand-inspired endeavors provide for receivers and givers alike.

A trusted and loyal community even appears to increase wealth for the individuals within it, according to Francis Fukuyama, political scientist, senior fellow at Stanford University, and author of *Trust: The Social Virtues and the Creation of Prosperity.*

Thus, you may want to consider both joining groups and undertaking hand action in the interest of finding happy moments, new friends, and a feeling of purpose.

LONELINESS, FEELING LOW, AND COMMUNITY

While you might be tempted to withdraw and avoid, especially if you feel downhearted, the awareness that a shared activity assuages loneliness might motivate you to plant yourself in a community endeavor. If you can overcome a brief breath of the unfamiliar, community engagement can distract your mind, shift your mood, and foster friendship.

One study of social life in America showed that half of all adults lack even a single close friend on whom they can depend. Over the years in my practice, I have learned that many people feel alone and ashamed of their loneliness. One simple but underused solution to loneliness is community connections. A chat with the clerk at the post office, sharing greetings and news when you meet a neighbor on the sidewalk, or talking to the café owner who's pouring your coffee can make you feel less lonely. This small step might pave the way to a better situation for you.

In a recent study reported by Michael B. Sauter and colleagues, Denmark ranked number one in the happiness arena. There is a strong sense of community among the Danish people, 97 percent of whom reported being able to rely on someone else besides a family member.

I once had a client who was an only child raised by a single mom who worked alone in an office. When he was sick, he went to the office with her. He told me that the worst thing about his childhood was the loneliness.

Here are some ways to handle loneliness:

- Volunteer for an hour. This helps others and gives you a sense of belonging and may inspire you to do more.
- Get involved in a community cultural organization.
- Chat with the people at the local farmer's market, coffee shop, or post office. It can lead to something more.
- Even if it is tempting to stay in, go out. One client told me that she went to an American movie alone in a foreign country and sobbed during a sad scene. The boy sitting next to her stopped her afterward and asked her to meet him the next day at a café. She made a new friend.
- Join a self-help group that can support you as you cope with a situation, an illness, or a psychological challenge.

There are many places where you can engage in activities that include both community and working with your hands:

- Pottery studios
- Knitting stores
- Film clubs
- Sculpture classes
- Community gardens
- Organic farming co-ops
- Sewing circles
- Shared artist spaces
- Construction or wood workshops
- Library events
- School projects

A word about virtual communities. If you can't find a place, space, or group in your town that provides comfort but you have an interest, mission, or ideology, you might find a community on the Internet. We hope that you will join the Creativity Cure community. Research from New York University and Michigan State University suggests that online communities can be a great way to connect with like-minded others who share your interests, especially if there aren't too many in your immediate vicinity. In Chapter 9 we will help you find ways to have a few in-the-flesh friends, too.

A FEW MORE WAYS TO THINK ABOUT YOUR HANDS

1. Let Your Hands Do the Talking: Nonverbal Expression

Psychotherapy (sometimes also known as the "talking cure") has long been a powerful form of rehabilitation. Insight, expression, and making past and present connections can relieve psychological burdens. Verbalization is healing in individual therapy or in groups.

When I was in fourth grade, a boy in my class lost his father in a car accident. He was crossing a street in a foreign country, was struck by a car, and was instantly killed. A few days later, the boy came back to school wearing a Harvard T-shirt. As we were standing on line to leave, our teacher asked him, "Is that where Daddy went to school?" The boy's head was down, but he suddenly lifted it up and nodded. Bringing it into the open seemed to help. Each day after that the teacher sat and talked with him for a few minutes while the rest of us ran on the playground. I hope wherever he is, he is okay.

In our current culture, for some there may be too much verbalization. Talking can become a defense against feeling, a way of not truly grappling with the problem.

Sometimes by talking we avoid experiencing. Talk can be a way to resist feeling fears, anxieties, disappointments, or desires. If talk is not helping, using our hands via crafts or other forms of handwork can be a way into the deeper self, the true experience. Musicians that Alton treats express themselves through their instruments. Dancers communicate with their hands as well as their bodies. Recently I saw a Parsons Dance piece called "Hand Dance" in which the dancers' faces and bodies were blacked out and only their hands were visible.

For some, physical expression is a finer, safer mode. Art therapy, music therapy, and occupational therapy are solid treatments that often take place in group settings, thus blending handwork and community. I met an Ecuadorian woman who told me that her mom, who was still in Ecuador, had become depressed. She was sent to a community treatment setting where working with clay was part of the treatment. "The feelings came out of the soul, through the hands, and into the work," she told me. After two months of this group treatment, her mother was better. The story reminded my client of her childhood, when she and her classmates were given scraps of material in school and instructed to make something. I could see the life in her face when she told the story. She used her hands and leaned toward me as she spoke.

A client once told me that in her previous analysis she had never missed a session and was rarely late. She went four days per week for many years. She said, "One day I was feeling happy. I was working on wallpapering my closet with a couple of my friends. I just couldn't stop even though I felt guilty about being late. When I went to my session, my therapist said, 'You missed part of your session for a reason like that?'"

While it can be important for the sake of your health to attend your sessions if you are in therapy, it is also true that if working with your hands and with other people helps you feel freer, stronger, more independent, and better able to create joy in your life, you may not need the therapy sessions as much. If you are connected to a few people through a shared activity, it can help with your mental health.

Dr. Druss told me, "When a patient cancels because they are doing something very engaging"—such as laying tile on a kitchen floor, as my client Kelly did one day—"it is a sign of progress."

Ideas to Grapple With

- Has it ever been easier to do than to talk?
- Might it be better to express your self in a nonverbal way, to make something?
- Can you become completely absorbed in a project and find that your state of mind changes even if you have not talked with anyone about a problem you might be having?
- What kinds of experiences have you had quietly working alongside others? Do you feel comforted or crowded?

Hold this thought: Hand use and creative engagement can provide solace or a solution that verbalization may not. It may offer a way to be part of a team or group.

---

2. Meaningful Handwork and Self-Direction

Which types of handwork are meaningful to you and which are not? How do you decide? This is an individual matter. Ask yourself which home improvements, hobbies, or professional tasks give you a sense of mastery and pleasure and why. Consider which endeavors produce an outcome or product that enhances your life or the life of your loved ones. When you think about it, you might realize that they have a component of self-direction.

Activities that allow for self-direction as opposed to following orders are excellent for True Self and Creative Capacity. Self-direction is when you go with your feeling, instinct, or intuition. It is not following the stated path but rather forging your own. It involves a bit of risk. If you improvise when you cook by experimenting with your own combination of ingredients, play an instrument by making up a riff, or even take a walk and deviate from your usual route, you are employing self-direction. You may not always be able to create a situation in which you can be self-directed, but do it when you can, because as we said, it helps with clarity, identity, self-knowledge, confidence, and joy. As we said earlier, jazz musicians felt most content when they improvised.

My client Catarina came from a family of architects and said that all her parents did on the weekends was improve their house. They repainted radiators and refurbished shelves. They built rock walls, dug trenches, cut hedges, and planted. Bushes and flowers layered in color and height made their day. They reveled in self-direction.

Ideas to Grapple With

- What activities do you engage in that involve self-direction and creativity?
- Do you struggle with starting tasks or projects that are self-directed and have unclear guidelines?
- Might you feel best guiding yourself? Might you feel best having guidance? A mix?

Hold this thought: Self-directed endeavors can bring great joy. And perhaps your community can benefit from your innovations.

---

3. Turn the Mundane into the Magical

Which mundane activities have meaning for you? Only you can decide that. If picking up your kids' clothes makes you feel good because you are tending to, beautifying, and organizing their lives, that is great. When you think about it, there is a lofty aspect to this type of caretaking. Once I was bemoaning some mundane tasks I had to perform on behalf of a sick relative when I was pressed for time. My friend Catherine touched my hand, looked me in the eye, and said, "You are doing God's work." It made me feel so much better.

As my client George, a stay-at-home dad, said, "There's cooking and there's throwing a meal on the table." When you toss a meal in the microwave, it is efficient, but you might feel debilitated by another act of drudgery. And while a prolonged session in the kitchen may fill your sink with pots, it may also fill your mind with interesting associations, daydreams, memories, or ideas. (Paradoxically, too, scrubbing the pots can put you in a better mood, especially if what you prepared was an offering for others.) When you mix and mash, stir and pour, scrub and rinse, you have used your hands in multiple ways. You have given your mind a chance to wander in the presence of flowing water, even if it comes from a faucet.

My friend Mary Anne lit candles, placed flowers, played Chopin, and used cloth napkins every night for the family dinners she made from scratch. This was after taking the bus all the way across to the West Side and back for the cuts of meat she wanted. I was intrigued that she could not get what she was looking for closer to home, but maybe the effort involved was the point—maybe the traveling and the careful preparation made her feel purposeful and pleased.

My friend Dylan taught himself to be a fine chef by studying cookbooks, frequenting ethnic markets, and asking the shopkeepers about how to use various spices. He threw great dinner parties once a month for friends and people in the community whom he wanted to get to know. He does sometimes turn the sports channel on in the kitchen while he is sautéing the shrimp.

Ideas to Grapple With

- What happens when you have to perform tedious or mundane tasks?
- In what ways can you make them pleasurable?
- How does creating something for others—family, friends, or neighbors—affect the process?

Hold this thought: Find grace in the mundane.
Invite some people you would like to get to know
to share in what you produce.

---

4. Penmanship

Research has shown that penmanship is linked to the development of intelligence, but according to a recent article in the *Wall Street Journal,* penmanship can also foster community links. One woman wrote handwritten notes to members of her online community during her forty-five-minute subway commute, to make her contacts "real and 3-D." One of Alton's old friends requested that for his birthday Alton write him a handwritten letter on real paper with real ink. His profession involves reading typed scripts for movie companies and coping with a deluge of emails, and he told Alton he missed the handmade, personal feel of penmanship. Alton chose to write the letter with a fountain pen, as he claims this style of pen, in which the ink flows freely onto the paper with little pressure, is kindest to the hand.

Alton says his fountain pens often become a point of discussion with patients, because the pens remind them of their parents, grandparents, or childhood. However, handwriting with any kind of utensil is a form of self-expression. For years people have expressed their uniqueness, neatness, free-mindedness, and connection to others via handwriting.

Mastering first the block style of writing and then cursive is a great source of pride for children, and when it is taught in a classroom setting, it can be a source of community experience. Writing style can evolve into a means of self-expression and communication; as calligraphy, it can even be an art form.

The State of Indiana has recently passed a law eliminating the requirement for children to learn cursive writing in the classroom. This has catalyzed some questions and concerns. My client Judy says that her handwriting is so even and lovely, it causes others to exclaim, which tickles her. It makes her feel special and draws others to her.

Ideas to Grapple With

- How often do you write things by hand?
- What do you prefer to handwrite? To type?
- How has your penmanship changed over the years?
- Do you enjoy writing carefully, briskly, or sloppily?
- When you have to sign something, do you dash it off, or do you carefully form each letter?

Hold this thought: Handwriting can be a form of creativity and self-expression.

---

5. Crafts, Habits, and Imperfections

How do we make meaningful hand use part of our lives? It is not only about picking up a knitting needle or hammer when you are depressed. If you are depressed, crafting something will seem like a pretty superficial answer, and you might not feel motivated to do it. This is not to say that manual habits are not a solution, because they are. Developing certain hand habits *before* you become depressed provides a comforting routine on which you can fall back. It can offer both something to do and people with whom you can do it. The routine is about forming healthy, helpful habits. If you have habits in place, you are less likely to be buffeted about by difficult circumstances. Habits give you something to hold on to, even if you do it imperfectly.

Let's visit imperfection for a second. Making what we can, however imperfectly, is empowering, because it is an expression of the self. It makes use of where the self is in that moment. The next rendition might be more advanced, but a growth process has begun. The imperfections that you allow in wood products or woven items can somehow be intriguing and cozy. Have you ever responded to a certain beauty in imperfection that was more compelling than an overly manicured self or product? We are attracted by a bit of wildness or a "sweet disorder," which can bewitch "more than when art is too precise in every part." Natural settings, natural selves, and natural products appeal to us, despite or even because of their imperfections.

Before she died, my father's mother crocheted each of us a bedspread. I was given the one that was four-fifths white and one-fifth cream. The rest were uniformly colored. "I was losing my eyesight," apologized my grandmother. But I truly love the asymmetry of it. When I look at it, I feel happy. It is interesting to look at the flaw, remember the story, and conjure up the person in your mind. (However, I must confess, I did wonder why, of the four girls who got them, I was chosen to receive the one with the defect. At first I wanted the one with the perfect pink rosettes.)

Ideas to Grapple With

- What reaction do you have to flawed pieces?
- Why are they acceptable in some situations but not others?
- What flawed products do you love?
- Did you make them or did someone else make them for you?
- Did it involve a solo or group experience?

Hold this thought: If the outcome represents
something that is real and interesting and that
involves a story, it will have lasting appeal.

Beauty is truth, truth beauty.

—JOHN KEATS, poet

6. Handling One's Profession: A Few Thoughts About Surgeons from a Psychiatrist's Point of View

I interviewed with a general surgeon when I applied for medical school. He likened the lights in the operating room to the lights of the stage. He said that when surgery starts, all is still and a "sacred experience" begins. The team members, gowned, masked, and capped, are ready for their tasks and click into deep concentration. According to several books I've read and surgeons I know (including my husband), the practice of surgery is highly conducive to peak experience, or flow.

I have often wondered how one can enter any kind of flow when the responsibility is immense and the stakes are high. However, it seems that deep concentration, immersion, creativity, and the ability to improvise are crucial to flow, and because in surgery unpredictable things can happen—the surgeon encounters anomalous structures, atypical anatomy, excess bleeding—thinking on one's feet, finding alternatives, and knowing the body so well that one can find another way are essential.

People who genuinely enjoy working as surgeons may well find mundane, repetitive hand activity to be a soothing counterpoint to the tension and drama of surgery—a source of Mind Rest. Alton recently asked one of the applicants for a fellowship what the applicant did for pleasure outside work. The candidate replied that he had been trying to perfect a single beef curry recipe for an entire year. He tweaked it every Sunday, made a big pot, and ate it for the entire week. He told Alton he had just about gotten it to where he wants it. And Alton has a sweeping habit, which I confess sometimes used to get to me—such as when we would be getting ready for a party and he would be sweeping leaves at the edges of the yard when I thought he should be slicing tomatoes. But sweeping, he tells me, relaxes him. A few years ago, when Alton's sister was dying, he would occasionally disappear for a while and could be found sweeping the garage.

Ideas to Grapple With

- Which aspects of your professional or personal life create flow?
- Do you like being part of a work team, or do you work best alone?

Hold this thought: If someone (including you) is in flow, free thought, or a deeply relaxed state, don't interrupt it with a nonessential like tomato slicing.

CONCLUSION

Be conscious of your hands and how they influence your mind and mood. Think about how you can create an intersection between handwork and being part of a team or community. Even if you feel you do not have time for do-it-yourself endeavors, handwork, or hands-on care, remember the psychological benefits; it might influence what you decide to do in the future.

SUMMARY

In this chapter we explored your hands and community. We covered how handwork alone or with others has the potential to move your mind and lift your mood. We discussed do-it-yourself activities. We covered penmanship, nonverbal expression, self-direction, imperfection, the mundane—and surgery.

FIVE-PART PRESCRIPTION: WEEK FOUR

From Head to Hands

INSIGHT (10–20 MINUTES A DAY)

Throughout this chapter, you have considered your hands. Now it is time to take it out of the mind and onto the page.

Here are your prompts. Remember, do not edit. Write freely and record all of your responses. Let details flow from your mind, through your hands, and onto the page without second-guessing them. Do not try to make it wonderful. Just let whatever emerges emerge. No one will see this, so you do not have to feel self-conscious. Think about your senses, your body, and how you felt when specific events occurred. Let go, wallow, whatever. We will lift you up when it is time.

Write about when you experienced:

- Weak handshakes
- Crushing grips
- Wounded fingers, hands, wrists, arms
- Learning to write
- The challenge of cursive
- Hurtful letters written to you
- Being told to wash your hands
- Slapping
- Pinching
- Clenching
- Gripping
- Nail biting
- Dry hands, cold hands
- Unfinished projects
- Having no hand to hold
- Not being able to participate in a team project

MOVEMENT (15–30 MINUTES A DAY)

In this chapter, the Movement Enhancement we are going to add to walking is hand use. Continue your walking, but take about ten minutes for your upper limbs—weight lifting—before or after you walk. Lifting weights builds muscle, tendon, and bone strength. It increases metabolism and burns calories. You can use soup cans, heavy bookends, or stones if you do not have hand weights. A rubber exercise band is also a good tool. Alton says:

Biceps

The biceps is the muscle on the front of your upper arm that bends your elbow.

Put the weights in your hands (or hold a rubber exercise band in your hand while stepping on the other end). Stand with good posture. With your elbows at your side, bend your elbows against the resistance of the weights. When you are able to complete three sets of six to ten repetitions each, then increase the weight or resistance.

Triceps

The triceps is the muscle on the back of the upper arm. It is easy to strengthen your triceps muscles, because you can use your own body weight. You can do upright pushups against a wall, angled pushups against your kitchen counter, or pushups on knees or toes on the floor.

Start with a few repetitions against the wall and then gradually increase the repetitions. When upright pushups become too easy, move to the counter or floor.

Shoulder Muscles

The shoulder muscles include the big deltoid muscle and the rotator cuff (four muscles joined together). These muscles move the shoulder to position the hand in space. The muscles around the shoulder blade—trapezius, latissimus dorsi, and rhomboids—stabilize and move the shoulder blade. These muscles are important for posture.

To strengthen the rotator cuff, loop a rubber exercise band around a doorknob and hold the two ends in your hand. With your elbow at your side and bent ninety degrees, rotate your arm outward and inward against the resistance of the band.

To strengthen the trapezius and rhomboids, hold two weights in your outstretched hands above the level of your shoulders and try to bring your shoulder blades together. Then move your arms in small circles until you start to feel a mild ache. After a short rest, do this exercise again, for a total of 3 or 4 minutes. (There are many Internet resources for rotator cuff and shoulder strengthening, including these orthopedic websites suggested by Alton: www.scarsdaledocs.com, www.cvstarrhandsurgery.com, and http://orthoinfo.aaos.org.)

Activities You've Done Before

Or, as before, try swimming, rowing, skating, skiing, spinning, dancing, yoga, weight lifting, running, mowing grass, raking leaves, or shoveling snow.

MIND REST (5–10 MINUTES A DAY)

Hand activities—crafting, constructing, or creating—are restful for the mind, as you know. Repeating a mantra as you lift weights or just counting your repetitions is also a way to experience Mind Rest at the same time.

Our new suggestion for this chapter is deep breathing. Deep breathing, as performed in yoga or other meditation practices, is excellent for Mind Rest. Singing, which is all about the breath, is also good for Mind Rest. My voice teacher once told me that if she did not vocalize each day, she felt out of sorts.

Here is a singing exercise, which involves deep breathing that you can use for Mind Rest. Lie on the floor and put five heavy books on your lower belly. Breathe in on a count of five and lift them up. Then hold them for a count of five. Now let the breath out on a count of five while you lower the books. You can practice this without the books and rest your hands on your lower belly instead. You can daydream or concentrate on not letting the books fall. After you've done this three times, sing while you put the breath beneath the tone and let it out slowly with the sound.

Or, as before, lie on your bed, do nothing, putter around, sit in your favorite spot, listen to music you enjoy, or sing anything (sing "Ah" if you don't know the words).

Or meditate. Say a mantra (a repeated phrase—whatever feels right, from a prayer to a rhyme). Avoid all but your own thoughts and let them go where they will.

YOUR OWN TWO HANDS (20–40 MINUTES A DAY)

The new suggestion for this week is writing a letter by hand. "Writing a letter out of the quiet mind passes the real self along," says John Freeman, author of *The Tyranny of E-Mail*.

Consider how you like to write.

- Do you like cursive, print, or a combination?
- Might you add a drawing, a sketch, a tiny design, or a splash of paint? What does the paint smell like?
- What about the paper? Do you prefer one with texture? What paper is around you? A brown paper bag? The other side of your kids' discarded drawing?
- Should you use all the space on the paper? Not necessarily. As Gary Schneider, a photographer, told our daughter Caroline while he was examining her handmade book, the "white space is just as important as the image."

What is your artistic or creative wish? The one that has been floating around your mind for a long time? What is that thing you always wanted to do? It's time! You must make a commitment now to your Creative Hour, at least five days per week if you want to make the fantasy a reality. Here we go.

Look at the original list you made in Chapter 3. We are going to ask you to commit to the long-standing creative dream that you have not acted upon. Write out the concrete steps you will take this week to make it happen: what calls do you have to make, what materials do you have to buy, what changes do you have to make in your schedule, and what might you have to forgo to honor your Creative Hour, when you'll move from dreaming to doing? Success is all about establishing a creative habit.

- Sign up for a class.
- Collect or buy materials.
- Find a partner to keep you on track, one with whom you can check in, or one who will work alongside you.
- Make a schedule by knowing exactly when you will work on your project. (Set your Creative Hour in stone in your mind, so you cannot slip away and not do it. If you must miss it, then you have to find another time.)
- Accept that you will not be as on top of other things for a while. Live with a few loose ends.
- Figure out how to get other tasks done and make your Creative Hour a priority.
- Let people know you will be a little less available.
- Decide ahead of time how you are going to react to your first wobbly efforts (I suggest doing so with kindness and the rational critic). Do not be surprised or thrown by initial ineptitude, should it occur, and be ready with a way to deal with your disappointment, such as "I am learning and I showed up." (Process, process, process, not product.)
- Deal with your guilt about whatever it is you are not doing and whomever it is you are not attending to, and keep going.
- Be ruthless about showing up for your Creative Hour.

The difference between those who create and those who do not is the carved-out time, the concrete steps, and the consistency. Establish your habit, show up, stay put, do what you can do, and do not deviate from this routine. If you must miss, make it up. An hour a day or at least five hours per week is best. Let's make it happen.

MIND SHIFT (10–20 MINUTES A DAY)

Our goal for this week is to delve deeply into the internal experience of hand use. Gaining self-awareness in this area is useful and might lead you to start new habits, or it might shift the way you spend your day. Hands are about warmth, welcome, connectedness, construction; many good things. Let us uncover the positives.

Here are your prompts. Consider:

• Good handshakes
• Comforting grips
• Strong fingers, hands, wrists, arms
• People to whom you have written nice letters
• Beautiful script
• Kind letters or notes written to you
• Clean hands with neat fingernails
• Holding hands
• Touching hands
• Caressing
• Soaking hands
• Warm hands
• Pleasurable projects with others
• Someone reaching out
• Community connections that made you happy
• Worthwhile habits
• Creative projects that are going to come to fruition

I hope you are thinking about your hands a bit differently or that you will start to find ways to use them that you had not tried before.

Freud said, "We require civilized man to reverence beauty wherever he sees it in nature and to create it in the objects of his handwork so far as he is able." In the next chapter, let's take our hands, our bodies, and our buzzing minds to the best place they could possibly be: nature.

7

Creativity, Nature, and Exercise

The High Line stretches one's gaze—out to city or riverscape and back to blooms or butterfly. . . . In the process, the psyche also glides, between general and personal, blurred and crisply present. . . . [It] allows one to feel elevated in spirit, aloft in a garden in space.

—DIANE ACKERMAN, writer

MATTERS AT HAND

How do nature, exercise, and Creative Capacity intersect? In this chapter we will show you research that documents how outdoor experience fosters physical health, psychological well-being, and an unimpeded mind. We will also share information that explains how exercise produces some of the same benefits as being in nature. Though nature and exercise may seem to be two separate and distinct areas and routes to wellness, we entwine nature and movement in the Creativity Cure because it's easy to incorporate them as a combination and get the benefits of both. Also, some clients have told me that they are more inclined to exercise if it can be outdoors. Moving outdoors can catalyze the coming into being of your True Self and Creative Self, allowing your Creative Capacity to unfold. Sitting outside or exercising indoors counts, too, but if it is easy for you to meld nature and exercise, you could be in for some serious pleasure.

WHAT CAN NATURE DO FOR CREATIVITY AND HAPPINESS?

Not only does hiking through the woods, strolling along the shore, or running around a park shape your body, but studies also show that the creative mind takes shape in nature. Research shows that children use their imaginations more in green environments, and perhaps this has implications for the development of Creative Capacity in adults as well.

- Dr. Stephen R. Kellert of Yale University, in his book *Building for Life: Designing and Understanding the Human-Nature Connection,* documents research on the importance of nature for the development of creative and cognitive capacities. "Play in nature," he writes, "particularly during the critical period of middle childhood, appears to be an especially important time for developing the capacities for creativity, problem-solving, and emotional and intellectual development."

- Professor Robin C. Moore of North Carolina State University, author of *Natural Learning: The Life of an Environmental Schoolyard* and an expert on children's play and learning environments, says, "Natural spaces and materials stimulate children's limitless imaginations and serve as the medium of inventiveness and creativity."

- Studies by Professors Andrea Faber Taylor and Frances Kuo of the Landscape and Human Health Laboratory at the University of Illinois demonstrated that green areas foster more creative play in children than do manufactured playgrounds. A study in Sweden showed that asphalt playgrounds fostered interrupted play, whereas natural settings induced narratives that had meaning, depth, continuation, and imagination.

- Dr. Louise Chawla, associate professor at Whitney Young College, has studied children, the environment, ecstatic moments, and nature. She posits that five-sense experience outdoors is beneficial for all people and a source of creativity as well as health. Chawla says, "Most of these benefits are great human advantages, whether or not we make our way in the world as creative thinkers."

While these studies focus on children, the findings could be significant for adults as well because much of creativity has to do with play, and natural settings will help us adults "play" in our own way. Trekking across a natural landscape, we might daydream, hum, invent a recipe, or come up with a hypothesis rather than skip. Then again, skipping is possible. Nature invites you to leap over logs, smell honeysuckle, jump a puddle, pick up sticks, skim stones, take in a sunrise, ogle a rainbow, or pick a raspberry and pop it in your mouth. It engages your five senses and your imagination as well as your muscles.

Recently, *New York Times* reporter Matt Richtel and five neuroscientists took a "primitive trip with a sophisticated goal." They spent days in the wilderness to study how nature might reverse the effects of technological immersion and to see if nature could help produce clearer thoughts in their minds. Richtel described the "rhythm of the trip: As the river flows, so do the ideas." The scientists seemed enamored of this unusual method of study.

Nature is also a source for transcendent moments of happiness as well as creativity and fitness. Marghanita Laski, a British author and journalist who studied ecstasy and published a book on the subject, found that triggers for peak experiences include water, flowers, mountains, sunrises, and springs—natural phenomena. In the words of poet Emily Dickinson, "The soul should always stand ajar, ready to welcome the ecstatic experience."

Recently, Alton and I shared a mountain house with four friends and cousins, and I was writing in my room when I heard some scary shrieks. My mind produced a grizzly. I ran outside to find my companions perched at different spots on the hill behind the house gasping, holding their hands to their mouths, and aiming cameras—at a double rainbow. Such sights get you going and as it turns out, can even help you overcome stress.

WHAT CAN NATURE DO FOR HEALTH, HEALING, AND CREATIVE CAPACITY?

According to Dr. Peter H. Kahn Jr., associate professor in the Department of Psychology at the University of Washington, director of the Human Interaction with Nature and Technological Systems Lab, and author of *The Human Relationship with Nature: Development and Culture,* many studies document that exposure to nature reduces stress in adults. Professor Nancy Wells from the College of Human Ecology at Cornell cited similar findings in children and says, "Our study finds that life's stressful events appear not to cause as much psychological distress in children who live in high nature conditions compared with low nature conditions." I'll bet you intuited this, but it's great to discover that science backs up what you know inside.

One reason that stress reduction can foster Creative Capacity is that if our worries diminish, we can be more receptive to inspirations from within and from outside. Even if you start by taking it all in from your deck chair with your sun-brewed tea and just-plucked sprig of mint, it is a step in the right direction. Research suggests that the sun can be a source of healing as well as inspiration.

What about the sun? Should you avoid it for fear of burns and cancer risk or embrace it for the sheer delight of warmth and light? A little sunlight is good for both your body and mind because it elevates mood, converts vitamin D (which strengthens bones) to its most active form, energizes the immune system, and helps you sleep better at night, according to a recent article by Deborah Kotz in *U.S. News and World Report.* Patients get better faster in hospitals when they have a room with a view to the outside, according to Esther Sternberg, MD, author of *Healing Spaces: The Science of Place and Well-Being*. Sunny or cloudy, dry or drizzly, outdoor exposure is good for us.

Richard Louv, author of *Last Child in the Woods: Saving Our Children from Nature Deficit Disorder* and adviser to the National Scientific Council on the Developing Child, has coined the term "nature deficit disorder" to describe the effects of insufficient doses of nature. While an absence of nature can cause depression or anxiety, a healthy dose of nature can combat these painful conditions as well as others such as attention deficit disorder. He says, "Nature experience can relieve some of the everyday pressures that may lead to childhood depression." Building forts or tree houses, skipping stones off a lake, weaving dandelion stems into a crown, or just being in the sun are more than leisure or even creative activities; they are essential for wellness.

Nature is solid medicine.

WHAT ELSE CAN NATURE DO FOR YOUR MIND AND BODY?

Because natural environments often demand walking, running, lifting, shifting positions, or clearing your path, they provide more opportunities for movement—movement you may not even be aware of. Just by grabbing a walking stick (or carving one), reaching for a wildflower, kicking the dirt off your shoes, or swatting a mosquito, you have bent, stretched, flexed, and extended more than if you were curled up in front of the nature show on TV with your microwaved cup of green tea. You also bend, reach, lift, and push indoors, but domestic efforts may not inspire you to sprint to a weeping willow, leap over patches of mud, or turn a cartwheel—as our son's teacher apparently did on the playground. (Her fan club is growing.)

According to Richard Louv, "a growing body of research links our mental, physical and spiritual health directly to our association with nature—in positive ways." However, even if you are aware that natural settings are good for you, it is easy to deny this truth when you are driven in your devotion to your work or tasks that demand much indoor time. Work, family commitments, and other responsibilities can lead you to shortchange your body and to forgo outdoor explorations that could change your life for the better.

Did you know that nature also has a great impact on your cognitive ability? According to recent studies by Marc Berman and colleagues at the University of Michigan, "simple and brief interactions with nature can produce marked increases in cognitive control." In an interview with *Wall Street Journal* reporter Shirley S. Wang, Berman said, "Performance on memory and attention tests improved by 20% after study subjects paused for a walk through an arboretum." Busy streets did not have the same effect. The arboretum appears to have relaxed the mind and made it receptive. One can deduce that Creative Capacity would also be sparked by an arboretum, forest, beach, park, or garden, because the relaxed mind lets the unconscious rise up. If you keep this truth in the forefront of your awareness, you will be more likely to choose nature when you can. Keeping nature in mind will help you.

TERMS TO GRASP

Peak Experience

A peak experience is a self-actualizing, self-justifying moment with intrinsic value. It involves excitement, feelings of intense happiness and well-being, wonder, and awe. It may also involve an awareness of transcendental unity or knowledge of higher truth, as suggested by Dr. Abraham Maslow, father of humanistic psychology.

Ocnophile

An ocnophile is someone who is hesitant and clingy; a shrinking being.

Philobat

A philobat, by contrast with an ocnophile, is a daring, motivated, leaping being.

PEOPLE WHO CHANGED

Evelyn

My client Evelyn, a buyer for a clothing store, says that holding her balances longer in yoga and running up the hills in the park on her way home makes her feel proud. The bushes, trees, and grass in the park are important to her after being inside all day. She resisted exercise for many years, but when she made it part of her daily life, her mental state improved. In our sessions together, we spoke about the value of movement, and she tried to find a form that kept her motivated. She feels freer and happier when she exercises outdoors.

What Evelyn hands us: Even if you think you
are not an exercise person, you can become one.
Try doing it outdoors.

Brian

My client Brian, a highly accomplished student, aces tests, publishes articles, and studies up to sixteen hours a day. He receives endless reinforcement for his academic successes. But Brian was riddled with anxiety when I first saw him. One night between class and home, he found himself shaking uncontrollably on a busy street corner. He did not know why. At times he felt so lonely he could not focus his mind. This sent him spiraling into a panic state. The panic eventually made the studying impossible, and a vicious cycle ensued.

The summer after we first met, Brian spent time in the Adirondack Mountains with family friends. He stopped studying at 5:00 p.m., ran with their golden retriever through the evergreens, and cooked dinner over a wood-burning stove for his hosts while playing indie music. He told me that the best thing about this summer was running beneath those trees. Exercising provided great relief.

What Brian hands us: Exercise changes your state of mind. Trees have an effect on your well-being, whether they're in the deep woods or around a city park.

Paulina

Paulina had always resisted jogging because she didn't enjoy it. In fact, she said, she hated it. She tried running with her best friend, because her friend said it was the greatest exercise. Once she ran around the local school track with her sister, but two big barking dogs burst out of the woods and chased them. When she moved to a new city, she tried joining a running class, but even with the others' support she just could not maintain the commitment to the three-day-a-week schedule.

Paulina spent her workdays at a keyboard and felt bored with her job. Lying in bed watching television and eating takeout after a sedentary work shift provided both short-term comfort and long-term malaise, and it added troubling poundage. When she went home for her ten-year high school reunion and met her brother for dinner the night before the reunion, he said, "You have an ass like a horse." She decided to start moving.

This time, with the help of the 5PP, she tricked herself into the effort by spending her Saturdays walking long distances to neighborhoods she wanted to explore. Then she began walking faster. She combined pleasure with practicality, distraction with determination. She studied the mechanics of power walking, practiced the technique, and added an evening walk in the park before dark. Watching people while keeping her pace was interesting. The habit was reinforcing because she felt fit and more energized. She soon increased to three days per week, sometimes four.

She lost the weight she'd gained, and she bought some new clothes that made her feel like a leggy colt instead of a lumbering horse. Her energized city hikes led to adventures, discoveries, and a healthy dose of sunlight.

What Paulina hands us: If your inertia becomes painful enough, you just might be motivated to move and change who you are. If one form of exercise doesn't appeal, do not force it. Find another that does. And get a little bit of sun, even or especially if you have sighed often that day.
You can turn it around.

If you have been tempted to pass over the Movement section of the 5PP, let's take a closer look at what might be holding you back or keeping you inside. Sometimes you avoid your physicality because of unknown fears. You might even avoid aspects of the outdoors based on incidents you do not remember or inclinations you never quite understood.

Dr. Michael Balint, a well-known psychoanalyst who wrote extensively about human relations, fear, and anxiety, coined two terms for one's relationship with adventure: "ocnophile" and "philobat." These terms derive from the Greek roots *philos*, "to love"; *acrobat*, "to walk on one's toes"; and *ocno*, "to shrink back, hesitate." The ocnophile shrinks back, hesitates, and clings, whereas the philobat leaps forth into daring, exciting action. Which one are you? If you think you are an ocnophile, this matter can be addressed, but first you have to identify your reasons for reluctance. You do not want you to miss out on the peak experiences that physical experiences in nature can provide for you.

- Do you feel uncomfortable outdoors? Why might you?
- Do you dislike the sensation of sand between your toes or mud in your sneakers? Try walking along a manicured path in a park.

- Might you feel physically unsure? Amble along a brambly, uneven path to increase your surefootedness.

- If you feel too overweight or cumbersome to even take a stroll, let those feelings motivate you instead of hold you back. Say a mantra instead of thinking these thoughts. Walk where you can behold a natural scene that is more attention-getting than these concerns.

- Are you afraid of getting hurt from stumbling on rocks or branches? Pick an even path with good light, slow down when you need to, and look around. You will stumble less if you move more. With a few outdoor treks your confidence will build.

- Did you once fall off the monkey bars and have the breath knocked out of you? Climbing is not necessary. There are other options.

It is important to contemplate your resistance. Be curious about your misgivings. If you try to force yourself to overcome them before contemplating the reasons for your hesitation, you might not win the battle. Sometimes a childhood incident can become lodged in the psyche and distorted into a much scarier situation than it needs to be. Maybe you fell out of a tree or into an ice-cold lake and now you feel hesitant. Some of us (philobats) are psychologically predisposed to get back on the horse that throws us, while others of us (ocnophiles) might simply avoid the horse in the future. We want you to win, so try to get to the bottom of it. Then again, if you get nowhere by thinking, just open your front door and step out.

My client Maria started a daily outdoor stretch class at age eighty-four. It is her new job, providing a routine, a purpose, and a source of pleasure. Like Maria, you can find your own way to combine movement and the stimulation of nature. You can work with your truth, your preferences, your fears, or your distastes to get you to a safe place, physically and psychologically.

STRENGTHENING THE SOURCE: GET YOUR BODY READY FOR ADVENTURE

Now we are going to focus exclusively on the benefits of exercise and leave nature aside for a moment. If we can first strengthen your body, you might be more inclined to go outdoors, discover your inner philobat (leaper, darer, doer), and have transcendent moments.

Research from countless medical journals shows that exercise strengthens your heart, protects against memory loss, helps you stay at a healthy weight, reduces stress, lifts mood, enhances learning, increases immunity, and strengthens bones. Exercise prevents, treats, and even reverses physical and psychological illnesses. The benefits are astounding. Exercise, especially outside, primes you for peak experience and creative adventure. When you look at all the hard-to-ignore advantages, maybe you will find it easier to bound out the door in your cross-trainers.

FIVE REASONS TO BE PHYSICAL

Running! If there's an activity happier, more exhilarating, more nourishing to the imagination, I can't think of one.

—JOYCE CAROL OATES, writer

1. Exercise Decreases Depression

John Ratey, MD, notes that exercise is "one of the best treatments we have for most psychiatric problems."

A growing body of evidence, including a study by Duke University psychologist James A. Blumenthal published in the *Archives of Internal Medicine,* shows that pulse-pounding exercise at least three days per week for thirty minutes is a solid treatment for depression. It is as effective as the antidepressant sertraline (Zoloft), and the benefits last longer, according to a study in *Psychosomatic Medicine* by Dr. Michael

A. Babyak from Duke. Because it naturally boosts the neurotransmitters norepinephrine, dopamine, and serotonin, which ameliorate both anxiety and depression, exercise has the same impact on the brain as medication.

Citing a large volume of research, John Ratey, MD, Harvard psychiatrist and author of *Spark: The Revolutionary New Science of Exercise and the Brain*, asserts that:

- Norepinephrine wakes up the brain and enhances self-esteem.
- Dopamine improves mood, motivation, sense of wellness, addiction management, and the attention system.
- Serotonin combats sadness, impulse control, and slipping confidence.

Dr. Stephen Ilardi, author of *The Depression Cure: The 6-Step Program to Beat Depression Without Drugs*, says, "There are over one hundred published studies documenting the antidepressant effect of exercise. Activities as varied as walking, biking, jogging, and weight lifting have all been found to be effective. Exercise changes the brain." There is no question that if you can get yourself to move regularly (especially with trees around you), you can feel better.

Ideas to Grapple With
- What is the impact of movement on your mood?
- How might exercising outside be more cheering for you?

Hold this thought: Exercise increases feelings of contentment and wellness, especially with a view.

---

2. Exercise Increases Pain Tolerance

Exercise makes you less susceptible to pain because it stimulates the release of endocannabinoids. Endocannabinoids are naturally produced substances that influence appetite, pain, mood, and memory, providing a mild natural high. Endocannabinoids decrease depression and increase pain tolerance, according to recent research in the *Journal of Neuroscience and Neurophysiology* by Dr. P. B. Sparling from the School of Applied Physiology at Georgia Tech. Exercise also builds immunity—making you less susceptible to illness—and helps you recover faster should a bug make its way into your bloodstream.

It helps to know the science about exercise so you can feel great about your effort.

Ideas to Grapple With

- What do you think about your pain tolerance, physically or psychologically? Is it high, low, average? Does the sea or a swath of trees make you forget about the pain?
- Do you fear discomfort, illness, or body damage? Might certain settings make you feel safer or more courageous? Which ones?
- How have you typically dealt with this fear? Avoidance? Plunging in?

Hold this thought: When you feel free, strong, and unencumbered, you are better able to focus your mind on subjects that interest you, or let your mind go where it will.

---

3. Exercise Makes You Smarter

Research has shown that the mind works better when the body is robust. "The point of exercise is to build and condition the brain," says John Ratey, MD. Ratey cites a school in Naperville, Illinois, with a novel fitness program; the students there achieved much higher than expected scores on international math and science tests. Their contentment and success have been attributed to the school's creative, unique approach to cardiovascular fitness.

Other researchers have validated that vigorous exercise makes you smarter. Because exercise increases brain-derived neurotrophic factor (BDNF), a natural protein also humorously referred to as "Miracle-Gro for the brain," it bolsters cognitive ability. Dr. Carl W. Cotman, professor at UC Irvine School of Medicine and director of the Institute for Brain Aging and Dementia, has linked exercise to increased BDNF and reports that the promulgation of this protein improves learning capacity.

Recent research by Dr. Kirk I. Erickson, assistant professor of psychology at the University of Illinois at Urbana-Champaign, has shown that aerobic exercise can augment memory in older individuals by enlarging the hippocampus. Shrinkage of the brain with aging was once assumed to be inevitable. According to a recent study in the *Journal of Applied Physiology* by Michelle W. Voss, a researcher from the University of Illinois, a sedentary lifestyle leads to inferior academic performance, poorer memory, and the inability to multitask.

"Exercise is medicine," says Dr. Ilardi.

Getting out there in your new Nikes will alleviate depression, enlarge your brain, spark your memory, and help you handle stress. It's hard to ignore the evidence, right?

4. Exercise Provides Euphoric Moments

You may have heard that exercise releases endorphins that produce the famous "runner's high." While there is controversy about the biochemistry of this post-exertion peak, there is no debate that it exists. If you run, you might feel euphoric, crave the effect, or become "addicted." While transcendent moments may not last, their number and amplitude increase when you make exercise a habit.

The writer Haruki Murakami, author of *What I Talk About When I Talk About Running*, writes, "Most runners run not because they want to live longer, but because they want to live life to the fullest." You do not have to be a runner. Any form of exercise will benefit you.

Ideas to Grapple With
- When have you had euphoric moments, peak experiences, or even transcendent ecstasies?
- Were they associated with movement or nature, or both?
- Elaborate on such an experience.

Hold this thought: Exercise provides euphoric moments.

Here are some things to think about:

- What might a new exercise habit do for you? Do you think you can motivate yourself if, say, flowers fleck the path, or brisk walkers pumping their arms pass by? If you have been following the 5PP walking plan, might you be inspired to rev up?
- Do any of the health concerns we mentioned relate to you?
- If you are already familiar with the benefits of working out and are not physically active, have you wondered why? What is happening inside you with regard to the shoulds and can'ts?
- Would an iPod with sounds of water help you get moving?

Hold this thought: Do not think; move.

---

5. Exercise Fosters Creative Capacity

Exercise fosters Creative Capacity because movement relaxes and frees the mind. When your body is moving along in a rhythm, ideas can emerge. Instinct, spontaneous thought, and free association are the warp and weft of a Creative Self and a True Self, and exercise allows them to occur. The active body releases the mind, allowing problems to be solved, innovations to surface, and thoughts to collect.

There is an indirect relationship between the active body and Creative Capacity. The linking factor is the passive mind. *An active body leads to a passive mind, which is the essence of Creative Capacity.* A passive mind is a mind that allows thoughts to go where they will without trying to control them.

Many creative people attest to the importance of exercise for their creative lives. Creativity Coach and writer Gail McMeeken in her book *The 12 Secrets of Highly Creative Women* reveals that exercise is one of the secrets. According to Joyce Carol Oates, the long walks of the poets Wordsworth, Coleridge, and Shelley are linked to their creative output. A writer friend told me that when she heard that Virginia Woolf and Stephen King "walked their books," she felt more justified in shutting the lid of her laptop and hiking the trail that winds through our town. Physical exertion relaxes the mind and increases effectiveness.

The passive mind also plays a role in athletic skill. With too much directed thought, athletes may stop hitting the ball, and then they may stop winning. Trusting in the ingrained movements formed from thousands of hours of practice leads to excellence. Habit delivers in a powerful way. "The idea is that when you have a highly honed skill, when you are in the zone, when your actions flow out of you rather than being generated by you, then you are acting at your best; the worst thing you can do in this kind of situation is to get in the way of whatever is going on," in the words of philosophy professors and authors of *All Things Shining*, Hubert Dreyfuss and Sean Dorrance Kelly.

We can take a leap and say that both Creative Capacity and athletic brilliance rely on a well-conditioned body that takes the lead, honors habit, and allows intuition to surface. The important idea is that when you master the body, let it respond, give it space, go with instinct, go where it will, and do not second-guess where it takes you, great things will happen. Powers and possibilities will emerge.

Ideas to Grapple With

- Is there somewhere you can go to take long walks in the wild (or the wild mind)?
- Have you ever come up with a great idea when you were out of breath or your pulse was beating? What was it?
- Was there a peak experience in which you felt happy about being alive and that all was well? What were the circumstances?

Hold this thought: Physicality will increase your Creative Capacity. Embrace the wild in all its forms.

As I run I tell myself to think of a river. And clouds. But essentially I'm not thinking of a thing.

—HARUKI MURAKAMI, writer

WAYS TO GET YOURSELF TO MOVE

Just in case you need an extra boost:

- Say, "no choice, no choice, no choice."

- Realize how bad you feel about not being who you can be, doing what you can do, and doing what you once loved to do outdoors. Bad feelings are excellent motivators.

- Find a form of nature that feeds you and incorporate it into the effort. If you can't get outside or near a window, then do sit-ups in front of a nature program on TV; it can prime you for another time.

- Realize that your physical self does not have to mimic or reflect someone else's. You can be you and do it your own way, with your own natural style, in your own time. You can, of course, absolutely and with self-esteem, start slowly, like a small shoot or a tiny seed. We are permitted to grow and change at any age.

- Realize you will feel great after the first step, just for overcoming all the nos and naysaying. Getting over the hump is huge, a major puddle you've jumped.

- Plan on a reward, but not something that you will regret, that you will feel guilty about, or that will make you feel as if you undid the good. Think of rewards that will help you maintain a good feeling, such as a trip to the local lake with friends, rock climbing, or even sitting on a rock on a sunny day with someone you can talk to.

- Don't think, just do.

- Let a natural setting carry you.

"I Am Too Attached to My Computer to Get Up"

Much of the Creativity Cure involves transforming core identity, bolstering physical and mental health, and creating happiness by using natural forces. When we are slumped over keyboards and surrounded by screens, our senses are not sufficiently stimulated, and our bodies lie fallow. This can lead to malaise, low-level depression, and a shut-in, shut-down, isolated self. While certain applications and games allow you to move your body, the many sensory benefits of full-bore physicality are in short supply. So let's get up and go back to nature.

What Is the Best Landscape for You?

We need to talk about what settings are the most stimulating for you. This is not about being picky or a prima donna, but rather about attunement and choices that nurture. If you have limited free time or vacation, you want to be aware of how to best use it, how to get the most out of it. Dr. Peter H. Kahn Jr. says that the psychological effects of preferred landscapes are quite real.

It's important to identify your chosen natural environment because the right setting matters and is not always obvious. A place that others find thrilling may not move you, but you may never have acknowledged this. One client said to me, "For years I went sailing with my father and then one day I woke up and realized I never liked it. You have to jump around pulling lines and hoisting sails, and just when you think you can lie down and relax, you have to switch sides to balance the thing and duck to keep your head from getting slammed." She liked to be with her father, but sailing wasn't a pastime she particularly enjoyed.

Let's consider the elements within you and outside you. First of all, are you a woods person, a beach person, a mountain person, a desert person, or a lake person? Before you read on, write down the first answer that came to mind: _____

Now let's think about it some more.

- What's your ideal landscape? Even if you cannot always get there, it is good to identify it because you can always find everyday substitutes for the ideal—for example, tomato plants that you grow in your yard instead of the field of plum tomatoes you passed while on your bike in Tuscany.

- Is one setting more likely to transform your mood, calm you, or move you than another?

- Which settings are most likely to help you forget about the minutiae of life?

- Do you like warm or cold settings? Would you rather be in ski boots or flip-flops?

- What childhood memories of natural settings are meaningful, pleasurable, and worth carrying on?

Consider your body in these settings and whether you are most content:

- At the beach with small lapping waves or with large crashing ones
- In your backyard, on your terrace, or in a community garden, alone or with others
- In the mountains with lakes, creeks, rivers, moss, and ferns
- On a basketball court or tennis court, perhaps with a periphery of trees
- In a desert with searing sun
- On a city bike path or a mountain biking trail
- Walking on a moor in a muggy rain, or even through a city park
- In the open plains under a vast broad sky of uninterrupted blue

Is your answer still the same as it was above? The bottom line here is to ask yourself: "What does my favorite natural environment do for me? How can I maximize my exposure? And how might I incorporate it into my Movement plan?"

CONCLUSION

Moving your body, in whatever way you can, is a route to happiness, as is experiencing nature. The higher the pulse, the greater benefit. Exercise leads to psychological and physiological fitness. We do not want to push you (well, maybe we do, but only at a pace you can handle), but we do want you to be aware. If medical and scientific data do not motivate you, then forget about these important facts for now. But go take a walk anyway. Get some sun. Let the combination of nature and body heat fill, soothe, renew, and energize you.

SUMMARY

In this chapter, we covered the relationship between physicality, nature, and Creative Capacity. We talked about exercise, settings, and double doses of healthy behaviors.

FIVE-PART PRESCRIPTION: WEEK FIVE

From Active Body to Relaxed Mind

INSIGHT (10–20 MINUTES A DAY)

Let us suggest some prompts that will stir up feelings, then allow you to sift through them and let them settle down. Write freely, with full inner responses. Don't leave out important details even if they make you shudder. You can shudder, you can be upset; it is okay. You are not there right now. You are with this book, the page, and your layered mind. That is a good place to be because whatever it is or was can be altered. That is why you are writing about these experiences. When we work through, repeat, recall, and gather the effects in the aftermath, the painful memories transform and have less negative power.

This week try to write outside in a park, on a porch, or in an outdoor café. If that is not possible at this moment, then find a room with a view of nature. If you can't do that, then tack up some inspiring nature scenes in your writing space. Write about when you experienced:

- Feeling bloated, big, cumbersome, unable to move
- Physical pain
- Bodily harm
- Fear of an aspect of nature: waves, woods, ice, rocks, mountains, heights
- Your inner ocnophile
- Refusal to embark or enter
- Laziness, sloth, or lack of motivation
- Pressure to be physical when you did not want to
- Not wanting to get off the couch or the bed

187

MOVEMENT (15–30 MINUTES A DAY)

This chapter has been all about movement.

- Where are you with movement now? Are you satisfied with where you are?
- Are there new possibilities in natural environments that seem achievable for you?
- Have you been able to take it to another level? If so, was it painful or rewarding or both? If not (which is fine), what do you think is holding you back?
- Did considering your past exercise experiences in nature shift your perspective at all?

Even if you do nothing else, do not rule out exercise and movement in a natural setting. If you cannot or will not exercise now, then catch up with your moving self later—it's in there, and can handle it.

As Movement Enhancement, can you add on to your walking, pace, posture, and distance by starting to jog or to run, however slowly? Can you jog or run for half a block or a minute or two? Try it and walk as you need to; try to acclimate. Can you go farther? Try a different route, new scenery? If you are breathing harder and sweating a bit, that is good.

A new suggestion for movement: find a place in nature such as a city park, a beach dune, a forest, or even a fire escape with a pigeon, and do some stretches. Perhaps a red-tailed hawk, a coyote, or a turtle will appear on the scene. If you have no access to a natural setting at this very moment, go into a gym and try to skip the machines near the TV; find a machine that allows you to see outside, whether your view is rooftops or tall trees, and see if the vista does anything for you, such as spark childhood memories or new thoughts. Seek out and integrate nature into your exercise routine as best you can.

Or, as before, try swimming, rowing, skating, skiing, spinning, dancing, yoga, weight lifting, running, mowing grass, raking leaves, or shoveling snow.

MIND REST (5–10 MINUTES A DAY)

This week's new suggestion is to find some green. Do an outdoor chore. As you do the work, be aware of your deep breathing; feel the energy in your arms or legs or back muscles. See if you can somehow be in touch with the many parts of your mind and body. Stop and take a look at both what is around you and inside you. If you see a lawn, a sunset, or an undulating cityscape, that's great. What you behold does not have to be beautiful to inspire or to move you. Let your mind wander.

Try yoga (it is possible to find an outdoor class in some places). I once took a yoga class in which the teacher encouraged lounging on the mat for almost the entire class. She said, "Not doing is just as important as doing." I could not agree more. However, this class made you *feel* as if you had taken an exercise class, when your real self knew that you had not done anything. It was more about the passive mind.

Or, as before, lie on your bed (an outdoor hammock is even better), do nothing, putter around, sit in your favorite spot, listen to music that you enjoy, or sing anything (sing "Ah" if you don't know the words).

Or meditate. Say a mantra (a repeated phrase—whatever feels right, from a prayer to a rhyme). Avoid all but your own thoughts and let them go where they will. Try moving your meditation outdoors, where you can focus on the sounds: the rustles, the chirps, the croaks.

YOUR OWN TWO HANDS (20–40 MINUTES A DAY)

How can you enhance the full sensory or full body experience by using your hands? How can your hands help you to intersect with nature?

This week's new suggestion: today, try to find and enter a place in nature that you have been curious about or physically drawn to, and see what is there for you to use as material for a project. Driftwood for a sculpture? Shells to display in a decorative way? Ferns for a bouquet? Perhaps there is a hand activity that requires strength or skill such as chopping wood. Even if you are inexperienced, can you give it a try or have a friend teach you? Perhaps you can go chop down your own fresh holiday tree (or bush, or branch).

My friend Lisa decided to learn to weld one day even though she had never so much as donned a welder's mask or held a blowtorch. She made metal chairs with a leafy design for her fiancé's outdoor porch. They stood straight and tall as a tree and didn't wobble. My cousin told me he has long wished to do the same exact thing. I once knew an artist who made massive wood and metal sculptures.

We can combine or entwine whatever works.

Don't forget to check in for your Creative Hour:

- Did you set up your Creative Hour time?

- Did you enact the commitment to turn dreaming to doing by taking the concrete steps to work your Creative Hour into your week?

- Are you starting to solidify your creative habit?

- What happened this week or what will happen with your project?

- If you began, how was the initiation? How do you feel about it?

- Were you excited, bored, overwhelmed, underwhelmed, or disappointed in your own production? (Writers often comment about how the page does not reflect the wonderful things that were in their head, so you are in good company if that is what is happening.)

- How are you going to make yourself continue if these initial forays do not make you feel pleased with yourself? (You always get credit for honoring habit.)

You are not allowed to quit, because you are starting to develop.

MIND SHIFT (10–20 MINUTES A DAY)

Look at your past Insight writings. You were there; now you are here. Even if you cannot change physical realities in the moment, you can visualize or imagine other realties. There is no reason why you cannot adopt positive thoughts or imagine settings that offer solace. A woman told me that when she had to undergo an MRI for her spine, she thought about running along the beaches in Costa Rica, where she grew up, and those thoughts calmed her down. If these images have a place in your mind, then that makes it more possible for them to be part of your life somehow, someday.

Are you still in that outside writing place? If it is rainy and gray, can you find a muffled, muggy beauty in that? Here are your prompts.

Write about when you felt:

- Strong
- Fast
- Smart
- Your inner philobat
- Determined and consistent
- A pleasant exhaustion
- Inspired, transcendent, in awe of a natural phenomenon
- Invigorated, energized, peaked by a natural setting
- A euphoric moment after physical effort or in nature
- That pain is not a problem and that you can control the fear
- Healthy, relaxed, okay
- A peaceful surrender
- Good in the grass, field, sun, or drizzle
- That you reached a physical goal
- Lean and mean
- Effective and light
- A secret delight
- At peace in a natural setting
- Like dancing, skipping, jumping or leaping over a mud puddle just because

Now that you are fit or trying to get there, which is just as good, let's jump into other forms of refinement.

8

Creativity and Self-Mastery

We are in bondage to the law in order that we may be free.

—CICERO

MATTERS AT HAND

You have been working through the Creativity Cure for several weeks now. You have excavated psychological issues, addressed your hands and body, and contemplated how nature and community can affect your well-being. In therapeutic processes, the goal is to strengthen and move forward. In creative processes, you express your inner life, shape it into a product, and, as an added plus, further your psychological development. Thus both creative and therapeutic endeavors facilitate self-repair and enhanced experience. In this chapter, we cover self-mastery. Self-mastery is useful for your project as well as for yourself because if you are discriminating about what you do as well as who you are, you maximize your chances for success.

In this chapter we are going to explore the five aspects of self-mastery: compromise, humility, restraint, self-reliance and self-possession, and selection.

WHAT IS SELF-MASTERY?

Self-mastery is a positive form of self-control. Measured behavior helps you adapt to your circumstances, get along with others, and employ your most effective self. Self-mastery means being able to contain momentary impulses so you can direct energies toward loftier interests, long-term goals, sublimated acts (turning raw feelings into refined outcomes), and the greater good, for you as well as others. It means not being a victim to yourself (or others) and not succumbing to self-destructive acts, but rather using self-awareness to make healthy choices. This, of course, also serves those around you. By making you less susceptible to undermining impulses, self-mastery provides an equilibrium that leads to a calm, sturdy sense of self, baseline contentment, and more happy moments.

Self-mastery can enhance your Creative Self. Because you feel "safe" with yourself—not fearful of your own excessive, out-of-control, or destructive behaviors—you are willing to let your mind go where it wants to go. You can indulge in reverie because you know that a temporary loss of control or regression in your mind might lead you to discover something exciting, fresh, fun, or useful. When you trust yourself, True Self can emerge and Creative Capacity can flow. If you know your fantasies will not lead you to untoward action, you will restrict your mind less.

Self-mastery involves an inner compass that is built upon self-knowledge. You cannot develop your own brand of custom-designed self-mastery unless you have the deep awareness that tells you how and when to be strict with yourself and how and when to be lenient. Everyone has a unique recipe for self-mastery based on individual traits and tastes. When you understand yourself, the strictures and freedoms you outline are manageable. Because your choices are rational, attuned, and sensitive, you are more willing to comply with your very own regime. People with self-mastery have an easier time adapting to unexpected situations and getting along with others.

The behaviors we adopt can either entice or repel others; they can allow us to forge ahead or fall apart. When you are the master of yourself, life is easier. You can stand strong, find your way, and focus on engagements rather than recoveries. You have inner authority—a combination of surety, clarity, calm, and rational thinking—which makes you both effective and appealing. Studies have shown that personality and character are greater predictors of success than test scores. Self-mastery is not rigid control but rather using drives, passions, energies, inclinations, and even conflicts to enhance your happiness and to get along with others.

Self-mastery is:

• Being in charge of yourself
• Knowing how to take care of yourself
• Creating a congenial situation for all concerned

WHAT DOES SELF-MASTERY HAVE TO DO WITH CREATIVITY?

We have defined self-mastery as a way of managing yourself, but what is the relationship between self-mastery and creativity? It's pretty simple. There are times when you have to look at yourself with a critical, objective eye and make a decision about what to do or not to do. The same applies to your product or project. Control, restraint, the ability to discard ideas or outcomes to which you may be extremely attached, and a critical and analytical eye are key.

First you let go, employing your True Self to express what is beautiful, disturbing, confusing, or moving to you through your body, with your mind, or with your hands.

When you evolve from True Self to Creative Self, you shape, hone, consider, and deliver a final product that is evocative of you. Your Creative Self takes what your True Self has expressed and sublimates it (turns it from raw to refined) into a concrete outcome. After the free expression of the True Self, the Creative Self employs the rational critic's eye to chisel out a meaningful distillation.

In psychoanalysis we have an expression, "regression in the service of the ego." In the beginning of an analytic treatment the "rules" are to show up for sessions and to say whatever comes to mind, with no editing or judgment, however messy, raw, unbecoming, or controversial it may be. If you feel safe, you will show the True Self. The goal of the analysis is to understand who you are in a deeper way and whether the choices you are making are working for you. Ideally, you will decide to maintain healthy habits and discard self-defeating ones. By the end of a productive treatment, you should feel stronger and clearer about who you are, what you want to do, and how you can do it. Ideally, you will like yourself more, be able to communicate effectively with others, and be able to experience more satisfying moments.

A creative process has a similar trajectory. Raw, messy, incoherent, chaotic expressions emerge, and then you turn them into something that works, that makes sense, and that has meaning to you. Going from Insight to Mind Shift is another way of transforming an untoward inner narrative into a more tenable one, or to master and contain what may have felt overwhelming.

I have observed that there is a parallel process between psychoanalysis and writing. Psychoanalysts like to use the metaphor of Michelangelo creating his statue of David to refer to the analytic process of chipping away at stone-like layers of unhealthy defenses (self-protective behaviors) and forms of False Self to allow the spontaneous, authentic, beautiful being to come forth. I have often thought that the reason so many written drafts of an article or book are necessary is that each one gets you a bit closer to the truth of what you are trying to say.

In the first chapter, we gave you several definitions of creativity. Now we are going to expand the definition a bit because at this point in the Creativity Cure you are ready to think about the next step. Here are two more definitions of creativity that allude to self-mastery and the mastery involved in producing something.

The first definition of creativity includes:

Divergent thinking: expansive, open thinking that can involve
   unusual combinations
Convergent thinking: turning an objective eye to your subject,
   filtering, and deciding what to discard and what to include

Another definition of creativity comes from Dr. Robert J. Sternberg, creativity expert, Tufts psychology professor, and author of many works on the subject including *Successful Intelligence: How Practical and Creative Intelligence Determine Success in Life*. According to this view, creativity involves:

Synthetic ability: the ability to generate new ideas and make connections between ideas or groups of things that often go unnoticed by others

Analytical ability: the ability to think critically, evaluate ideas, accept or reject hypotheses, and anticipate outcomes, responses, or problems

Practical ability: the ability to turn ideas into practical steps and to communicate the value of one's innovations to others

While earlier chapters focused on mental and physical freedom, this chapter discourages a complete letting-go. Now that you are freer with your mind and Creative Capacity is part of you, you will learn how to discriminate in the ways you expand your inner energies and express your ideas. Some conscientious withholding is healthy and useful for you. In this chapter, you will establish anchoring forms of self-mastery.

TERMS TO GRASP

Self-Mastery

Self-mastery involves positive, useful self-control.

Inner Compromise

Inner compromise is finding a balance between passion and practicality. Inner compromise is freeing.

Humility

Humility can be defined as modesty or respectfulness.

Restraint

Restraint involves not acting on your immediate impulse; withholding action.

Self-Reliance and Self-Possession

Self-reliance involves acting independently, while self-possession involves thinking independently.

Selection Capacity

Selection capacity refers to the ability to choose or to discriminate.

Narcissistic Injury

A term coined by Freud but developed by Heinz Kohut, psychoanalyst and father of self-psychology, "narcissistic injury" is used to refer to a fragile, wounded sense of self wherein the feeling of self-worth is easily threatened.

PEOPLE WHO CHANGED

Scott

Scott is a lanky, wealthy, likable thirty-year-old man from Maine. He has achieved everything a parent could want: Ivy League degree, sailing trophies, and excellent manners. Scott attempted suicide at age twenty-two by swallowing a bottle of Vicodin tablets. In spite of his accomplishments, he felt depressed, purposeless, and tormented. He felt disappointed in himself because in spite of his gifts, he could not find contentment or focus on a career goal. He did not want to follow the family trend and work on Wall Street. Something was missing.

"What is wrong with me?" he asked.

He loved his parents, but they were fragile. Scott's mom is an engaging socialite who feels more at ease after four drinks; Scott, on the other hand, feels awkward at festivities because it is hard to banter with people he does not know. He feels self-conscious and sometimes blushes. He thinks that his dad, a "descendant of the ruling class" and a once high-earning but now unemployed executive, is embarrassed about his lot. Scott feels his parents are troubled inside and disappointed in their lives.

After two years of treatment, Scott decided to apply to become a clinical psychologist. Volunteering in a Big Brother program one summer was an eye-opening experience. In college, he had studied the work of Erik Erikson, an expert on identity and a man who named himself after himself, having had an absent father. This self-created thinker captivated Scott at the time and had stayed in the back of his mind.

When Scott was able to understand his own dark side, he no longer felt swept away by angst. Directing empathic energies into his work was healing for him. Through awareness of his inner life, he found identity, direction, and a way to manage himself.

What Scott hands us: Depression can decrease when we understand, own, and direct our inner life effectively—when we have self-mastery.

Phoebe

My client Phoebe trained in business, reached a high level, was laid off, and is happier now as a restaurateur. "Even if you make it to the top, if what you are doing doesn't involve true interest or talent, you won't last," she says. Phoebe believes that in business, her greatest ability was finding out-of-the-box solutions, brainstorming, and interacting with clients. When she was promoted to a managerial position at her old company, she felt bored and bedraggled. Designing events was a compromise that allowed her to use her strongest skills in a new way without returning to an industry that hadn't been a perfect fit. She may not be climbing the corporate ladder, but she has created a niche that makes her happier.

What Phoebe hands us: If the top position does not tap into True Self, it may not be worth it. Self-possession, knowing who you are, knowing what suits you best, and actualizing it will provide more happiness than an impressive position that creates daily angst or pressure because it does not feel natural.

GETTING A HANDLE ON CREATIVITY AND CHARACTER

Character is destiny.

—HERACLITUS, philosopher

I once read that self-betrayal or self-destructive acts are the highest form of immorality. At first glance such a statement would seem to advocate egocentricity. However, people who do not take care of themselves, who are not responsible for themselves, whose behavior is unexamined, and who are not in control of their actions cause pain for others as well as themselves. If you practice enlightened self-care, then you are more capable of caring for others. Self-mastery is a form of self-care and includes awareness, compromise, humility about limitations, restraint from hurtful actions, a sense of how to select things, and self-reliance or self-possession.

FIVE WAYS TO GET A GRIP ON SELF-MASTERY

1. Capacity for Inner Compromise

*When you are aspiring to the highest place, it is honorable to reach
the second or even the third rank.*

—CICERO, philosopher and statesman

As we've seen, inner compromise involves a balance between your
practical needs and your passionate desires, such that you come out on
top whatever the circumstances. Inner compromise involves the ability to assess your situation and find a way to adjust to it without losing
your True Self. The capacity for inner compromise means that you can
make the best of things given who you are, what you want, and what
you are handed. It is about being flexible and finding opportunities
even if they are hidden under a rock.

When you accept limitations, assess risks, know what you can tol-
erably forfeit and what you can realistically achieve, and integrate your
skills and knowledge with your desires, you have achieved inner compromise. If you balance what is fitting and sensible with desires and
impulses, however impractical or unachievable, your passions infuse
your actions and you end up in a satisfying place. When you stretch
for something that is possible for you rather than impossible, you have
made a healthy choice. You have to adapt your urges to the situation.
For example, you might have to decide to wait for what you truly want
rather than settling for gratification in the moment.

Inner compromise might involve being at peace with something
different from your original ideal.

My client Olivia, who trained for a national ballet company in
Houston when she was a child, said that her dream was to be a dancer,
but she was dropped from the company because her body did not
grow into the proper type. Sometimes what you thought you wanted
would not have been best for you, and the second choice, a seeming

compromise, is better. While her original fantasy was to be a prima ballerina, she adapted to physical realities and to the gradual insight that the rigors of a life in ballet might be overwhelming. Becoming a modern dancer—her body type would have been acceptable in this situation—did not feel like the right compromise. Instead she switched gears completely and became an elementary school teacher, a profession that was about nurturance, and this fulfilled her in a different way. The time spent in ballet training was not wasted because it kept her toned and taught her self-discipline, which she could apply to other forms of learning. The choice to be a teacher involved an inner compromise that allowed her to live a stable, safe, pleasurable life.

For my client Giselle, law school was a lifelong goal. She was a good student, but when she took her LSAT she did not score in the top range, which immediately ruled out several schools. Still, she applied to them. Each time she received a rejection letter she was shocked and devastated. Eventually, she accepted the inner compromise, attended a fine school, and now has a gratifying job. She likes her coworkers, as they are not ruthlessly competitive.

My client Rebecca told me that when she was fifteen, she looked in the mirror at her broad shoulders and said, "I am not beautiful. I will probably never have a boyfriend or get married." She envied slight girls sauntering to the beach with a bevy of boys carrying their bags. Rebecca felt that she had better find something else to do. She became a volleyball champion, found friends among her teammates, and found a husky boyfriend on another team.

Olivia, Giselle, and Rebecca embraced what they had, eschewed an unrealistic ideal, and came out ahead.

Inner compromise can be applied to what you produce as well as who you are. When you design products, projects, programs, parties, and functions, sometimes you have to compromise on what you are able to do. There may be financial restrictions or limited material. You may not have many choices. If you are innovative and can adjust, find a way to use the non-ideal, and let your imagination override your frustration, you have served the Creative Self and employed self-mastery.

To help achieve inner compromise, understand your wishes, ideals, and dreams. Don't hold back. This is a time to be grandiose. Indulge the lofty vision.

Now, assess your situation practically, financially, and with respect to your responsibility to others. Think about what is achievable or how you might work it out or compromise so you can come close. This might seem like a simple answer, but it takes psychological strength to enact it. Some people feel humiliated or injured by not achieving their ideal, and they feel that anything that falls short is shameful. This leads them to approach plan B with ambivalence or resentment. Such an attitude, in turn, can defeat the next phase of engagement. Try to embrace the compromise, and it might turn out to be just the situation that allows you to flourish. Be curious about how you came up with your ideal in the first place. Was it your true preference, or was there an external influence that steered your inner knowledge or intuition? Maybe your priorities were not lined up properly or you were swayed by an outside force.

Let the ideal feed the real. That is usually good enough as far as satisfaction goes.

Ideas to Grapple With

- When has a compromise or a second choice turned out to be the best outcome for you?
- When has facing the truth about your situation and making adjustments allowed you to succeed?
- When has it ever been unsettling but ultimately a relief to just be yourself and perhaps choose to do something that is natural for you but less impressive to others?
- What elements about yourself once gave you pause, but now you consider them quirky, special, or just "normal" after all? Have you been able to integrate these qualities and find a way to work with them? In what ways might they have strengthened your position?

Hold this thought: Inner compromise is a way
to be creative and resourceful, and
to achieve self-mastery.

---

2. Capacity for Humility

Humility helps with Creative Capacity, the True Self, the Creative Self, and the creative habit, according to choreographer Twyla Tharp. Humility is *not* assuming you know more than you do, or that you are grander than you might be. It is being at peace with the fact that you need to learn some things. Having self-esteem is good, but it is best for your self-image to be grounded in reality. You may not be a whiz at all subjects, which is fine. Whatever you may lack, you can probably learn, but if you do not care to learn it, that is your privilege as an imperfect person.

Humility protects you because it makes you prepare. You do your homework. Humility is the opposite of grandiosity, wherein a person inflates his or her importance, expertise, appeal, or feeling of entitlement. People with an unhealthy dose of narcissism tend to be grandiose. Grandiose persons put forth less effort because they assume they are superior, and they can fall hard from this perch.

My friend Regis sent me an email with a comment about bumptious colleagues. I did not know what the word "bumptious" meant, so I looked it up. It means "sniffy, chesty, toplofty, and overweening," and I wrote back to inform Regis of what I had learned. He replied, "*Toplofty* made my day." Sporting a bumptious persona can become an insidious form of self-torture. Such an attitude does not manifest true self-esteem, as that can come only from serious effort and self-knowledge.

Grandiose people accumulate deficiencies because the learning process feels demeaning for them. If you have a robust sense of self, you can tolerate the idea that in some areas you are weaker than others. People with narcissistic injury (a fragile, wounded sense of self) are often grandiose and find it very hard to admit any weakness, flaw, or imperfection in themselves. It can be hard for them to acknowledge abilities or talents in others, which can compromise their relationships. These are the same people who find learning difficult because they cannot tolerate *not* being an expert from the get-go. They are also the ones who find it hard to be accountable. Wellness requires a deep acceptance of the self both as it is and as it can be, given one's nature and the circumstances. It requires the capacity for humility and effort.

Be willing to admit that you don't know everything. It is okay to say, "I don't know." Willingness to not know, to be curious, and to be wrong will take you far. Some people are loath to say "I don't know," "I don't know what *hubris* means," "I never saw *The Godfather*," "I have never been to Paris," or "I don't know how to ski."

Alton and I have both observed that clients and patients always seem surprised and relieved to hear us say, "I don't know, but I will do my best to figure it out." It is best to leave your hubris at home, say "I don't know," and then go find out what you need to know.

But why is not knowing so shameful? People often lie about it. But doing so is unnecessary. When someone says, "Well, gee, I don't know," or "I never learned that," do you not feel more curious, respectful, or motivated to share?

"There are no stupid questions," said your kindergarten teacher.

Maybe you disagree. Maybe there really are some stupid questions. Maybe because someone just wants to shoot her hand up, or to be heard, or feel included, or discharge anxiety, she blurts out queries without forethought. Rather than growing frustrated with the questioner, consider what prompted the question.

Modesty and respect for others will serve both you and those around you. For one thing, these traits attract other people, whereas bombast and pomposity repel people. Humility is all about being your True Self, deficiencies included. Because people can sense sincerity in your personal presentation, others may be drawn to you and see you as trustworthy. Humility is acknowledgment of your True Self, admitting who you are and what you do and do not know. Covering it up and pretending to be something or someone else usually backfires.

Humility is great for creativity because if you knew it all, if you had all the answers, if you could just plug in a solution from your all-knowing head, then you would not have an interesting process with an unusual outcome, and you would probably miss out on some delightful surprises. As you know, process is often where the joy lies.

As far as your creative process goes, be comfortable with "I don't know," loose ends, and no answers. Muddle around for a while. Finding something that works, feels right, and makes sense to you after a murky period is exciting. *When you are comfortable with being puzzled, and are observant and receptive, excellent solutions surface.* Your Creative Self is deeply enriched by "I don't know."

Dr. Druss once told me that the ability to be curious and puzzled in the treatment room, to not know, takes you to deeper places with your client.

Suggestions for cultivating humility:

- Take a rigorous inventory of yourself in private or with someone you trust.

- What is it that you think you are supposed to know that you do not? Do you really have to be an expert on this subject?

- What are the knowledge-deficient areas that make you feel self-conscious?

- Practice admitting them by saying, "I know about this, but I don't know about that."

- See what happens inside when you say "I don't know."

- Does saying "I don't know" make you anxious because you imagine someone with haughty disdain, someone who makes fun of you, someone who rejects you? Does the irrational critic rear its barbed head?

- What can you do about that? Imagine potential responses and understand your inner reaction.

- Can you look someone straight in the eye and say, "I don't know about that, but it sounds like you do. Tell me more"?

Convey an interest. Why not? It could be intriguing for you. Let someone else share his or her excitement and expertise.

- Be a good listener: it can be fulfilling as well as giving.

- Now, play with the idea (in your inner mind or with a trusted other) of saying that you saw something, read something, or did something that you actually did not—lying about the matter to save face. What is the inner feeling associated with doing this? Do you feel more or less safe?

I once had a client who told me in the first session that she was a pathological liar. I thought, "How am I going to handle this? How will I know when she is telling me the truth?" It was tempting at first to try to distinguish truth from fiction, but then I gave up because it was almost impossible. We talked about it, and I told her I wasn't going to be able to distinguish for sure, although I did note that a pause, a wait for a reaction, a certain look, seemed to follow certain stories. Eventually we developed a trust and together tried to figure out why she might be tempted to exaggerate or lie about her accomplishments. When our rapport deepened and she had the sense that she could be valued for her real qualities and talents (which were numerous), the tall tales ceased.

Ideas to Grapple With

- When have you felt embarrassed or ashamed for not knowing something?
- When have you felt afraid to make or reveal a mistake?
- When have things worked out in spite of the mistake?
- If you admitted to the error in judgment and came clean, how did you feel afterward?
- When might you have exaggerated to impress? How did you feel afterward?

Hold this thought: Remain humble, ask questions,
and say "I don't know" sometimes. This is
a form of self-mastery and
fosters creativity.

3. Capacity for Restraint

This spring, I took our children Nicholas and Caroline to a butterfly room at a museum: three hundred butterflies, warm light, lush plants, rising steam, chrysalises, identification charts, delighted faces, and joyous exclamations. I thought, "What would it be like to work in a place where people start beaming the second they enter?" Where there is unadulterated, unrestrained, fresh-faced pleasure every day?

I told the grinning Nicholas and Caroline not to stick out fingers and encourage landings. They mostly restrained themselves, but a few times they could not resist the temptation to touch the butterflies.

The guard told me that not only do people try to hold the butterflies, but they also try to steal them. The day before, he said, a woman had put one in her purse. When she purchased a card at the gift shop, it flew out and landed on the cash register. I asked him if that was considered a crime, and what is done in such a case. The guard shook his head, shrugged, and said in a soft voice, "The way I like to put it is that some people are immune to moral embarrassment."

Rather than being immune, as this woman was, know when you should restrain yourself, or when you have gone too far and should even feel a little shame. Clients have told me about risky, unrestrained behaviors involving driving, drinking, drugs, hook-ups, infidelities, Internet involvements, and thefts that have shaken them up. In the moment, they found it easy to deny, minimize, or compartmentalize their actions—to put the risk factor in a box in the mind and seal it up completely. Risky behaviors and bad choices are as common as they are human, but if you can maintain a little anxiety about the consequences it can protect you as well as others.

Teaching yourself the benefits of long-term gratifications over short-term ones is very useful for self-mastery. Your inner dialogue might go something like this: "I want it now, but if I restrain myself, I will be better off." Teaching yourself to comply with good sense even when you want to defy it (perhaps rebelling is a thrill) will deliver a much better chance for happiness. If you need a group, a sponsor, or a friend to help you restrain and contain, that is an excellent way to go.

A little restraint goes a long way for the health of your True Self and Creative Self because delayed gratification usually fosters a more satisfying long-term result.

Suggestions for fostering restraint:

- Think about when you have done something you wished you had not, or got caught, or felt ashamed. Don't judge, but let yourself feel the ramifications.

- Use this feeling to motivate yourself to choose differently next time.

- If you can hold off the impulse to intrude or even speak at times, see where it gets you. Often if you hold off for the first minutes, it will become easier.

- If you have a need to defy, rebel, be different, challenge authority, say no or even "screw you," or take risks for the sake of asserting your independence, be aware and find a way to channel your feistiness into refined action. You will be better off. For example, if you have an abundance of aggression, hit the *ball* hard, not the gas pedal.

- Guide your actions with inner awareness and a smidgen of anxiety, as this will help you keep yourself and others safe.

Ideas to Grapple With
- What does the word "restrain" mean to you? How do you define it?

- When have you been so moved by beautiful things that you could not resist the urge to have, hold, take, or purchase them, when perhaps it was best to restrain yourself?
- What experiences have you had with restraint that were torturous? Uplifting?
- Which of your behaviors have been hard to live with?
- What experiences have you had with holding your tongue that helped you? What about when blurting out that something or someone hurt you?
- When have you violated another and gotten away with it? When have you gotten caught? What was that like?

Hold this thought: Restraint often enhances your situation. Take risks that have the potential to better your situation, not worsen it.

---

4. Capacity for Self-Reliance and Self-Possession

The only true joy is self-possession in the face of adversity.

—BOETHIUS, philosopher

Fortune is fickle, to paraphrase the philosopher Boethius, but self-reliance and self-possession will hold fast. Self-reliance is being able to act independently, and self-possession is being able to think independently. When you have self-reliance and self-possession, you are more likely to have fulfilling days. You are the master of yourself. Self-reliance and self-possession are based on following inner inclinations, having the capacity for self-direction, being able to self-soothe, and being able to find alternatives within your own mind. They are all about inner reassurance and resourcefulness. If you have a rational critic inside you and can find a way to reinforce yourself in spite of scathing criticism or rejection, you are much better able to move on.

For example, it is great to be a standout, a star, or a soloist, to be the acknowledged one. But often that experience pales in comparison to the one you have when you conquer cracks in your register, tighten the wobbly vibrato in your voice, and hit the high D effortlessly in the privacy of your own room. Such moments are the essence of a good, ordinary life that can, if you let it, include peak experiences. Independence from evaluation by others can protect you when outer reinforcement is not forthcoming. This is self-possession.

Self-possession is also useful for the Creative Self. When you honor and trust your own mind and your independent thoughts, you are better able to commit to and pursue your creative instincts. You are able to go your own way. Sometimes you are marching to your own drummer, especially if others do not quite understand what you are doing, but if you can tolerate a bit of this, it is worth it.

Self-reliance, because it is all about independence and resourcefulness, will also help you push through your process, develop your own method, and complete the task. If you do not wait for others to rescue you, you will find a way even if it takes a while. And in the end, creating your own solution will make you happy.

> Authentic happiness is always independent of external conditions.
>
> —Attributed to EPICTETUS, philosopher

Suggestions for cultivating self-reliance and self-possession:

- Find ways to get where you want to go without asking for help, but be patient with yourself. Test yourself and see how well you tolerate the independence.

- Study the map and see where you end up.

- Honor your inclinations, as wispy as they may seem. Ask yourself, *Why does this passage make me uncomfortable? Why do I get very emotional when I see this?* and so on. When you really understand your inner reactions—what you like, what you don't like, and why—it is easier to develop self-possession. Some people really have trouble knowing what they truly think and feel.

- Explore artistic, intellectual, athletic, and domestic areas so you can uncover your own vision and express it. Respect your pace of progress.

Ideas to Grapple With

- When have you been able to stand strong in the face of rejection or severe criticism?
- When have you been devastated or crushed or lost confidence because of an outside evaluation? How might you have had a different response? What perspective on the matter might have helped you?
- What experiences have you had with self-reliance? When have you had to forge ahead with no help or support? What was that like? How did you manage?
- How are you dependent and how are you self-reliant? In which ways do you have a mind of your own and in which ways do you prefer to follow others? Were there times when you followed others and regretted it?

Hold this thought: Self-reliance and self-possession are excellent tools for happiness and creativity.

---

5. Capacity for Selection

Creative decisions are more likely to bubble up from a brain that applies unconscious thought to a problem.... It is much harder if we are under a deluge of data.

—SHARON BEGLEY, writer

We have become victims of excess. Excess stuff, bought because it was a "good deal," because it was cheap, or because commercial pressure got the better of us, can burden or even wall us in. Advertisements and peer pressure can make us purchase things we neither need nor want. Suffocating accumulations overwhelm us. In our current culture, the ability to rule things out is a survival technique. It seems counterintuitive to have to put things out of the mind rather than put things in, but because we are inundated with junk mail, telephone solicitations, images, messages, requests, and spam, selecting what we focus on is an important strategy, a modern-day life skill. In the words of William James, "The art of being wise is the art of knowing what to overlook."

In ninth grade our daughter Chloe wrote and illustrated a story called "Olive the Greedy Mouse." Two mice scurry into a well-stocked house, gathering all manner of items and bringing them back to their tiny mouse hole. Soon they have so much stuff in their little mouse hole that they can no longer see or hear each other, or even move around. They are paralyzed by their relentless pursuit of possessions. Greed leads to a total disconnection between them, a total loss of mouse humanity. The moral, which you already know, is that less is more and relationships will do more for you than accumulations.

I once told a client who enjoyed eating a whole bag of Oreos in one sitting that the experience of saying no to the last two cookies was a good start, the first flex of inner muscle. Instead of completely caving in, she could maintain a tiny grip. For her the true goal was not fewer cookies or losing weight but rather beginning to build an identity as someone who can say no.

Jim, Alton's dad, always says: "We have everything we need. We really don't need anything else."

Less is more.

Selection capacity is the ability to rule out most things and decide on just a few that are right for you, things that enhance your situation rather than cluttering it up. Selection capacity is more important today, as we are inundated with images on the Internet, inexpensive and appealing items to buy, and a plethora of television channels.

Those with good selection capacity can protect themselves from an endless and distracting onslaught.

In medicine, physicians are trained to formulate what is called a differential diagnosis, a list of all the ailments a person could have, from the most obvious to the most obscure. After careful testing, examining, and getting to know the patient, the physician winnows down the choices, arrives at the most likely diagnosis, and then institutes the proper treatment. At first, though, open-mindedness is important for thorough exploration, since you want to cover all the bases.

Applying this method of ruling things out, starting broad and ending narrow, to your personal matters can be lifesaving. When you have a careful thought process about your choices, tastes, instincts, likes, and dislikes, you are more capable of ruling things out with inner conviction and ending up in the right place or with the proper item. You'll also end up pleased instead of distraught. Selection is not easy for some people. They are seduced and overstimulated by many things and then begin to doubt their own minds.

Improved self-awareness leads to a far easier time with selection.

Selection capacity is good for the Creative Self because when you are discriminating, clear, and self-aware, you can choose well, commit to your project, and feel good about your process. You can refine and streamline what you present to others. You'll feel a sense of control, wholeness, and completion because what you have constructed is a distillation of you and what is meaningful to you.

"Look, listen, and feel." This is what doctors are taught in the context of doing a medical exam. Pay attention to your senses as you observe. Wait for something to start to make sense in your mind, for the answer to be clear. Listen for the inner clues and let them float around for a while. If you act too quickly, you lose the opportunity to know yourself. Wait and let options fall away until the true preference, based on your individual tastes and true identity, surfaces.

Ideas to Grapple With

- When have you felt overwhelmed by choice or when did you feel clear about your selection of items, friends, lovers, or career choices?

- When have you rushed to grab something, and ended up with things you did not want or need, and wished you hadn't?
- When have you ruled out certain possibilities without fully exploring them?
- Do you feel impatient and anxious just waiting and letting the right answer come to you?
- Can you say no?

Hold this thought: The capacity to select and discriminate is useful for self-mastery and creativity because restraint helps you clarify what is truly meaningful for you.

CONCLUSION

In this chapter we explored the concept of self-mastery. The bottom line is that when you have self-awareness and self-control, you feel lighter and better. While the purpose of this chapter is not to proselytize about character, if you practice self-mastery you will build character as well as inner strength, an independent mind, and the capacity to do without. This makes you less dependent on things you may not be able to control. Your inclinations and identity will be clear to you.

SUMMARY

In this chapter, we explored character and outlined aspects of self-mastery. Self-mastery includes capacities for compromise formation, humility, restraint, self-reliance and self-possession, and selection. We spoke about the risks of overstimulation.

FIVE-PART PRESCRIPTION: WEEK SIX
Swept Away to Self-Mastery

INSIGHT (10–20 MINUTES A DAY)

What choices have you made that trouble you and make you feel unhealthy or out of control? Write with abandon—no control, no restraint. Regress, be messy, and let whatever spills out spill. Restraint is useful for other parts of your life, but for your private revelations, let go. Write about when you felt:

- All over the place, swayed, swept away, swept up
- Out of control
- In trouble
- Bigheaded, overblown, grandiose (though it is true that a bit of vanity or grandiosity can help bolster confidence)
- Inelegant
- Unclear
- Purposeless
- That you behaved in an embarrassing manner or exhibited poor manners and felt bad about it
- Overwhelmed by emails or objects

Because too much input disorganizes the mind, and responding can become a stultifying task, we may begin to feel out of control. In order to respond to everything, we have to skip around and thus sacrifice breadth for depth. According to Nicholas Carr, author of *The Shallows: What the Internet Is Doing to Our Brains,* this creates a culturally induced form of attention deficit disorder and anxiety.

For the second set of Insight writings, think about how overstimulation affects you and leads you away from self-mastery.

- How does excess input make you feel or think?
- Are you frenetic, anxious, or depressed because of the overload? Unable to prioritize?

- Do you feel connected to many but somehow less involved?
- Have you felt that you must change your ways, that you must purchase a flashier car, the latest flatscreen, phone, or something else?
- Have you worried that who you are or what you have is not acceptable?
- Instead of self-possession, self-reliance, and self-mastery, are you ever pulled toward comparing or competing?

MOVEMENT (15–30 MINUTES A DAY)

When we have mastered a technique such as running, jogging, or walking, then we are in a position to be creative with it, change it, make it new and novel, make it our own, or turn it into something else. When we have self-mastery, posture, alignment, and prowess, we are free to innovate and create, to choreograph our very own Movement plan.

The Movement Enhancement for this week: Can you run more than you walk? At least as much as you walk? Can you run, walk, run, walk, run, walk, and then run more?

Can you make your movement new in some way? Can you change directions? Can you stop and add arm exercises, sit-ups, ballet positions, or yoga postures while focusing on a spot in front of you?

Can you add a separate and new form of movement, and try to master the very basics? Try to make yourself a little uncomfortable so you can see how well you can tolerate the feeling? (You can if you have a mind-set that is patient, accepting, and a little bit brave.)

Or, as before, try swimming, rowing, skating, skiing, spinning, dancing, yoga, weight lifting, running, mowing grass, raking leaves, or shoveling snow.

MIND REST (5–10 MINUTES A DAY)

We all have "passive longings." This is a psychoanalytic term that refers to the need to let someone else handle it so you can hang out. Passivity and healthy dependence are an essential part of the human experience. While effort, action, and self-mastery are crucial, sometimes you have to indulge. You just have to stay in your pajamas.

For my friend Despina, pajamas are the perk of her job. She translates the dialogue in foreign films, so she can sit in her house in her pajamas all day with her dog at her feet.

I have heard from a few friends and a couple of clients that the day they each stayed home in their pajamas was the day they felt happy and calm.

Even if we fear sloth, we can still be psychologically victorious via the passive position, with pajamas or without. Really. When you slow down and take care of yourself, you are better equipped for challenges.

My children's pediatrician is named Dr. Barney Softness. This is his real name, and there is always something useful about the incidental comments he drops, such as "Your kids just need to hang out with you." I had asked him whether I should sign up three-year-old Chloe for multiple classes in disparate locations, as the whole enterprise felt sort of stressful. His comment relieved my guilt about not "doing" and also made me realize that a relationship can further a mind in ways that formal lessons might not. Conversations over the kitchen counter or while raking the leaves can be worth a whole lot. When I told my friend Sara, who was running all over Manhattan in cabs to get her kids to the "right" classes, what Dr. Softness had said about hanging out, she started to cry.

For Mind Rest, hang out—with a friend, with your family, and perhaps in your pajamas. Commit to rest and relaxation, in spite of the wagging finger you envision. It will prepare you for the harder stuff involved in self-mastery.

Or, as before, lie on your bed, do nothing, putter around, sit in your favorite spot, listen to music that you enjoy, or sing anything (sing "Ah" if you do not know the words).

Or meditate. Say a mantra (a repeated phrase—whatever feels right, from a prayer to a rhyme). Avoid all but your own thoughts, and let them go where they will.

YOUR OWN TWO HANDS (20–40 MINUTES A DAY)

Alton's dad, Jim, says, "I like to do as many things for myself as I can."

This chapter was about self-mastery. We are going to try to keep you on track to meet your True Self and Creative Self by assessing whether you are taking concrete steps. Sticking with the concrete steps through thick and thin is a form of self-mastery. Grappling, scratching, mixing it up, and plugging your way through, as messy and as unglamorous as it can be, is how you get to the higher place.

For your Creative Hour check-in, think about these questions:

- Do you feel you want to change course with your project? Are you honoring your commitment even if the experience has not peaked at this point?

- How is that going? What have you noticed? Do you love what you are doing? Do you just like it? Are you not sure? Do you feel eager to get back to it or obligated?

- If slow learning is involved, can you stick with it? Sometimes things click into place all of a sudden. You didn't think you were getting anywhere and then one day you realize that you were absorbing knowledge and developing unawares.

- Are you engaging, muddling through, and tolerating ineptitude by feeling great about the fact that you have made a big change by taking this step? We are overemphasizing this in the interest of helping you develop a taste for delayed gratification, because that is a crucial part of self-mastery and contentment.

- Recall that character and personality are great predictors of success, and think about how that applies to you.

- What is your goal? Can you keep a visual image of it?

- How do you define success with regard to your particular
goal? Must you have notoriety? Would mastery be enough?
Do you have to have public acknowledgment or money?
Or do you simply need an end result that pleases you
and only you?

- Can you separate out the pleasure factor from the impressing-
others factor in your mind? Can you pursue your goal for
reasons other than what others will think?

- Can you make this project be about self-mastery and mastery
of a craft, body of knowledge, or art form for itself, because
that is a fine thing to do, because it is a quiet and dignified way
to be with yourself and others with whom you cross paths?

- Now that you have practiced divergent (playful, experimental)
thinking, can you apply convergent (selective, objective)
thinking to your efforts? (Refer back to page 196 for a
refresher on divergent and convergent thinking.)

- Your efforts thus far have been synthetic—they have involved
putting together different pieces. Can you now turn an
analytical and practical eye to your project and see what you
think of it, employing your inner rational critic?

MIND SHIFT (10–20 MINUTES A DAY)

Look at your Insight Writings. Sometimes things are out of control,
either within you or outside you. If you had perfect restraint all the
time, you would be too controlled. Focus on knowing when to hold on
and when to let go. Freud talked about the rider riding the horse rather
than the horse riding the rider. Let us gather, hold, and contain.

Write about when you felt:

- Pleasantly humble
- Content with compromise
- In control

- Self-reliant, self-possessed
- Refined, graceful, grateful
- Self-contained
- Neat, clean, clear, orderly
- Punctual and pleased
- Accountable, responsible, careful, and free
- Purposeful
- Able to exhibit grace unobserved
- Self-mastery

Now let us see how we can move from self to other, from inner mastery to outer contribution. True Connections is our next stop and, in many ways, the most important one. We are happier people when we are involved with others or making a contribution.

9

Creativity and True Connections

When you choose your friends, don't be short-changed
by choosing personality over character.

—W. SOMERSET MAUGHAM, writer

MATTERS AT HAND

There is almost nothing more fulfilling than being your True Self with a true friend. Few things compare to feeling treasured, free, and accepted in spite of your foibles. True Connections to friends and loved ones are based upon empathy, loyalty, and kindness—a feeling of emotional safety. A clear identity helps, too, because if you are your True Self, you are more likely to find someone you can relate to and to attract like minds. Showing the True Self enhances relationships because while your authentic characteristics may not appeal to everyone, those whom they do attract are those with whom you can create a solid connection. Authenticity augments True Connections, and True Connections augment authenticity and creativity.

How so? When you find real friends with whom you can be spontaneous, truthful, and vulnerable, show the dark side, the true side, the edgy side, or even the ugly side, there is trust between you. Trust facilitates deeper conversations, and substantive conversations foster creative thought and discovery. True Connections enhance the True Self and the Creative Self because the depth in the interaction allows unconscious, rough-edged material to emerge.

Research has shown that friendships can help us recover from illness, deal with stress, face challenges, assuage loneliness (which causes depression), increase happiness, and enhance mental health. In one study on breast cancer, women with friends, with a support network, were four times more likely to survive. Research has shown that friendships can protect against heart disease and cardiac arrest.

In another study, students asked to climb a hill with a heavy backpack perceived the hill as less steep if they could face it with a friend. The longer the duration of the friendship, the less daunting the hill seemed. Having a couple of trustworthy friends moves you forward and takes you deeper into your True Self because friends help you face challenges, take risks, and uncover hidden parts of yourself. If you do not have to hide your vulnerability, if you can expose your real self, you are poised for a creative existence. True friends, with whom the organic self arises, foster Creative Capacity because you talk about what matters to you.

Friendship is a valid medical treatment. Research has shown that true friendships change our neurochemistry. When women experiencing stress seek solace from friends, the connection causes oxytocin, a calming hormone, to be released. According to Ethel Person, MD, eminent psychoanalyst and researcher, a trusted companion or confidant can be the cornerstone of creative output.

Forming True Connections is a great do-it-yourself therapy as well as a foundation for a creative life. The idea that a little help from your friends lets you survive or thrive is true. However, learning how to build and maintain real friendships can be a challenge, especially in a culture that fosters superficial social links. You might know that real friends matter, but you may still resist taking steps to solidify your relationships. You may be afraid to make a gesture or build a relationship because you fear rejection. But reaching out and following up is worth the psychological effort. With a bit of assistance, you can over-come mild social anxiety and bring stronger, truer connections into your life along with the attendant benefits.

In order to have a True Connection to someone else, you must first have a True Connection to yourself. You achieve this by understanding your requirements both large and small as far as relationships are con-cerned. Your needs are a condensation, representation, and expression of significant inner matters, past and present. If you don't smile much, maybe you need to be around people who make you laugh. Or maybe you need to be around people who welcome dark or intense conversa-tions. One client, a nurse and mother of four who managed medical trauma daily, told me that it was hard to be around moms who didn't work outside the house because she felt like crying sometimes, and she worried they would be put off by her intensity.

Some people are devastated if their birthday is overlooked; others could not care less. One client told me that her sister was outraged if no one made the drive to the airport to pick her up; to her, taking a cab felt like a rejection. My client, however, actually preferred to have a period of alone time in the cab before she faced the family holidays.

She usually called her best friend before, during, and after these holiday visits. Her friend finally told her, "I don't think you should go back to that house. You get totally depressed, and it takes you two months to get over it." My client's friend gave her the support and hon-esty she needed.

There are many options for True Connections. You can have a trusting, safe, abiding relationship with a friend, spouse, boyfriend, sibling, parent, cousin, teacher, counselor, or adviser. The important thing is to understand the nature of your relationships with different people. Some dynamic, interesting, or charismatic people can be very seductive but are not that reliable. Even if they are not the most loyal or trustworthy people, you can still enjoy their company. Just teach yourself not to get too attached in order to protect yourself.

I bring this up because I have seen several clients over the years who fall for friends or lovers who appear to care about them and say tender, complimentary things in the moment but then disappear, torment them, or do not commit. This is injurious and hard to get over. Some people spend months wondering what happened and saying "What did I do wrong?" over and over in a ruminative fashion.

You did not do anything wrong. It is not *about* right or wrong, but rather about real self, authenticity, compatibility, and the possible shallowness of the other. (Narcissistic people are prone to seduce and abandon.) Even if you could have summoned up a behavioral plan to entice your paramour or friend to stay, if it isn't or wasn't your natural way, it wouldn't last and probably would not be worth it.

It helps to be careful about with whom you share the real feelings, worries, wishes, past troubles, and present concerns. When you are selective about your attachments, it solidifies your identity and preserves your capacity to be vulnerable with another—to trust. With fewer defenses (self-protective mechanisms) against the fear of a broken heart, you will have a greater chance of happiness. Do I sound like a mother warning you to avoid the "bad crowd"? Sorry, I can't help it. It's not so much about good or bad behavior but rather about kind or cruel disposition. Some people have sadistic traits. The ability to discern who is truly capable of love, loyalty, compassion, and generosity will protect you. Exposing yourself in a relationship only to find out that it was not reciprocal is so painful. The real and true support, the right emotional connections, the loving people are out there. If you find them, they can help you flourish creatively and otherwise. They can help you be healthy. A few transgressions or insensitivities are inevitable. You just have to determine your tolerance level and be aware of the kind of teasing that is okay with you.

Social connection helps push the brain in an antidepressant direction, turning down activity in stress circuitry, and boosting the activity of feel-good brain chemicals like serotonin and dopamine.... We need to ... place our relationships at the very top of the priority list. Truly, nothing in life matters more.

—STEPHEN ILARDI, psychologist

Here are some questions to ask yourself about True Connections:

- How safe do you feel with this person?

- Do you feel you have to edit, hold back, or walk on eggshells?

- Can you expose matters that are troubling you, or that you are excited about, without fear of being betrayed? Do you feel safe and trusting or are you worried when you share things that are really important to you? Do you somehow feel unsettled after revealing issues that are on your mind?

- Are you constantly trying to read the other person to see if he or she is still with you?

- Do you have the sense that the other person is on your side? Would she or he be happy if you failed?

- Are you so preoccupied with pleasing another person that it is making you anxious or worried?

- Does the other person retaliate or act in a mean or snide way if you do not measure up to his or her standard? How does that make you feel? (Clients have told me that they have been told by significant others that their pores are too big, their belly is too fat, or their feet are pigeon-toed.) People say what they want to say. You just have to decide how you feel about it and how you want to handle it: snap back, walk away, overlook it, comment on the callousness, and so on.

- Could you call if you were stuck, alone, or needy in some way?

- How loyal might this person be? How important is loyalty to you?

- Maybe you choose charming personality over loyal character. What kind of impact has this choice had on you?

Here is what you want to think about for True Connections, creativity, and a potential partnership:

- Can you expose your flawed work to this person?
- Will this person critique rationally and without malice and help you grow?
- Will this person stimulate your mind or the work in a helpful way?
- Is there a free-flowing, easy dialogue between you?
- Do you laugh together?
- Does the collaboration feel easy and natural?
- Does this person help you discover things you might not have discovered on your own?
- Does this person bring out parts of you that others do not?

> A relationship is a physiological process as real and as potent
> as any pill or surgical procedure.
>
> —DAVID SERVAN-SCHREIBER, MD, PHD

REVIEW OF TERMS

True Connection

A relationship that bolsters and supports your True Self is a True Connection. It is a reciprocal, healthy relationship.

Empathy

Empathy is the ability to understand and identify with another's feelings or situation.

PEOPLE WHO CHANGED

Brianna

Brianna is a nineteen-year-old college freshman. She has had trouble making close friends ever since her best friend of three years dropped her when she was thirteen and became friends with a girl with a "mean streak." They chided her for wearing her treasured jeans two days in a row. They bullied her about her hair, the car her mother drove, and the fact that her father was an immigrant. Still, she wanted to be accepted, so she tried to win affection by offering them trinkets, by tolerating their jabs, and by sharing her party dress, which came back crumpled and stained. She was so concerned about acceptance that it was hard to focus on schoolwork or extracurricular activities. Brianna evolved into a fearful, inhibited, and guarded person. As a teen, she spent hours watching reruns of movies involving vampires. She worried that she would never have real friends.

The first time she experienced true friendship was when she went to college. Her first roommate became her best friend. They were both interested in stories about the supernatural as well as interior design. They chatted about many subjects while lounging on their twin beds and shopped for a rug together. When Brianna stopped trying to be accepted, she found a True Connection. Friendships, she says, are more important to her than anything.

"I know what it is to be lonely," she told me.

What Brianna hands us: The environment that fosters your True Self can heal early wounds. You are more likely to find True Connections with worthwhile others if you are not too anxious to please; this elicits cruelty or disdain in some people. A clear identity and strong interests lead to enriching interactions.

Jean-Paul

Jean-Paul, a twenty-seven-year-old chef from Montreal, came to me because he had recently moved to New York and was having trouble meeting people. When he invited new acquaintances to a dinner party hardly anyone responded to the email. He felt completely alone and embarrassed after this attempt, because it had taken courage to reach out in the first place. He was a self-conscious and insecure person. At times, he was tempted to move back home, where he would not have to face strange situations, but the thought of living with his reclusive parents was troubling. I wondered if he had somehow developed a social anxiety by osmosis (seeping in of the family pattern), because they, by his description, were estranged from *their* community.

In our sessions we tried to understand his social fears. Sometimes he felt so stiff and worried when he was with others that he neglected to convey interest in them, to ask about them. He couldn't relate in an easy and natural way, which made him seem aloof. Though he was awkward, he was eager to connect. He was easily injured, sensitive to every glance, gesture, or body posture, and often interpreted these actions in negative ways. It was hard to concentrate on his cooking when he was feeling deflated.

We worked on his sensitivities and tried to thicken his skin. He made friends with a hostess at his job, and they decided to throw a party together for coworkers and friends. Everyone was impressed with the mutual cooking effort and it was fun.

What Jean-Paul hands us: If you can overcome the initial awkwardness and tolerate the discomfort, you might meet someone you can relate to. If you are clear about your creative interests and stick with them, you will find like minds.

GETTING A GRASP ON THE "BEST FRIEND" FANTASY

The wish for a "best friend" is common. Have you ever met someone and thought that this person could be your best friend? This wish can be a way of saying, I want to be totally understood, accepted, and treasured. I want someone who values me above others. I want to be the one and only. It might be an unconscious wish to merge in symbiotic bliss and unconditional love, as we did as infants. But as it turns out, symbiosis is not always bliss. Even infants need space, and unconditional love may not be a good idea if someone can't resist hurting you. You can still love that person if you must, but maybe you should focus your deepest affections elsewhere.

At any rate, it is possible that you have a wish to coalesce, to merge, to have a singular bond that solves all your emotional needs. This wish is fine, but perhaps you can gratify it through a variety of friends or involvements if your "best friend" has not yet shown up. Doing so will also keep you safe, because while a few people do depend on a lifelong, loyal best friend, sometimes this singular relationship can shatter. The end of a friendship can be devastating, but having connections to others will buoy you.

The bottom line is that being your True Self in the presence of another and being treasured, adored, and respected is important for you. And it is possible. It can be one special person or a few, and the right connection can lead to a creative sounding board or collaboration.

HANDLING FAMILIES, FRIENDS, AND
TRUE CONNECTIONS

While family can give you confidence and support, sometimes they may also be the source of troubled relationships. Understanding how early relationships shaped you is useful, but you don't want to become mired in persecutory memories.

If you come from a family that lacked True Connection, you may repeat by putting up with people who devalue you. As Freud said, when we do not remember (understand, work through, achieve insight), we repeat. You might need to change friends and your inner template of what you look for in a friend.

The other day, I had lunch with my friend Shinhee, and she said (she is also a therapist), "I deleted all my borderline friends today." Friends who turn on you, friends who display unpredictable or irrational cruelties, friends who punish or disappear or retaliate, and friends who "joke" that you have fat thighs or that your prom dress is ugly may not be worth it.

People who are afraid to be lonely put up with torture. People who have been bashed around can have a high tolerance for more pain. They do not consciously register assaults, but they feel them deep down and it whittles away at their self-esteem. If you can make the pain conscious and fully feel it, you can change, even if you have to withstand loneliness during the evolution-revolution. A little loneliness is good for creativity and self-respect and for discovering what you really think and feel. You may discover that you do not want to put up with degradation anymore, which is excellent for True Self robustness.

If you are drawn to destructive people because of an early life blueprint, you need to cease and desist. Past determines present, but the Creativity Cure is about understanding the past in order to make better choices in the present. There is so much literature on destructive, twisted, romantic relationships, but the wrong friends can be just as bad. The right friends can expand your life and set you on a lighted path. They help you feel safe and free enough to become creative. Many a Creative Self has risen out of loss, trauma, or betrayal. As you know, a sense of a loving other within is necessary for Creative Capacity, and the right relationships can provide that for you.

Whenever my necklace is twisted and tangled, I stick it on Alton's desk, in front of his computer. He is very patient about untangling it, but what is even better is that he cannot resist the urge. So even if he has a hundred emails to answer, he has arrived home at 11:00 p.m. after putting together a shattered hand, and he has to get up at 6:00 a.m., I always find my necklace sitting on my bathroom counter ready to put on.

Find someone with the ability to love.

HANDLING BULLIES

Bullies can be deceptive and clever. They can slyly provoke you until you explode, and then it's you who takes all the heat. Bullies who claim victimhood, or people who exaggerate their persecution and convince bighearted others of their plight, can wreak havoc, because they manage to obfuscate the truth. Bullies can be covert as well as overt. They can be the menacing disguised as the meek, or the deranged disguised as the righteous. There are school bullies, family bullies, neighborhood bullies, and work bullies. Some people get off on scapegoating, devaluing, or making others feel desperate for a few kind words from them. That is their privilege, but you are not required to hang around.

My cousin John always says, "I refuse to live in a world where the insane inherit the earth."

Bullies can attribute their unsavory, untoward, aggressive characteristics to others as a way of not dealing with their own problems. This is called projection. To project means to ascribe our own characteristics, thoughts, wishes, needs, or behaviors to someone else in an attempt to manage or disown them. My client Mia, who is consistently bullied by a relative, reduced to tears or frantic outbursts, and then accused of heinous acts she did not commit, decided to tell the relative, "I can no longer be the receptacle for your unwanted characteristics," when she encountered her at the next family celebration.

Some people would rather blame and demean themselves than separate from a destructive other. Staying with that person can feel easier than facing the loss or emptiness without him or her. But your True Self, your Creative Self, emerges when you exit that relationship, and there are many other ways to fill the void left by a damaging person.

In many ways, happiness depends on relinquishing destructive attachments. For some people, understanding that "you can't go home again" is the key to psychological survival.

CREATIVITY WITHIN FAMILIES

While we are focusing on friends in this chapter, it's important to note that projects with spouses, children, and other family members can enhance your Creative Self. Doing projects together is a great way to have a positive, connected family experience. There is something uniquely fulfilling about your Creative Self in the company of those to whom you feel a strong bond.

Maybe you can carve out a couple of hours per weekend with your children to:

- Build a fort
- Plant a garden of edible food and serve it
- Design a flower bed
- Construct a wooden sculpture from pieces you found on a walk
- Make a sculpture with shells, stones, and other beach discoveries
- Press wildflowers and identify them
- Walk through the woods, take pictures of trees, birds, and animals, and then identify them when you get home
- Collaborate on another kind of photographic essay
- Pick berries and make a pie
- Cook dinner together and let the kids make what they make, with messes and mistakes (the process provides more than the dish)
- Sketch sunsets with pastels because they blend and smudge in a sunsetty way

Establish some creative rituals. What is comforting for children is the routine and predictability of this special time, not how much time it is. If the shared event is in their minds all week, then the connection is occurring in an ongoing way, not just at the designated hour. They will carry the togetherness within. Rituals create solace.

With members of your family of origin you might:

- Design a shared or inherited space together
- Plan extended family meals and have everyone take a different task from cooking to decorating the table
- Make a book of old family photographs
- Make a playlist of music that was meaningful to the family over the years
- See what you can make out of what you find in the basement or attic, and laugh while remembering
- Begin a creative tradition such as an annual extended family hike, dinner, and discussion of a subject (take notes and read the comments next year)
- Write down what everyone is thankful for at Thanksgiving and see how it compares year to year
- Maintain meaningful rituals

With a spouse or partner you could:

- Repaint rooms
- Redesign your home
- Read the same book and discuss ideas
- Take a dance, art, writing, or photography class together
- Hang out and see what happens as you ponder the backyard (try to *not* talk about the kids)

THE "HOLDING ENVIRONMENT"

D. W. Winnicott coined the term "holding environment" to refer to a nurturing situation in which the True Self can be expressed. While his work on the Holding Environment referred to infants and mothers, we can apply this idea to finding a healthy fit in friends, lovers, and places you frequent. Though in psychoanalysis we strive to help people become strong and adaptable by altering the inner life, there is no question that some settings will suit your inborn temperament and your tastes far better than others.

Chloe and I were visiting a college to which she had been accepted, and we met a panel of students. Two of them said that what they liked best about their school was that there is always someone to talk to. All three said there is someone to support you if you have had a bad day. One said that when she goes home for vacation, she watches television to pass the time and cannot wait to get back to her dorm since there is always a door to knock on. Another said that she does not even know how to hook up the cable in her dorm. This young woman teared up when asked about graduating. At that point Chloe turned to me and said, "Okay, Mom, sign me up."

The nurturing situation, or the holding environment, is critical for cognitive and emotional development. You may have had a great one while you were growing up or you may not have. Either way, whether you mimic the past or reinvent it, it is good to establish a holding environment that makes you feel both protected and free. With all the challenges and unpredictability you face, it is important to establish a safe place, a haven. How can you do it? Identify what makes you feel safe and whole. This is unique to you. Consider these questions:

- Is it a home environment with a log burning in the fireplace, the aroma of cinnamon apples, and your family around? A certain room?

- Is it a particular neighborhood place, with or without certain friends present?

- Is it a café in another town with people talking and the smell of coffee? Maybe the bustle and anonymity comfort you.

- Is it with close friends at their summer house, where you feel relaxed, safe, and open? Or at your favorite vacation spot? Can you figure out why you like it, and try to re-create a bit of it in your everyday life if you cannot get there often?

- Is it a place with people from your childhood? Where is it and who is there?

- If it does not exist, or if you lost it, how would you compose it anew and with whom?

- How can you make a holding environment a regular part of your life?

My friend Cate told me last night that her place is Paris, where she used to live, but because of multiple responsibilities, she rarely goes anymore. Still, just thinking about her former life there helps her recapture the identification and a sense of a holding environment.

GETTING A GRASP ON TRUE CONNECTIONS

1. True Friends and the Good News

With real friends, you can share the good news as well as the bad. If you are telling someone only your bad news, you need to wonder why. If friends have their own good news, successes, and pleasures, they are more likely to be okay with you having yours. If your friend falls apart when you share good news, she may not be where she needs to be in her own life, so you may want to refrain from sharing the details with her and talk about them with someone else. In a true friendship, the caring outweighs the competitiveness. A true friend wants the best for you and will create a connection that facilitates True Self and Creative Self.

My client Tristan told me that he had received two awards for a film he made, but he did not want to tell anyone. He also got an agent for his book, but he did not want to tell anyone about that, either, because telling might jinx it.

Ideas to Grapple With
- Have you had a friend who is excited to hear your good news?
- Can you think of a friend or two with whom it is difficult to share good news? Why do you imagine this is the case?
- Do you have any close friends with whom you still have to edit yourself?

Hold this thought: True friends
can be genuinely happy for you.

2. Friends with Excellent Insight

There are kind comments that anyone can provide, such as "Great intro," "Nice sentence structure," "Beautiful couch," or "Loved the rice dish," or sympathetic comments such as "I am sorry for your loss" and "Too bad about the babysitter wrecking the car." But empathic, good insightful comments from a true friend can be transformative. Sometimes a true friend can see you more clearly than you can see yourself. They may articulate what you cannot, and this can be lifesaving. They can point out the truth, and because you know that they have your best interest at heart, you are able to hear, trust, take in, and consider it instead of defend or deny. You can use the insight to better yourself or your situation. And you will do the same for your friend, because usually such relationships are reciprocal. The trust and depth between you allows the True Self and Creative Self to surface.

Ideas to Grapple With

- Has a friend ever made a comment that changed your course?
- Who is that friend who can make you laugh when you are about to cry?
- When you are with a friend who really gets it, what does that do for your mood? Your feeling of optimism or motivation?
- Have you had painful differences but maintained the friendship in spite of them?

Hold this thought: People who understand you
can help you see the truth and work with it.

3. Real Friends and Virtual Friends

A word about Internet relationships. Superficial connections may be fun and stimulating, but some in-the-flesh interaction is best for True Connections. New research shows how the Internet encourages fabrication. By maintaining and projecting a manufactured self, we avoid true development; we airbrush the truth.

Hyperconnectivity, or being all over the place with many parties at once, can be fun for a time, but it can also be harmful. Hyperconnectivity creates a false sense of connectedness. If we rely on the number of virtual "friends" we have on social networking sites for satisfaction, we may not develop actual friends who know our flaws and love us anyway. Quantity is not quality. Constant connectivity to many can take time away from your True Connections with a few, because instead of taking a walk with a companion you may be tapping the keys of your computer. Staying in touch with dear friends over the Internet is great. There is no risk if you know them well already. But there can be a risk if you have never actually met in person.

Many people have a fear of intimacy, and online connections can be a perfect way to avoid it. If you do not have to work through your fear by meeting people in person and risking discomfort or even the possibility that some of them may not be that interested in you, you are more alone than ever when the virtual relationship falls apart. You can survive not wowing people, not having a freshened-up, unflawed picture of yourself floating around. By projecting perfected images of yourself to online friends, you may start to feel intolerant or ashamed of the real you. Without authentic expression, we can become depressed.

However, there is another side to the story. According to recent research, there are circumstances in which online connections can fill in when in-the-flesh interactions do not suffice. Some people who do not fit into their school, community, or workplace—people who cannot mingle comfortably, who are very fearful, or who are even ostracized—can find others to feel close to via virtual contact on blogs or networking sites. Ideally, they will work to overcome their social anxiety, but in the meantime, online connections can help them feel bonded during otherwise lonely or isolated periods. Belonging to an online community can also shore up identity, as communication about shared interests fosters a strong self. In the end, a five-sense, in-the-flesh, flaws-disclosed friendship or romance will provide the most fulfillment, but at times we have to settle for a respectable replacement.

Find someone who loves you, the real you (it is an achievable goal), because expressing your real self, your ideas, and your true thoughts is important for creativity and happiness. The Internet can also be great for helping you *maintain* a True Connection to someone you have bonded with in the flesh but cannot see often.

Ideas to Grapple With

- Have you ever had a true friend? Why was this person a true friend to you? What was it about this person's qualities or the way you spent time together that made it work?
- Do you have many virtual friends? What kind of impact does this have on you? Is it fun to have a big number?
- Do Internet friends interfere with time for in-the-flesh friends, or do you have a good balance?
- Has the Internet helped you maintain True Connections in any way?

Hold this thought: True Connections are based on your true, flawed, but fine self.

---

4. Fear of Loss or Betrayal

Sometimes a person you believed to be true betrays you. Things fall apart. You evolved, the other person regressed, or both. Or somehow you were accused of violating the other person when you were doing nothing of the sort. Finding a way to live with loss or our own choice to end relationships that are replete with misunderstandings is key for the True Self and Creative Self. Even if you initiated the leaving, in your unconscious mind it can feel as if you were abandoned. Maybe you were, at least emotionally, and that is why you left.

Continual dialogue with the other about their transgression is a form of hope. But sometimes it is a mistake to prattle on with someone who has no capacity for insight. You try, you believe, you hope; you think you can have an impact if you just explain it in the right way, from every angle. But people with no capacity for insight will not get it. They will try to make it all about you. In this case, you have to move to the offense even though they are using everything they have to keep you on the defense. If putting their problem back into them so that they can deal with it does not work—when the dialogue is at a dead end—give up. When you do, you will be free. When you are less dependent on making things work out with such people, you will go your own way and become your True Self and Creative Self.

Ideas to Grapple With

- Try to remember a frustrating dialogue (as described above) that you have had. What transpired?
- What friends have you lost? Why? What happened? What was going on in your life at this time?
- Did you keep pushing or talking to achieve a reconciliation, an understanding, to save it? That is okay, because it was kind of you to imagine that they were capable of change.
- Did you finally give up, and was it really painful? Was it worth it?

Hold this thought: It is better to let go of toxic attachments. Better to lose bad connections in the interest of creative development.

---

5. Internalized Relationships

There is another kind of connection that involves internal relationships, relationships in the mind. These can be with people you have

known and loved, or even with people you have never met. Dr. Rita
Charon, pioneer of narrative medicine, writes about her electrifying
internal relationship with the long-deceased author Henry James. She
writes that sometimes just recalling a quote from one of his works can
bolster her inner life.

Chloe recently asked me why I do not have anything that belonged
to my father, who died when she was twelve. I told her that someone
swept up all his belongings one afternoon and took them away.

Chloe said, "Doesn't that upset you?"

I said, "No, not really. I don't need the stuff because I had him."

To be sure, I do miss the picture of him that was taken during
World War II, where he is standing in uniform under cherry blossoms
in China with his arm around a friend. But see? That picture is embla-
zoned within me.

Ideas to Grapple With

• Even if people who were dear to you are gone, they are not
  completely gone if you conjure them up inside, through what
  they gave you or taught you or how they inspired you.

Hold this thought: True Connections live on
internally and give you strength and succor.

---

6. Setting

Setting is important for conjuring up internal relationships and
unconscious material so that True Connections can come alive
within. Certain places shut you down and others open you up. When
a setting opens you up, it allows your unconscious to roll out and the
internalized relationships to rise up. Sometimes being in a particular
space—private or public, home or foreign, familiar or novel—fosters
connections with loving figures from the past in a good way. The
setting catalyzes the right inner life situation. If you find the place

where you feel free, then supportive, internalized, beloved persons come to you.

My client Isabel says that writing in cafés is fine as long as the people sitting next to her are not having too interesting a conversation. Sometimes she cannot tune out what is being said. She prefers to write at home with her partner, each of them in a separate room.

Sometimes silently sharing the same room has a very nurturing effect. Shared creative space can be very useful for creative growth. Even if you are just side by side quietly working on your own projects, whether it is jewelry making, writing, or flower arranging, the sense of the other in his or her own deep place, concentrating and inventing, is useful.

For some people, one of the big hurdles with regard to a creative life is the fear of loneliness. Solitude may be necessary at times, but it can be nice to feel the physical presence of a companion. One of my clients attended a weekly writing salon at a friend's apartment, which was comforting for him. The group worked while they were there together but did not share material.

When I hear Alton tapping away in the next room, I think better.

Ideas to Grapple With

- Place matters. What is yours?
- Are there several?
- Where do you feel safe? With others you know or don't know? Alone?
- Is it a dark, soothing setting with books and club chairs?
- Is it a modern, light, uncluttered café?
- Is there a low hum or a cheerful banter in the surround?
- Who appears in your inner life when the setting is right?

Hold this thought: The proper conditions
conjure up True Connections.

---

7. Privacy

Privacy is important for True Connections, because privacy protects intimacy. Intimacy does not involve a complete togetherness or merging, but rather sensitivity to another's requirements for space as well as closeness. If boundaries are violated, if private space is intruded upon psychologically, physically, or socially, there is little possibility for True Connections. It is a good idea to understand how and when you need space, what you like to share and what you do not. Spend time with those who are at ease with your requirements involving privacy and merging.

When I was in analytic training, a colleague had just completed his personal analysis. (To be a psychoanalyst, you undergo a treatment yourself.) We were gathering books after class when someone asked, "How does it feel to be done?"

He said, "It's nice to be able to have private thoughts again."

I found this interesting. If the goal of analysis is autonomy, spontaneity, mental health, and freedom, then private thoughts should be part of the process. Choosing to keep something to yourself, even in therapy, can be quite reasonable. I once had a therapist who misunderstood so much and said so many off-base things that I really regretted talking to him.

I do not want my clients to feel forced to reveal things to me. I like to ask questions, but they know that they do not have to answer them.

Once my father told me, "Never completely hand your mind over to someone else." He had read many books about psychoanalysis but had not undergone the process himself. Still, he loved the ideas and imparted them to me over cups of Lipton tea.

Recently, Alton and I went to a conference with our friends Lee and Bob. Lee and I are both working on books. We discovered that we both write in bed, keep a stash of almonds nearby, and exercise when stuck. On day one we decided we would retire to our respective rooms and convene at dinner. On the plane home, sitting side by side, Lee watched a movie and I wrote, then I watched a movie and she wrote. It was so nice not to chat.

Over the years with clients, the matter of maintaining mind privacy within the context of an intimate relationship has often arisen. Concerns are:

- Should you share all with your partner?
- Should you keep certain feelings, thoughts, comments, or even experiences a secret?
- Is not revealing all a form of betrayal?

While tenderness beneath honesty is certainly a good idea, complete honesty can be harmful at times. I'm not advocating unfaithfulness, but rather faithfulness with good boundaries. You are less inclined to drive another person away if you are respectful of his or her needs and of what makes him or her happy. Merging too much—not giving the other space, time, and privacy—can corrode a good connection. Let the other do what he or she needs to do, even if you are not in on the plan. You do not have to share all experiences, interests, or thoughts. Privacy is not for the purpose of deceit or deception, but for respect, longevity, and intimacy.

Ideas to Grapple With
- When have you revealed too much?
- Have you ever regretted a comment you made? What were the circumstances?
- Did you ever share an extended silence? How was this experience?
- When might you have stopped a loved one from having an independent interest and why?
- Why might it be important to you to have complete togetherness, or no breathing room?
- How would you describe your requirements regarding privacy and merging?

Hold this thought: Privacy can enhance rather than interfere with True Connections. People can bond in silence. Unconscious communication exists.

---

8. Lunch Is the Most Important Thing

When I asked my mother what she missed most about retiring from her forty years as a professor, she said, "Lunch with friends is the most important thing." She ate with the same group of four women five days a week for many years. They talked about unruly children, their field, and the mystery of academic promotions.

As we have discussed, research reveals the importance of friendships for wellness, recovery, stress, and a feeling of confidence and safety. Friendships are also good for distraction and for making you laugh in the midst of a major headache. Some researchers have explored the idea of laughter as a healing phenomenon. We share this with you to encourage you, even if you are super pressed for time, busy, and stressed, to spend time with friends or develop some new friendships (join an organization or invite someone to meet you in a casual way) and laugh a little. Or cry if you need to. Medically, socially, psychologically, and often intellectually, it's great for your health.

Ideas to Grapple With

- Have friends drifted away as you have evolved? That might be okay, but you might want to reconsider if you are where you want to be professionally and if you feel bereft friend-wise.
- Is sharing meals important to you? How might you make this part of your life?
- How do you define social and professional happiness? Can you find a balance?
- How can you make the development and maintenance of friendships a priority?

Hold this thought: Lunch with friends nurtures
True Connections.

---

9. Creative Partnerships

Duos work well if the core relationship is solid. We covered collaboration in the beginning of the chapter, but we will touch upon it again because a creative partner can be the difference between succeeding at a creative life or not. Some people just need an other to bring out their True Self, their Creative Self.

My client Helena was having a hard time. She planned a party for her dad and no one showed up. Her roommates moved out, leaving her responsible for the rent. One month she drank daily lattes, purchased two sweaters and an iPod, and spent so much that she did not have funds to make it to the end of the month.

Meanwhile, she had to prepare for and write an article. She was having trouble doing anything at all. So she spoke to a friend who gave her this advice: "This week, carve out time each day to read. Pick out a specific book you like and show up to do it at the time you designated, in the place you decided." (No choice, no choice, no choice.) And then she told her, "Call me when you need to talk."

She did, a few times. It helped. The conversations with this friend helped her clarify her thoughts and come up with interesting ideas in addition to keeping on track.

Some people work best in creative partnerships, whether it is in composing music, collaborating on a book, writing a screenplay, or cooking. In fact, the need for the partner can be so crucial that one cannot experience the Creative Self without this alter ego, this connected other. You can be stimulated, catalyzed, and brought forth by the particulars of the other's mind. If you think you may do better as part of a duo than as sole agent, it is important to recognize this. You want to discover and act upon what suits you best. People can go for years not realizing that a simple change in approach, based on self-awareness, can make all the difference.

Ideas to Grapple With

- Is there someone you would like to work with, but you refrain from reaching out to them?
- What happens if you ask for help?
- Might your mind feel freer, more stimulated, more creative with a partner?
- Is there someone who brings out the best in you and in your Creative Self?

Hold this thought: Know that if you ask, there are people who would be interested in helping or collaborating with you.

---

10. A Word About Differences

The characteristics of those with whom you can form True Connections may surprise you. You can be similar to someone deep down but seem so different from them on the surface. Different politics, different religions, different ethnicities, and different backgrounds may not matter if you share other interests or if your intrinsic values or qualities are similar. Tiny gestures and a step into the unfamiliar can create rich connection. And empathy helps to strengthen the connection. Empathy helps.

Ideas to Grapple With

- Have you ever felt close to someone with whom you thought you had nothing in common?
- Who was that person, and what was that like?
- What experiences have you had with closeness that surprised you?
- When have you assumed someone was not your type and then learned differently?

Hold this thought: What you are looking for
may show up in a surprising place.

HOLDING ON TO YOURSELF WHEN
THE CONNECTION IS BAD

Sometimes you have to override, or try to override, the influence of the other in a duo. Depending on your personality—whether you feel better complying or defying—this can be painful.

When I was a resident, I saw an unusual five-year-old child: bright, disconnected, but somehow connected all the same. As a resident, you are assigned to a supervisor and expected to take care of the patient as a partnership. You evaluate the patient alone, then with your supervisor, and then discuss the case before deciding upon the diagnosis and treatment and meeting with the family.

My supervisor for this case saw the child for an hour and decided he was autistic. I had also spent an hour alone with him, and I told my supervisor I did not think he was (I happened to have pored over the criteria with a fine-toothed comb the day before).

We argued. He was vexed.

We met with the family, and he handed over the autism diagnosis. The parents sobbed. It was terrible.

It turned out that the boy did not have autism but rather Asperger's, which has a far better prognosis. My supervisor was removed from the case. He wrote in my evaluation that I could not accept authority.

Why am I telling you this story? It is usually adaptable, mentally healthy, and a sign of good judgment to be deferential and to not incite your supervisor. Just agree and think your own thoughts in private. Do not strut, show off, or assert yourself inappropriately. Respecting your superiors, assuming they are in a position of power for a reason, and not challenging their thinking is usually a good idea. You can ask some questions. You can learn some things.

But I couldn't help it in this situation because certain diagnoses are overwhelming for people and you want to be sure before you definitively tell someone that they have a certain condition. It was very uncomfortable to persist with my argument after he told me, with disdain and annoyance, that I was wrong. Asperger's was not in the textbook at the time. He never looked me in the eye again.

The point of this? As much as you should try to get along with others, see their point of view, put yourself in their shoes, and respect authority, when your True Connection to yourself or another is screaming for attention, then probably you should listen. The boy just did not seem autistic, because when he played with me, I felt a True Connection.

Ideas to Grapple With

- Do no harm.
- Think before you speak, and speak up if your concern is pressing.

Hold this thought: Your True Connection to
your own mind is important.

GRAPPLING WITH SOCIAL CONSCIENCE AND COMMUNITY CONNECTIONS

We covered community connections before, but I want to take it a step further here and bring up social conscience, because having a social conscience is useful for creativity and happiness as well as for the betterment of others.

When I was nine, I held two fairs in my backyard to raise money for Head Start and the starving children of Biafra, respectively. We offered face painting and sold items such as old wire-rimmed eyeglasses and used toys. We raised nine dollars for one and eleven dollars for the other, and we received a thank-you letter from Head Start. It was fine and fun, and I wanted to do it.

For the last three years, Alton has taken Chloe to Chinle Hospital on the Navajo reservation, where he volunteers. He sees patients and performs surgery while Chloe helps out by interacting with the patients and filling syringes for Alton's injections. (Alton and Chloe are both part Blackfoot.)

The point here is that True Connections with friends, lovers, family members, and others is important for you. But you can also connect with other people through an ideology, a belief system, a cause, a mission, or an idea. Sometimes there is something going on in the world that really matters to you or that can really matter to you if you learn about it. And you can find purpose, meaning, creativity, and satisfaction through your involvement in the cause. Altruism is considered a "healthy psychological defense," a mature and refined style of behavior. It is a sign of mental health.

Hold this thought: A cause can be a form of
True Connection.

CONCLUSION

True friends help your mental health and enhance your surroundings. If you do not have any now, you can find some. You can work on developing them. You can start casually and let it evolve.

SUMMARY

In this chapter we covered True Connections. We covered good news, insight, belonging, betrayals, loss, virtual friends, internalized relationships, settings, privacy, differences, lunch with friends, and creative partners. Social conscience came up, as did the matter of authority figures.

FIVE-PART PRESCRIPTION: WEEK SEVEN

From Loneliness to True Connection

INSIGHT (20 MINUTES A DAY)

Relationships are the basis of many forms of success, psychological, professional, and otherwise. We know this, and yet too often we forget it. Write about:

- Troubled relationships
- Difficult friends
- Inner circles or popular crowds
- Cutting peers, scapegoating, bullying, rejection
- Isolation, avoidance, feeling guarded
- Secrets
- Explaining, justifying, desperately trying to make others see, unsuccessfully
- True friends
- Disloyalties, betrayals
- Haughty, disdainful glances
- Cruel judgments

MOVEMENT (30 MINUTES A DAY)

For this week's Movement Enhancement, run all the way today. Even if it's just for a short distance, sprint and break free. While you are moving, think of who you treasure and who knows and treasures the true you.

Move with someone else and see how this affects you.

Or, as before, try swimming, rowing, skating, skiing, spinning, dancing, yoga, weight lifting, running, mowing grass, raking leaves, or shoveling snow.

MIND REST (10 MINUTES A DAY)

There are two new suggestions for this week. The first is to be with someone you care for and just hang out. The second is to be with someone and don't talk—engage silently, work in parallel.

Or, as before, lie on your bed, do nothing, putter around, sit in your favorite spot, listen to music that you enjoy, or sing anything (do it on "Ah" if you do not know the words).

Or meditate. Say a mantra (a repeated phrase—whatever feels right, from a prayer to a rhyme). Avoid all but your own thoughts and let them go where they will.

YOUR OWN TWO HANDS (40 MINUTES A DAY)

For your Creative Hour check-in, think about these questions:

- Are you continuing with your project? Are you keeping the schedule or making up for missed time? Good. The habit will be ingrained and then you will be changed.

- How is the work going? Can you apply a rational critic's eye and still feel free to explore and make mistakes?

- What obstacles are you facing at this point? What aspects are hard to master? Do you feel a shrinking back, like an ocnophile? Can you tolerate the difficulties, the areas of weakness, and keep going? Can you be curious about what is not working and try to improve it with rational, benevolent critique?

- Perhaps you are rather content with your progress. Is there a way to deepen, broaden, or immerse yourself more? Do you want to?

- Are other people around, or are you engaged in a solo expedition? What would it be like to make others part of your project? How would you do this? Would you want to sit side by side, go to a class together, chat after the session, or collaborate? How might a deep and lasting collaboration help you grow?

MIND SHIFT (20 MINUTES A DAY)

Might it be possible for you to share some of your Mind Shift writings or thoughts with a friend this week? If you feel too vulnerable to expose these matters in person, perhaps you can write a letter to someone who is important to you now or to someone you lost touch with who meant something to you. If you feel comfortable enough, try silently sharing your writing space with someone dear to you. You do not have to converse, but if that strengthens the True Connection, go ahead and put down your pen or close your laptop for a while. You will get back to it.

Things to write about:

- Feeling loved or loving
- Trusting or being trustworthy
- Inclusion, belonging
- Sharing good news with someone who was happy for you
- Confidences
- Positive memories, meals, gatherings
- Feeling understood, being understanding
- Feeling safe, open, honest, real, natural
- Feeling treasured, worth listening to, attractive
- Being forgiven
- Feeling accepted
- Feeling interested and interesting
- Feeling consoled
- Laughing
- Having a great partner or a true friend
- When life was good and why this was so

10

Creativity and Identity

That is happiness: to be dissolved into something complete and great.

—WILLA CATHER, writer

MATTERS AT HAND

The whole point of a therapeutic process is to help you feel better, to enjoy your life, to be happier. The Creativity Cure is a creative, do-it-yourself therapeutic process that is designed to make you more satisfied with your life and yourself through purposeful engagements that foster Creative Capacity. Creative Capacity leads you to your True Self and your Creative Self.

Aligning the True Self with your outer life—the friends you have, the work you do, the causes to which you contribute—allows you to be a happier person. Deep interest in your task will elevate your mood and expand your mind. Accessing and using your unconscious mind via Creative Capacity will lead to contentment. Happiness is about self-awareness, health, and the right kinds of involvements, tailor-made by you and for you.

You have completed the Creativity Cure. You wrote, considered, questioned, uncovered, discovered, emoted, moved, rested, used your hands, and then wrote and considered again. Whether your efforts have produced greater awareness, increased motivation, deeper understanding, peak moments, altered habits, or new thoughts, something has happened. Let us understand what.

- How has the Creativity Cure changed you: your habits, your thoughts, your understanding, your values, your perspective, your attitude, your desires, your tastes?

- What was easy to integrate or adopt in the 5PP and what was not? How can you approach the aspects that are less enticing to you?

- What insights, ideas, or anecdotes were useful for you, and do you know why they were so?

- How would you describe how you felt before you began and how you feel now?

- Which ideas or habits can you hold on to or use to get you through your day?

- Where are you with your Creative Self? How is your project going?

- If you skipped the Creative Hour part, can you do this at a later time?

- Will you continue with your current project and then find a similar one to keep your Creative Self alive and well and in action?

- Now that you have a greater ability to listen and heed what goes on inside you and use your Creative Capacity, how can you maintain this?

- What do you now think about your hands? Are you using them in a different way?

- Have you integrated more do-it-yourself into your life?

- Are you giving yourself Mind Rest as a regular reprieve?
- Has your relationship with your body changed? Are you exercising?
- What about relationships with others, either friends or community? Are you looking at these relationships differently? Do you feel optimistic about forming new relationships?
- How have you worked nature into your life?
- Are you beginning to feel better about aspects of your life, your work, your relationships, and your body?

The Creativity Cure is meant to help you find a way into yourself, out of your turmoil, and up to a healthier, happier position. While you cannot extinguish all ailments and predicaments, we hope you feel less fraught, more able to create, and more able to experience happy moments. The seven-week immersion you have completed should improve your situation, but to cement a lifestyle change and to ensure greater health and happiness, we encourage you to continue the 5PP indefinitely. If your engaging, purposeful activity reaches an end, find another. With an open mind and Creative Capacity, you will always be able to find interesting things to explore or people to be with. When you change who you are and how you think, you can change what you do and how you do it.

By now you should be writing, understanding, moving, resting, using your hands in meaningful ways, and offering yourself a better version of events—a positive perspective. Ideally, nature is part of your everyday life, whether it is through plants on a terrace or time spent in a forest or on the beach. If you have searched for True Connections, loyal friends, and interesting communities, you are following the regimen. If you realized that detaching from disquieting others was essential, that is fine. It is part of the Creativity Cure. Your healthier, happier Creative Self should be emerging, but to keep it primed, stick with the plan.

Let us review. Maybe you have some lingering questions.

CREATIVITY AND HAPPINESS

Creative processes take us to a deep place within. Because creative processes involve self-expression and self-repair, they meet a basic human need. Creative endeavors facilitate experimentation, improvisation, uniqueness, and original thinking, which are clear sources of fulfillment—some of the best things human experience has to offer. By fostering Creative Capacity, you are poised for creative processes.

Accessing Your True Self, Your Creative Self

Practice the 5PP because it is a way of staying in touch with your unconscious mind, your body, your needs, and your instincts—your Creative Capacity. It will help you solve problems, feel joy, and remain mentally and physically well. It will keep your finest physical tool, your hands, engaged.

If You Avoid Creative Habits

Even if you feel downtrodden, fearful, depressed, or anxious and all you want to do is avoid, you will feel better if you create, move, and use your hands to unleash your deeper self. Let Creative Capacity lead you to awareness, answers, and inspirations. Find the little spark or wisp within. Follow it. It is the way to relief.

Beware of Psychological Clutter

The can'ts, the shoulds, the irrational critic, and rumination can be managed, controlled, and put in their place. If you cannot remove clutter or diminish it, use it to deliver you to a higher place. Be more powerful than the clutter. Be authoritative with yourself. You can come out on top, on the right side of things, on your own side, if you hear all the parts of yourself and allow the rational critic to be the dominant voice in your inner life. If you do this, you will feel better.

Constructing Internal Resilience

Optimism, faith, benevolence toward yourself and others, and the ability to maintain core habits in the face of stress allow you to stand strong. To build strength, you have to get over the hump. Start with a tiny, tiny step and celebrate the change from not doing to doing. Even if everything in you is saying, "No, I can't, I won't, you can't make me, and if you try, I will dig my heels in further," agree with yourself that you can take a small step and then stop. Chances are that once you take that first step, you will want to keep going. If you maintain habits long enough, they become part of you and a resource to draw upon when you are in pain. Once the habits are part of you, you can rely on them to move you through.

Remember to Use Your Hands

Hands, hands, hands. So simple, so profound. Whatever you can do that involves steps, constructions, and improvisations with your hands will help you. The hands are the window to the mind and your rich, creative inner life, which is a great place to hang out. Your inner life is your greatest resource for peace, joy, resilience, and creativity. When you make things, you feel good. You are interested and interesting. Elevated mood is linked to hand use. Fixing, repairing, constructing, and creating are paths to self-repair and happiness. Use your hands in a community project for a double boost of well-being.

Physicality

Movement, however slow, is essential for contentment. Vigorous movement can create euphoria. Movement is wonderful for physical prowess and Creative Capacity. It is essential for mental and physical health. Exercise remedies anxiety and depression, relieves stress, boosts immunity, protects bones, enhances cardiac fitness, influences cognition, and protects against musculoskeletal ailments. It is natural medicine.

In some situations, your body is a better guide than your mind. Athletes who overthink may lose their winning ways. Even if you are not destined for the Olympics, vigorous, regular movement will help you access your deepest, most empowered self. A doing, trained, disciplined body leads to "letting go" in the mind. Expanding your physical capabilities expands your mind. And that is how creative material emerges.

The Creative Self and the True Self are happier when you're moving than when you're lying on the couch, unless you are in Mind Rest. Vigorous exercise is a solid, valid medical treatment for anxiety and depression. Movement in natural settings, where your body is challenged, your mind is stimulated, and you are inspired by what you see, will produce peak experiences and creativity.

RELATIONSHIPS ARE THE ESSENCE

Find the right friends: supportive, sensitive, empathic people who get you or who are at least willing to listen. If you are very concerned about image, social climbing, celebrity acquaintance, or being seen in certain settings, then at least find someone you can really talk to in between events. Develop at least a few True Connections, and access those loved ones, present and past, who live within you. Keep your virtual contacts, but understand what they do and do not provide.

Stay away from people who hurt you. The hardest thing in life is to leave destructive relationships, but you can do it. We stay attached because we do not feel we can leave (when in fact we can). We feel guilty for leaving those we are supposed to love (whom maybe we do not love as much as we think we do). We tell ourselves it feels better to be with someone that we have known forever than to be with someone new. (New friends can become True Connections through the accumulation of casual, frequent, and tender interactions.)

Loyalty is a fantastic phenomenon, but it must be bred of mutual self-respect.

SELF-MASTERY IS EMPOWERMENT

Compromise by finding a balance between desire and practicality. Have your passions, but make adaptive choices.

Practice humility because it will make you work hard, engender respect, and take you where you want to go. It will make you more appealing to be around.

Refrain from actions that could harm you by pausing and honestly considering the consequences.

Expect refinement in yourself and in others. It is good to admire others. This does not diminish you. If you feel pleased with your own actions, you are much more likely to feel content.

Self-possession is having a mind of your own. This is a great source of strength and satisfaction.

Self-reliance is an age-old form of self-help. It applies to practical solutions as well as psychological self-soothing and physical ability. When you can rely on yourself, it gives you both inner power and outer panache. It is about being creative and resourceful, and thus being more content.

Say "I don't know." Doing so is refreshing. If you really have some defect in your knowledge base (most of us do) and it disturbs you, then take five minutes a day to learn about the subject. I say five minutes so that you will start and then have the choice to continue in whatever way you deem right. The initial act, however minuscule, can free you for lasting change. The tiny step can change everything because it represents a shift in identity.

When you expose yourself to new forms of stimulation, remember to hold on to your own mind, values, tastes, and views. You can learn, alter, adjust, and change, but do not lose yourself.

Be selective.

FIVE-PART PRESCRIPTION REVIEW

New behaviors follow from insight. When you have self-awareness, you make smarter choices. You can avoid futile effort or banging your head against a wall. If you try to change before you have gleaned some understanding of what is going on in your unconscious mind, you could be thwarted or have a terrible time of it. Unconscious resistance can undermine even a Herculean conscious effort. This is what "getting in your own way" is all about. Insight helps you know what you need to do and sets you on the proper path. But internal work does not take you all the way, and that is what the Creativity Cure is about. You need to build good habits, move your body, use your hands, and allow for passive moments.

If you want to change, developing new, positive habits—even the smallest daily dose—will transform you into someone else.

> We are what we repeatedly do. Excellence, then, is not an act but a habit.
> —ARISTOTLE, philosopher

INSIGHT

Keen self-knowledge leads to smart, sound choices. Writing about our experiences has therapeutic benefits, from the cognitive benefits of penmanship to the healing components of narrative expression. When you write down your inner experience and contend with your true reactions, you take care of yourself.

People talk about reinvention of self, but how do we do it? Reinvention starts with self-knowledge.

MOVEMENT

Get your body moving. If you are bored, insert novelty into the routine. If repetition calms you, then do it the same way day after day.

Know what circumstances are required for you to be consistent. What do you need to do so that you show up for your physical self?

If you feel too burdened to leave your problem behind while you move, then take the problem with you and contemplate as you move, starting slowly, with permission to stop. Give the worry its time, and then put it away. You can be in charge of it, not let it control you.

MIND REST

I know it is hard to find time to be passive or to give yourself permission to do so. Perhaps you find yourself saying, "There is no way that I can hang out or do nothing. Look at my list. Even if I spent the next two days not sleeping, I would not finish. You said to know my truth, and this is my truth."

Stop anyway.

Why?

Because you need to. Because "royalty doesn't rush around," in the words of famed choreographer George Balanchine. Now that you are in an elevated place, this statement applies to you. And because if you do, your tasks might feel less weighty.

Or because if you found out that you had a brain tumor, you might live differently.

Actually, not very long ago, in between the twins' classroom performance and attending a nursing presentation at my mother's assisted-living facility, I saw my doctor for dizziness. By itself the dizziness would have been no big deal, but I also had some eye symptoms that did not bode well. I was told to get an emergency brain MRI in the next two hours and see the chief of neurology at eight the next morning. Alton came in after finishing an operation and held my ankle while I was in the clanging MRI tube. I recalled that I had been in the same room holding my mother's ankle while she had the same scan six months before. I wore earplugs and meditated amid the deafening but strangely musical noises of the MRI machine.

After the scan and picking at a dinner we didn't much feel like eating, we ran into the neurology chief later that evening on the street, and he said, "It's normal!" I rested so well that night.

YOUR OWN TWO HANDS

If you take no other message from this book, take this: *use your hands.* Make, create, repair, cook, perform rote tasks, play an instrument. Your hands are very important for your happiness. We are affected by a cultural malaise that results from the overuse of computers and smartphones, and we have to make conscientious efforts to compensate. We have to be calculating about living naturally. Even if it means taking the long road or having a less polished product, go for it. Do it yourself if you can. This is about mental health. Keep your hands engaged.

MIND SHIFT

Consciously move to a positive position. Recall the gifts, blessings, and kind acts of others and yourself, and let them have space in your mind. We can shift the mood by changing the thoughts. We can change thoughts with practice. Remind yourself of how you contributed to good outcomes for others, within organizations, or for yourself.

Write down what it is about you that made these things happen—your traits, qualities, and character. Write. Always write.

TYING THINGS UP

Before we end, let me just say that even if you fix yourself all up, stuff still happens, and that is okay.

The other day, I was supposed to meet a girlfriend for Meatless Monday at The Red Hat, our local restaurant, and she never showed up. I sat on a bench in the sun outside and answered some emails. Then I left and bought Nutella and brioche for our French exchange student and ant traps for my mom, who is intolerant of any sort of insect. (When I told my mother about the mouse that had made its home in my dishwasher for two days, she said, "If I had a mouse in my dishwasher, I would move out.")

I then picked up a drawing from 1971 that had been sitting wrapped in thick white paper at the framer's for two months. Underneath the picture it says, "Happy Birthday, Carrie. You are eleven today. From all the boys and girls in your class," even though it was really just from my friend Robert. He used colored pencils on brown cardboard.

Just as I was about to sit down and revise this chapter, I received a call from Chloe letting me know that she had been in a car accident, along with our French exchange student and some other friends of hers. The car was demolished but no one was hurt. The rest of the day was spent speaking to police officers, the insurance company, the auto body shop, the other driver, the mother of the French girl staying with us (she was very understanding), and the girls who were in the car. I sent them to see Jennifer, who owns The Cupcake Kitchen on Main Street, in hopes that their memory of the event would be associated with cupcakes and not crumpled hoods.

Later I saw my friend Kirsten at the twins' soccer practice. She is a high-risk obstetrician, marathon runner, and mother of three. We talked about things we cannot control and how you just keep going.

You have to keep going. Muddle through and find a way even if you are tired, insecure, beleaguered, traumatized, fed up, or have a fever. Why? Because physical energy can be restored, inner states can be altered, and do-it-yourself approaches heal. Action breeds action and generates energy. Things can change if you take a step. The first step is all you have to commit to. Your biological urge toward health and your seeking, searching, able self who deep down knows a solution can be found will take you the rest of the way.

Stuff will happen:

- Someone becomes ill.
- A loved one turns into a lunatic.
- The car is totaled.
- You run out of money.
- You're late to the gig.

- You are not invited to an important event.
- Someone cheats on you or betrays the friendship.
- You receive an insulting critique or evaluation or a bad grade.
- The person never calls back.
- You lose your job or do not get the one you hoped for.
- You don't get into the school, club, or sorority.
- The diagnosis is scary.
- You oversalt the dinner party meal, drop it, or burn your hand.
- Your child is in trouble.

I get it. I have been through some things in the last ten years that have made me think the chairs should be switched in my treatment room. Alton has had his share of problems as well.

But you can have an intelligent response to stress, trauma, loss, angst, and disappointment. You can detach from the frenzy of hurtful events that threatens to swallow you up and focus on healthy habits, embrace absorbing distractions, and engage in creative pursuits that are both healing and productive. You can take your body into nature and start moving.

No one can take your mind from you. No one can stop you from finding purpose and options in spite of the predicament. You can control your attitude, direct your thoughts, sculpt your habits, forge your way, uncover your potential, find the people who will love you, and discover an interesting mission. You can create a life with many happy moments in spite of what happened to you. Creativity is part of who you are, and if you nurture, maintain, and continue to develop it throughout your life, it will provide many happy moments.

Sometimes you have to get moving even before you know where you are going, why you are going there, or what you are going to do once you get there. Many people need help to acquire the mental and physical position that allows them to "just do it."

Now you have it.

Acknowledgments

W E ARE GRATEFUL TO our patients for their stirring stories, compelling personalities, engaging thoughts, and for helping us develop *The Creativity Cure.* You know who you are!

Thank you to Susan Moldow, our publisher, and Alexis Gargagliano and Samantha Martin, our editors, for believing in the book, giving us the support to write it, and for kindness in the critique. Thanks also to Kelsey Smith for her kind assistance; and to the many others at Scribner who helped make this book possible, especially Dan Cuddy, Lauren Lavelle, and Wendy Sheanin.

Our agent, Jeanne Fredericks, and writing coach, Lisa Tener, ushered us through the early phases of development and we deeply appreciate their masterful guidance. They took us from dreaming to doing, and that has made all the difference.

Alton's parents, Jim and Arlene, fished, boated, built wood sculptures, chased lizards, caught butterflies, threw balls, and nurtured the twins for weeks at a time so that we could write. Love and gratitude to them and to Chloe, Nicholas, Caroline. Thanks to Carrie's mother, Florence, for a lifetime of insight and never laying guilt trips. And thanks to Carrie's father, Joe, wherever he may be, for being a careful listener and for saying many interesting and wise things.

A most special and deeply felt thank-you to our inimitable and ever-astute cousin John Erdman and to Carrie's singer soul mate and college roommate Wendy Sayvetz, for their unfailing attunement and for almost always picking up the phone. This effort and many others would not have been possible without them.

We are so fortunate to have had the support and input of certain longstanding friends and family members during the writing of this book, especially: Gibbs Bauer, Drs. Louis and Betsy Catalano, Drs. Dick and DuRee Eaton, Drs. Scott and Susan Ely, Ruth Greenholz, Thor Harris, Mark and Lisa Jennings, Dr. William Long and Maura Clark, Ann Papoulis Adamovic, John Ray and Dr. Harri Vanhala, Gary Schneider, and Dr. Todd and Lynn Sisto.

Acknowledgments

These friends and their ways of living have inspired us, shaped our thinking, and provided many happy moments: Steve Abbott, Betty Krulik and Tony Alvarez, Ken Bernstein, Marshall Bever and DOCTOR (as Marshall used to quip) Jerry Sullivan, Regis and Linda Boff, Tom Bullard, Paul and Kathie Boitmann, Tracey Calvan and Don Feary, Dr. Kirsten Lawrence Cleary and Andrew Cleary, Ray Culin and Janice Colella, Dr. Douglas Freedman, Dr. Jessica Halprin, Dr. Shinhee Han, Stephen and Cate Harty, Dr. Bryan Leek, Steve Lichliter, Dr. Peter Barnes Lindy, Dr. Will and Robin Martin, Greg Morey and Scott James, Sid Talisman and Alvin Novak, Amy Ormond, Jennifer O'Connell, Dr. Nicolas Patenaude, Sheri Pepper, Dr. Ray and Despina Raven, Dr. Kevin and Mary Anne Sanborn, Andrew Schulman, Graham and Lisa Winton, Bob and Lee Woodruff, Noel and Catherine Woods, and Dr. Ken Yamaguchi.

Here is a heartfelt thanks to Carrie's teacher Mary Carroll Moore and her fellow classmates at the Hudson Valley Writers' Center, for the invigorating discussions and the nonjudgmental atmosphere. We are grateful to RiverArts for sponsoring Carrie's dialogues with various artists on the creative process, and to the artists themselves for speaking openly about their lives: Richard Dresser, Don Feary, Marek Fuchs, Lisa Lynne Mathis, DeLaune Michel, Mary Carroll Moore, Amy Ormond, Kevin O'Rourke, Mary Ford Sussman, Mansheng Wang, and Tricia Wright. Also thanks to writer Allison Gilbert.

We hold dear what we learned from these physicians, teachers, and mentors: Nancy Assaf, Dr. Raymond Bernick, Dr. Richard Druss (thanks to Margery Druss for supporting the use of Dr. Druss's real name), Dr. Edward Foulks, Dr. Steven Glickel, Dr. Marianne Goldberger, Dr. Lucy Lafarge, Dr. Steven Roose, William Shain, and Dr. Barney Softness.

Thanks to Carrie's "lunch is the most important thing" Columbia colleagues: Dr. Brenda Berger, Dr. Lisa Goldfarb, Dr. Ann Maloney, and Dr. Elizabeth Schwarz, for years of laughter, lobster salad, and friendship.

We gratefully acknowledge the Columbia Center for Psychoanalytic Training and Research for a thrilling education, with a special note of gratitude to Joan Jackson and Judy Mars.

Thanks to Mike Dardano, for his early efforts, and to Brian Belfiglio at Scribner for helping us crystallize and promote the message. Emily Remes's careful reading and thoughtful suggestions were invaluable.

Special thanks to Gretchen Baisley, for her devoted care of our children, for her enormous heart, for her wonderful meals, and for showing up with groceries, unasked.

To Bruce Springsteen: There are no words, except maybe, as one of Carrie's Princeton classmates who hailed from New Jersey said repeatedly between 1977 and 1981, "You gotta see him in concert!" Thank you for making our message come alive in the preface and for your magnificent generosity.

Notes

1: Creativity and Happiness

3 *The poet Robert Frost said happiness:* Robert Frost, "Happiness Makes Up in Height for What It Lacks in Length," *Collected Poems* (New York: Henry Holt, 1939).

5 *Is not life supposed to be:* Henry David Thoreau, www.brainyquote.com /quote/quotes/h/henrydavid13266.2.html; Sigmund Freud, *Studies on Hysteria*, in *The Standard Edition of the Complete Psychological Works of Freud*, trans. James Strachey (London: Hogarth Press, 1995).

8 *While two-thirds of people:* Jonathan Engel, *American Therapy: The Rise of Psychotherapy in the United States* (New York: Gotham Books, 2008), xi.

8 *Studies by Irving Kirsch, PhD:* Irving Kirsch, *The Emperor's New Drugs: Exploding the Antidepressant Myth* (New York: Basic Books, 2010), 11. See also Mark Zimmerman, "Study Hints at Overuse of Antidepressants in US," Psychminded.co.uk, March 1, 2002; Mark Zimmerman, Jill I. Mattia, and Michael A. Posternak, "Are Subjects on Pharmacological Treatment Trials Representative of Patients in Routine Clinical Practice?" *American Journal of Psychiatry* 159 (March 2002): 469–73.

8 *For many, pills have the same effect:* Sharon Begley, "The Depressing News About Antidepressants," *Newsweek*, January 29, 2010.

8 *One in ten Americans: The Week*, August 14, 2009, and July 29, 2011.

9 *According to a Rand Corporation study in 2002:* Valerie Ulene, "Antidepressants: The Right People Aren't Always Getting Them," *Los Angeles Times*, May 11, 2009.

Notes

9 *Drs. Ramin Mojtabai and Mark Olfson:* Ramin Mojtabai and Mark Olfson, "Proportion of Antidepressants Prescribed Without a Psychiatric Diagnosis Is Growing," *Health Affairs* 30, 8 (August 2011): 1434–42.

9 *Dr. Jay C. Fournier and Dr. Robert J. DeRubeis:* Jay C. Fournier, Robert J. DeRubeis, et al., "Antidepressant Drug Effects and Depression Severity: A Patient Level Meta-Analysis," *Journal of the American Medical Association* 303, 1 (January 2010): 47–53.

9 *In a 2010 article by:* Benedict Carey, "Popular Drugs May Benefit Only Severe Depression," *New York Times*, January 6, 2010.

10 *Deepak Chopra, physician, writer:* www.oprah.com/spirit/does-self-help -really-work-deepak-chopra.

10 *Self-Help; with Illustrations:* Samuel Smiles, *Self-Help; with Illustrations of Character, Conduct and Perseverance* (New York: Oxford University Press, 2002 [1859]).

11 *A scientific study by Dr. Charles Limb and Dr. Allen Braun:* C. J. Limb and A. R. Braun, "Neural Substrates of Spontaneous Musical Performance: An fMRI Study of Jazz Improvisation," *PLoS ONE* 3, 2 (2008): e1679, doi:10.1371 /journal.pone.0001679.

11 *Even Freud said, "People who are receptive to":* Sigmund Freud, *Civilization and Its Discontents,* in *The Standard Edition of the Complete Psychological Works of Freud,* trans. James Strachey (London: Hogarth Press, 1995).

12 *Hephaestus, the Greek god of crafts:* Richard Sennett, *The Craftsman* (New Haven, CT: Yale University Press, 2008), 21.

12 *Dr. Kelly Lambert, a researcher and chair:* Louisa Kamps, "Crafting Happiness," *Whole Living Magazine,* June 2010.

12 *Clinicians and researchers:* Mihaly Csikszentmihalyi, *Flow: The Psychology of Optimal Experience* (New York: Harper Perennial, 1991). See also Kelly Lambert, *Lifting Depression: A Neuroscientist's Hands-On Approach to Activating Your Brain's Healing Power* (New York: Basic Books, 2008); "Stress Reductions Common Thread," *Journal of the American Medical Association* 274, 4 (July 26, 1995).

12 *According to Andrew Brink:* Andrew Brink, *Creativity as Repair: Bipolarity and Its Closure* (Hamilton, ON: Cromlech Press, 1982), 75.

12 *In the words of D. W. Winnicott:* D. W. Winnicott, *Playing and Reality* (New York: Tavistock, 1971), 65.

13 *Psychoanalysts Janine Chassegeut-Smirgel and Jean Sanville:* Janine Chassegeut-Smirgel, "Thoughts on the Concept of Reparation and the Hierarchy of Creative Acts," *International Review of Psychoanalysis* 11 (1984):

Notes

399–406; Jean Sanville, "Creativity and the Constructing of the Self," *Psychoanalytic Review* 74 (1987): 263–79.

13 *Further, accessing your creativity makes you:* Ralph Waldo Emerson, "Self-Reliance," *Emerson's Prose Works*, vol. 1 (Boston: James R. Osgood, 1875).

14 *"Creativity is allowing yourself to make mistakes":* Scott Adams, www.quote garden.com/art.html.

14 *"Painting is just another way of keeping a diary":* Pablo Picasso, www.quote garden.com/art.html.

14 *"Creativity is the process of bringing something new":* Rollo May, *The Courage to Create* (New York: W. W. Norton, 1975), 39.

14 *"Whatever creativity is, it is in part":* Brian Aldiss, www.answers.com/topic /creativity#ixzz1CR1kmndT.

14 *"Ideas are everywhere":* Twyla Tharp with Mark Reiter, *The Creative Habit: Learn It and Use It for Life* (New York: Simon and Schuster, 2003), 104.

14 *The psychologists and creativity researchers:* Mark A. Runco and Ruth Richard, eds., *Eminent Creativity, Everyday Creativity and Health* (Greenwich, CT: Ablex, 1997).

15 *Research by creativity and mood disorder:* Kay Redfield Jamison, *Touched with Fire: Manic Depressive Illness and the Artistic Temperament* (New York: Free Press, 1993). See also Nancy Andreasen, *The Creating Brain: The Neuroscience of Genius* (New York: Plume, 2005).

16 *In the book* Eminent Creativity, Everyday Creativity: Arthur J. Cropley, "Creativity and Mental Health in Everyday Life," in Runco and Richards, eds., *Eminent Creativity*, 240.

16 *What is remarkable is how:* Silvano Arieti, *Creativity: The Magic Synthesis* (New York: Basic Books, 1976), 344. See also Mihaly Csikszentmihalyi, *Creativity: Flow and the Psychology of Discovery and Invention* (New York: Harper-Collins, 1996).

17 *One of the most creative and well-respected psychoanalytic thinkers:* D. W. Winnicott, *Playing and Reality* (New York: Basic Books, 1971), 54.

19 *Freud did write about "ordinary unhappiness":* Freud, *Civilization and Its Discontents*, 29.

21 *The psychologist Mihaly Csikszentmihalyi:* Mihaly Csikszentmihalyi, *Flow: The Psychology of Optimal Experience* (New York: Harper Perennial, 1991).

25 *"It's like discovering that while you thought":* Anne Lamott, *Bird by Bird: Some Instructions on Writing and Life* (New York: Anchor Books, 1995), xxvi.

25 *Creativity, according to some:* Daniel Pink, *A Whole New Mind: Why Right-Brainers Will Rule the Future* (New York: Riverhead Books, 2005), 3. See also James Pennebaker, *Opening Up: The Healing Power of Expressing Emotions* (New York: Guilford Press, 1997); Thomas L. Friedman and Michael Mandelbaum, *That Used to Be Us: How America Fell Behind in the World It Invented and How We Can Come Back* (New York: Farrar, Straus & Giroux, 2011).

27 *If you can "jump over the chasm":* Merce Cunningham in an interview with Ann Papoulis-Adamovic, in "Epilogue: Merce's Meaning," unpublished, written permission granted for publication by Cunningham.

27 *"Whatever you can do":* Goethe, www.goethesociety.org/pages/quotes.html.

2: How Can I Cultivate a Creative Self?

29 *"Find a happy person":* Sonja Lyubomirsky, *The How of Happiness: A Scientific Approach to Getting the Life You Want* (New York: Penguin, 2008), 205.

30 *Engaging in an absorbing effort:* Mihaly Csikszentmihalyi, *Flow: The Psychology of Optimal Experience* (New York: Harper Perennial, 1991).

33 *The 5PP involves a process of "working through":* Sigmund Freud, *Remembering, Repeating and Working Through*, in *The Standard Edition of the Complete Psychological Works of Freud*, trans. James Strachey (London: Hogarth Press, 1995).

34 *"If we are to achieve the upper reaches of creativity":* Ethel Person, *Feeling Strong: The Achievement of Authentic Power* (New York: William Morrow, 2002), 262.

35 *Research has linked penmanship:* Gwendolyn Bounds, "How Handwriting Changes the Brain," *Wall Street Journal*, October 5, 2010. See also K. H. James and T. P. Atwood, "The Role of Sensori-motor Learning in the Perception of Letter-like Forms: Tracking the Causes of Neural Specialization for Letters," *Cognitive Neuropsychology* 26, 1 (2009); A. C-N. Wong et al., "Expertise with Characters in Alphabetic and Nonalphabetic Writing Systems Engage Overlapping Occipito-temporal Areas," *Cognitive Neuropsychology* 26, 1 (2009): 111–27.

36 *"I have forced myself to begin":* Joyce Carol Oates, in George Plimpton, ed., *Women Writers at Work: The Paris Review Interviews* (New York: Picador, 2007).

36 *A recent* Harvard Mental Health Letter: *Harvard Mental Health Letter*, July 2011.

36 *According to research by psychologist James Pennebaker:* James Pennebaker, *Opening Up: The Healing Power of Expressing Emotions* (New York: Guilford

Notes

Press, 1997). See also J. W. Pennebaker et al., "Expressive Writing and Its Links to Mental and Physical Health," in H. S. Friedman, ed., *Oxford Handbook of Health Psychology* (New York: Oxford University Press, 2011); Rita Charon, "The Self-Telling Body," *Narrative Inquiry* 16, 1 (2006): 191–200.

38 *"Ideally, insight enables"*: *Harvard Mental Health Letter,* September 2010.

38 *"Only when I'm given an actual"*: Haruki Murakami, *What I Talk About When I Talk About Running: A Memoir* (New York: Vintage Books, 2008), 22.

38 *Your love affair with the world:* Louise Kaplan, *Oneness and Separateness: From Infant to Individual* (New York: Simon and Schuster, 1978).

39 *Studies show that exercise:* Robert J. DeRubeis, Steven D. Hollon, Jay D. Amsterdam, et al., "Cognitive Therapy vs Medications in the Treatment of Moderate to Severe Depression," *Archives of General Psychiatry* 62 (2005): 409–16.

39 *"Working up a sweat":* John Ratey, "Psychoanalysis and Sports; Exercise, Mind and Brain," *American Psychoanalyst* 44, 2 (2010).

39 *Movement boosts serotonin:* John Ratey with Eric Hagerman, *Spark: The Revolutionary New Science of Exercise and the Brain* (New York: Little, Brown, 2008). See also J. A. Blumenthal et al., "Effects of Exercise Training on Older Patients with Major Depression,"*Archives of Internal Medicine* 159 (1999).

39 *Movement releases endocannabinoids and endorphins:* P. B. Sparling et al., "Exercise Activates the Endocannabinoid System," *Cognitive Neuroscience and Neuropsychology* 14, 17 (2003).

39 *Movement makes you smarter:* Gretchen Reynolds, "What Sort of Exercise Can Make You Smarter?," *New York Times,* September 16, 2009. See also C. W. Cotman and C. Engesser-Cesar, "Exercise Enhances and Protects Brain Function," *Exercise and Sport Sciences Review* 30, 2 (2002): 75–79.

39 *Sometimes you cannot maintain commitment:* A. Thomas, S. Chess, and H. G. Birch, *Temperament and Behavior Disorders in Children* (New York: New York University Press, 1968).

41 *Research indicates that flexibility and variety:* N. M. Glaros and C. M. Jandle, "Vary the Mode of Cardiovascular Exercise to Increase Adherence," *Journal of Sport Behavior* 24, 1 (2001): 42–62.

41 *Music that you like: Journal of Exercise Physiology* 13, 2 (April 2010).

41 *"Sometimes too much focus can backfire":* Jonah Lehrer, "Bother Me, I'm Thinking: Why You Should Drop That Espresso and Bounce a Ball Instead," *Wall Street Journal,* February 19, 2011.

42 *"A number of intriguing studies":* Sonja Lyubomirsky, *The How of Happiness: A Scientific Approach to Getting the Life You Want* (New York: Penguin, 2008), 242.

42 *Brain studies have shown:* Matt Richtel, "Growing Up Digital, Wired for Distraction," *New York Times,* November 21, 2010.

Notes

43 *"When I saw and realized that all"*: Booker T. Washington, *Working with the Hands: Being a Sequel to "Up from Slavery," Covering the Author's Experiences in Industrial Training at Tuskegee* (General Books, 2010 [1904]), 6.

44 *As we will cover*: Kelly Lambert, *Lifting Depression; A Neuroscientist's Hands-On Approach to Activating Your Brain's Healing Power* (New York: Basic Books, 2008). See also Frank Wilson, *The Hand: How Its Use Shapes the Brain, Language and Human Culture* (New York: Pantheon, 1998).

44 *When she studied the effects of hand use*: Lambert, *Lifting Depression*.

47 *"People who learn to control"*: Mihaly Csikszentmihalyi in Ronald D. Siegel, ed., *Positive Psychology: Harnessing the Power of Happiness, Personal Strength and Mindfulness*, Special Health Report, www.harvard.edu.

48 *The field of positive psychology has established*: Siegel, ed., *Positive Psychology*. See also Martin E. P. Seligman, *Authentic Happiness: Using the New Positive Psychology to Realize Your Potential for Lasting Fulfillment* (New York: Free Press, 2002).

48 *Benson has shown*: Herbert Benson, *The Relaxation Response* (New York: HarperCollins, 1975).

48 *"The greatest weapon against stress"*: William James, www.brainyquote.com /quotes/authors/w/william_james.html.

48 *Experts in positive psychology and cognitive-behavioral therapy*: Seligman, *Authentic Happiness*. See also Lyubomirsky, *The How of Happiness*.

49 *Cognitive-behavioral therapy holds*: Aaron Beck, *Cognitive Therapy of Depression* (New York: Guilford Press, 1979).

49 *In psychiatry, we use the phrase*: D. W. Winnicott, "Ego Distortion in Terms of True and False Self," in *The Maturational Processes and the Facilitating Environment* (Madison, CT: International Universities Press, 1960).

50 *"Man can alter his life"*: James, op. cit.

51 *"True happiness is a verb"*: Epictetus, *The Art of Living: The Classical Manual on Virtue, Happiness and Effectiveness*, trans. Sharon Lebell (New York: HarperOne, 1995), 85.

3: Creativity and Inhibition

55 *The False Self is the inauthentic self*: D. W. Winnicott, "Ego Distortion in Terms of True and False Self," in *The Maturational Processes and the Facilitating Environment* (Madison, CT: International Universities Press, 1960).

69 *You may feel so intoxicated*: Jean Sanville, "Creativity and the Constructing of the Self," *Psychoanalytic Review* 74 (1987): 263–79.

71 *If you want to be at the top*: Wendy Mogel, *The Blessing of a B Minus: Using Jewish Teachings to Raise Resilient Teenagers* (New York: Scribner, 2010), 51.

Notes

4: Creativity, Psychological Clutter, and the Well-Lighted Mind

86 *She wrote, "I turned upon her"*: Cited in Rozsika Parker, "Killing the Angel in the House," *International Journal of Psychoanalysis* 79 (1998): 757–74.

94 *"There is no happiness"*: William James, www.brainyquote.com/quotes/authors /w/william_james.html.

100 *Even Freud said that we worship external beauty*: Sigmund Freud, *Civilization and Its Discontents*, in *The Standard Edition of the Complete Psychological Works of Freud*, trans. James Strachey (London: Hogarth Press, 1995).

101 *"Use the disadvantage"*: Terry Gross, *All I Did Was Ask: Conversations with Writers, Actors, Musicians and Artists* (New York: Hyperion, 2004).

5: Creativity and Resilience

114 *Lee Woodruff, writer*: Lee and Bob Woodruff, *In an Instant: A Family's Journey of Love and Healing* (New York: Random House, 2007).

115 *I worked with Lily*: The phrase "inner gleam" is from Arnold Goldberg, MD.

118 *"No one has ever"*: Antonin Artaud, www.answer.com/topic/creativity#/822 /cr/kmndT.

119 *Stephen King, in an interview*: Fresh Air: Writers Speak with Terry Gross (Philadelphia: Highbridge, 2004).

120 *"Limitations are a blessing"*: Twyla Tharp with Mark Reiter, *The Creative Habit: Learn It and Use It for Life* (New York: Simon and Schuster, 2003), 124.

121 *We also covet the capacity*: Melanie Klein, *The Writings of Melanie Klein*, vol. 3: *Envy and Gratitude and Other Works, 1946–1963* (London: Hogarth Press, 1975), 176–235. See also Eric Brenman, "Cruelty and Narrow-Mindedness," in Roy Schafer, ed., *The Contemporary Kleinians of London* (Madison, CT: International Universities Press, 1997).

130 *It turns out that people are happier with effort*: Mihaly Csikszentmihalyi, *Flow: The Psychology of Optimal Experience* (New York: Harper Perennial, 1991).

130 *In* Rasselas, Prince of Abissinia: Samuel Johnson, *The History of Rasselas, Prince of Abissinia* (London: Penguin, 1976 [1759]).

133 *Research studies indicate that physical stamina*: Michalak et al., "Embodiment of Sadness and Depression—Gait Patterns Associated with Dysphoric Mood," *Psychosomatic Medicine* 7, 5 (2009): 580–57. See also Miers et al., "Peer Perceptions of Social Skills in Socially Anxious and Nonanxious Adolescents," *Journal of Abnormal Child Psychology* 38, 1 (2010): 33–41; Canales et al., "Posture and Body Image in Individuals with Major Depressive Disorder: A Controlled Study," *Revista Brasileira de Psiquiatria* 32, 4 (2010): 375–80.

133 *"The effect in sickness of beautiful objects"*: Florence Nightingale, *Notes on Nursing: What It Is, and What It Is Not* (Philadelphia: Lippincott, 1992).

135 *In the therapy field, there are about one hundred:* Martin E. Seligman, *Authentic Happiness: Using the New Positive Psychology to Realize Your Potential for Lasting Fulfillment* (New York: Free Press, 2002).

6: Creativity, Community, and Your Own Two Hands

137 *Because science has shown:* Sonja Lyubomirsky, *The How of Happiness: A Scientific Approach to Getting the Life You Want* (New York: Penguin, 2008), 131. See also David Brooks, *The Social Animal* (New York: Random House, 2011).

139 *As they began to make better tools:* Sherwood L. Washburn, "Tools and Human Evolution," *Scientific American* 203, 3 (1960): 63–75.

139 *According to Professor Richard Sennett:* Richard Sennett, *The Craftsman* (New Haven, CT: Yale University Press, 2008).

139 *According to Dr. Abraham Maslow:* A. H. Maslow, "A Theory of Human Motivation," *Psychological Review* 50 (1943): 370–96.

140 *"It is by having hands that man is":* Anaxagoras, *Anaxagoras Fragments and Commentary*, ed. and trans. Arthur Fairbanks (London: K. Paul, Trench, Trubner, 1898), 235–62.

140 *Making and using tools defined the rise:* John Eccles, *Evolution of the Brain: Creation of the Self* (New York: Routledge, 1989).

140 *Dr. Frank Wilson, a neurologist and hand expert:* Frank Wilson, *The Hand: How Its Use Shapes the Brain, Language, and Human Culture* (New York: Pantheon Books, 1998), 7.

140 *Antigone Sharris, an electronics instructor at Triton College:* Mokoto Rich, "A Summer Camp to Lure Girls into Manufacturing Careers," *New York Times*, August 19, 2011.

141 *In an article for the* New York Times: Alton Barron, "Like Athletes, Workers Need Conditioning for Computer Jobs," *New York Times*, November 4, 1999.

141 *Use of the hands for heaving and lifting:* Nancy Monson, *Craft to Heal: Soothing Your Soul with Sewing, Painting and Other Pastimes* (Tucson, AZ: Hats Off Books, 2005).

141 *Dr. Kelly Lambert, a neuroscientist and psychologist:* Kelly Lambert, *Lifting Depression: A Neuroscientist's Hands-On Approach to Activating Your Brain's Healing Power* (New York: Basic Books, 2008).

142 *Crafts, because they combine:* Monson, *Craft to Heal.*

142 *Studies indicate that handwork such as sewing:* Ibid. See also "Stress Reductions Common Thread," *Journal of the American Medical Association* 274, 4

Notes

(July 26, 1995); C. J. Limb and A. R. Braun, "Neural Substrates of Spontaneous Musical Performance: An fMRI Study of Jazz Improvisation," *PLoS ONE* 3, 2 (2008): e1679, doi:10.1371/journal.pone.0001679; Mark Frauenfelder, *Made by Hand: Searching for Meaning in a Throwaway World* (New York: Portfolio, 2010).

142 *Depression is essentially nonexistent among:* J. A. Egeland and A. M. Hostetter, "Amish Study, I: Affective Disorders Among the Amish, 1976–1980," *American Journal of Psychiatry* 140 (1983): 56–61. See also E. L. Schieffelin, "The Cultural Analysis of Depressive Affect: An Example from Papua New Guinea," in A. M. Kleinman and B. Good, eds., *Culture and Depression* (Berkeley: University of California Press, 1985).

143 *But hands are special:* Immanuel Kant, cited by Raymond Tallis in *The Hand: A Philosophical Inquiry in Human Being* (Edinburgh: Edinburgh University Press, 2003).

146 *Mark Frauenfelder, editor in chief:* Frauenfelder, *Made by Hand.*

146 *Other Maker Faires are springing up:* Julie Scelfo, "Kindergarten Shop Class," *New York Times,* March 30, 2011.

147 *"With our strengths and our minds":* Anand Giridharadas, "The Kitchen Table Industrialists," *New York Times Magazine,* May 13, 2011.

147 *Columnist Thomas L. Friedman and Johns Hopkins professor:* Thomas L. Friedman and Michael Mandelbaum, *That Used to Be Us: How America Fell Behind in the World It Invented and How We Can Come Back* (New York: Farrar, Straus and Giroux, 2011).

147 *Research has indicated that gardening:* D. Armstrong, "A Survey of Community Gardens in Upstate New York: Implications for Health Promotion and Community Development," *Health and Place* 6 (2000): 319–27. See also Geoff Herbach, "Harvesting the City: Community Gardening in Greater Madison,Wisconsin," 1998, Madison Food System Project Working Paper Series MFSP-1998-01; H. Patricia Hynes, *A Patch of Eden: America's Inner-City Gardeners* (White River Junction, VT: Chelsea Green, 1996); Hynes, cited in "Gardening—A Holistic Approach to Civic Health," www.huntingtoncommunitygardens.com/36.html; A. K. Hanna and P. Oh, "Rethinking Urban Poverty: A Look at Community Garden," *Bulletin of Science, Technology and Society* 20, 3 (2000): 207–16; Matthew Page, "Gardening as a Therapeutic Intervention in Mental Health," *Nursing Times* 104, 45 (2008): 28–30.

147 *Professor Dianne Relf of Virginia Tech University:* Emily Wallace, "Therapeutic Gardening: A Natural Approach to Health, Healing and Recovery," Huffington Post, May 25, 2011.

148 *Even caring for a plant:* David Servan-Schreiber, *Instinct to Heal: Curing Depression, Anxiety and Stress Without Drugs and Without Talk Therapy* (New York: Rodale, 2003), 170.

148 *The Edible Schoolyard, a program:* www.edibleschoolyard.org. See also Tara Parker-Pope, "Alice Waters Takes Kids Beyond Chicken Nuggets," *New York Times,* September 26, 2008.

149 *One study showed that diminished depression is a fringe:* E. A. Ross, T. L. Hollen, and B. M. Fitzgerald, "Observational Study of an Arts-in-Medicine Program in an Outpatient Hemodialysis Unit," *American Journal of Kidney Diseases* 47, 3 (2006): 462–68.

149 *Habitat for Humanity is a community-focused:* www.habitat.org.

149 *A trusted and loyal community even appears:* Francis Fukuyama, *Trust: The Social Virtues and the Creation of Prosperity* (New York: Free Press, 1996), 338.

150 *One study of social life in America:* M. McPherson, L. Smith-Lovin, and M. B. Brashears, "Social Isolation in America: Changes in Core Discussion Networks Over Two Decades," *American Sociological Review* 71 (2006): 353–75.

150 *In a recent study reported by Michael B. Sauter:* Michael B. Sauter, "U.S Doesn't Make Cut for Happiest Nations," 24/7 Wall Street from MSNBC, June 6, 2011.

151 *Research from New York University and Michigan State University:* Katelyn Y. A. McKenna, Arnie S. Green, and Marcie E. J. Gleason, "Relationship Formation on the Internet: What's the Big Attraction?" *Journal of Social Issues* 58, 1 (2002): 9–31. See also Nicole B. Ellison, Charles Steinfield, and Cliff Lampe, "The Benefits of Facebook 'Friends:' Social Capital and College Students' Use of Online Social Network Sites," *Journal of Computer-Mediated Communication* 12, 4 (2007), article 1.

151 *Psychotherapy (sometimes also known as the "talking cure"):* Owen Renik, *Practical Psychoanalysis for Therapists and Patients* (New York: Other Press, 2006).

152 *Recently I saw a Parsons Dance piece:* "Hand Dance," Parsons Dance, performed at Joyce Theatre, New York, spring 2011.

154 *In one study, jazz musicians:* C. J. Limb and A. R. Braun, "Neural Substrates of Spontaneous Musical Performance: An fMRI Study of Jazz Improvisation," *PLoS ONE* 3, 2 (2008): e1679, doi:10.1371/journal.pone.0001679.

156 *Research has shown that penmanship:* Gwendolyn Bounds, "How Handwriting Changes the Brain," *Wall Street Journal,* October 5, 2010. See also Katherine Rosman, "Stationery's New Followers," *Wall Street Journal,* August 25, 2011.

Notes

157 *This has catalyzed some questions and concerns:* Theodore Dalrymple, "The Handwriting Is on the Wall," *Wall Street Journal*, July 11, 2011.

158 *We are attracted by a bit of wildness:* Robert Herricks, "Delight in Disorder," in David Bergman and Daniel Mark Epstein, eds., *The Heath Guide to Literature* (Lexington, MA: D. C. Heath, 1984).

159 *"Beauty is truth":* John Keats, "Ode on a Grecian Urn."

159 *According to several books:* Mihaly Csikszentmihalyi, *Flow: The Psychology of Optimal Experience* (New York: Harper Perennial, 1991). See also Sennett, *The Craftsman*; Matthew Crawford, *Shop Class as Soulcraft: An Inquiry into the Value of Work* (New York: Penguin, 2009).

164 *"Writing a letter out of the quiet mind":* John Freeman, *The Tyranny of E-Mail: The Four-Thousand-Year Journey to Your Inbox* (New York: Scribner, 2009).

166 *"We require civilized man to reverence beauty":* Sigmund Freud, *Civilization and Its Discontents*, in *The Standard Edition of the Complete Psychological Works of Freud*, trans. James Strachey (London: Hogarth Press, 1995).

7: Creativity, Nature, and Exercise

167 *"The High Line stretches one's gaze":* Diane Ackerman, "Emerald Cities," *New York Times*, August 15, 2011.

168 *Dr. Stephen R. Kellert of Yale:* Stephen R. Kellert, *Building for Life: Designing and Understanding the Human-Nature Connection* (Washington, DC: Island Press, 2005).

168 *Professor Robin C. Moore:* Robin C. Moore and Herbert Hong, *Natural Learning: The Life History of an Environmental Schoolyard* (Berkeley, CA: MIG Communications, 1997).

168 *Studies by Professors Andrea Faber Taylor and Frances Kuo:* Andrea Faber Taylor, Angela Wiley, Frances Kuo, and William Sullivan, "Growing Up in the Inner City: Green Spaces as Places to Grow," *Environment and Behavior* 30, 1 (1998): 191–205.

168 *A study in Sweden showed that asphalt playgrounds:* Patrik Grahn, Fredrika Martensson, Bodil Lindblad, Paula Nilsson, and Anna Ekman, *Ute pa Dagis, Stad & Land* [Outdoor Daycare. City and Country] (Hasselholm, Sweden: Norra Skane Offset, 1997).

169 *"Most of these benefits are great":* Louise Chawla, "Ecstatic Places," *Children's Environments Quarterly* 3, 4 (1986). See also Louise Chawla, "Life Paths into Effective Environmental Action," *Journal of Environmental Education* 31, 1 (1990): 15–26.

Notes

169 *Recently,* New York Times *reporter Matt Richtel:* Matt Richtel, "Outdoors and Out of Reach: Studying the Brain," *New York Times,* August 16, 2010.

169 *Marghanita Laski, a British author:* Marghanita Laski, *Ecstasy: A Study of Some Secular and Religious Experiences* (Indianapolis: Indiana University Press, 1961).

169 *In the words of poet Emily Dickinson:* Emily Dickinson, "Part Four: Time and Eternity," in *Complete Poems,* available on www.bartleby.com.

170 *According to Dr. Peter H. Kahn Jr.:* Peter H. Kahn Jr., *The Human Relationship with Nature: Development and Culture* (Cambridge, MA: MIT Press, 2001).

170 *Professor Nancy Wells from the College of Human Ecology:* Nancy Wells and Gary Evans, "Nearby Nature: A Buffer of Life Stress Among Rural Children," *Environment and Behavior* 35 (2003): 311–30.

170 *A little sunlight:* Deborah Kotz, "Host of Health Benefits Attributed to Sunlight," *US News and World Report,* June 24, 2008. See also Stephen Ilardi, *The Depression Cure: The 6-Step Program to Beat Depression Without Drugs* (Cambridge, MA: Da Capo/Lifelong Press, 2009), 133.

170 *Patients get better faster:* Esther Sternberg, *Healing Spaces: The Science of Place and Well-Being* (Cambridge, MA: Belknap Press, 2009).

171 *Richard Louv, author:* Richard Louv, *Last Child in the Woods: Saving Our Children from Nature-Deficit Disorder* (New York: Workman, 2005), 3.

172 *According to recent studies by Marc Berman:* Marc G. Berman, John Jonides, and Stephen Kaplan, "The Cognitive Benefits of Interacting with Nature," *Psychological Science* 19, 12 (2008).

172 *In an interview with Wall Street Journal reporter:* Shirley S. Wang, "Coffee Break? Walk in the Park? Why Unwinding Is Hard," *Wall Street Journal,* August 30, 2011.

175 *Dr. Michael Balint, a well-known psychoanalyst:* Michael Balint, *The Basic Fault: Therapeutic Aspects of Regression* (Evanston, IL: Northwestern University Press, 1968).

177 *Research from countless medical journals:* John Ratey with Eric Hagerman, *Spark: The Revolutionary New Science of Exercise and the Brain* (New York: Little, Brown, 2008). See also K. I. Erickson et al., "Exercise Training Increases the Size of the Hippocampus and Improves Memory," *Proceedings of the National Academy of Sciences* 108, 7 (2011): 3017–22; Bruce McEwen with Elizabeth Lasley, *The End of Stress as We Know It* (Washington, DC: National Academies Press, 2002).

177 *"Running! If there's an activity happier":* Joyce Carol Oates, "To Invigorate Literary Mind, Start Moving Literary Feet," in *Writers on Writing: Collected Essays from the* New York Times (New York: Times Books, 2001).

177 *John Ratey, MD, notes that exercise:* Ratey, *Spark*, 7.

177 *A growing body of evidence:* J. A. Blumenthal et al., "Effects of Exercise Training on Older Patients with Major Depression," *Archives of Internal Medicine* 159 (1999).

177 *It is as effective:* M. Babyak et al., "Exercise Treatment for Major Depression: Maintenance of Therapeutic Benefit at 10 Months," *Psychosomatic Medicine* 62 (2000): 633–38.

178 *Citing a large volume:* Ratey, *Spark*.

178 *Dr. Stephen Ilardi:* Ilardi, *The Depression Cure*, 13.

178 *Endocannabinoids are naturally produced substances:* P. B. Sparling et al., "Exercise Activates the Endocannabinoid System," *Cognitive Neuroscience and Neuropsychology* 14, 17 (2003).

179 *"The point of exercise":* Ratey, *Spark*, 3.

179 *Ratey cites a school:* Ibid., 9.

180 *Other researchers have validated that vigorous:* Carl W. Cotman and C. Engesser-Cesar, "Exercise Enhances and Protects Brain Function," *Exercise and Sport Sciences Review* 30, 2 (2002): 75–79.

180 *Recent research by Dr. Kirk I. Erickson:* Erickson et al., "Exercise Training."

180 *According to a recent study in the* Journal of Applied Physiology: M. W. Voss et al., "Exercise, Brain, and Cognition Across a Lifespan," *Journal of Applied Physiology,* 2011.

180 *"Exercise is medicine":* Ilardi, *The Depression Cure*, 117.

180 *The writer Haruki Murakami:* Haruki Murakami, *What I Talk About When I Talk About Running: A Memoir* (New York: Vintage, 2008).

182 *Many creative people attest to the importance of exercise:* Gail McMeekan, *The 12 Secrets of Highly Creative Women: A Portable Mentor* (New York: MJF Books, 2000).

182 *According to Joyce Carol Oates:* Oates, "To Invigorate Literary Mind."

182 *"The idea is that when you have a highly honed skill":* Hubert Dreyfuss and Sean Dorrance Kelly, *All Things Shining* (New York: Free Press, 2011), 80.

183 *"As I run I tell myself to think of a river":* Murakami, *What I Talk About,* 23.

8: Creativity and Self-Mastery

193 *"We are in bondage":* Marcus Tullius Cicero, quoted at liberty-tree.ca.

195 *Studies have shown that personality and character:* Martin E. P. Seligman, *Authentic Happiness* (New York: Free Press, 2002).

195 *In psychoanalysis we have an expression:* Ernst Kris, *Psychoanalytic Explorations in Art* (Madison, CT: International Universities Press, 2000).

197 *Another definition of creativity comes:* Robert J. Sternberg, *Successful Intelligence: How Practical and Creative Intelligence Determine Success in Life* (New York: Plume, 1997), 191.

200 *"Character is destiny":* Heraclitus, www.brainyquote.com/quotes/quotes/h/heraclitus117863.html.

201 *"When you are aspiring":* Cicero, liberty-tree.ca.

204 *Humility helps with Creative Capacity:* Twyla Tharp with Mark Reiter, *The Creative Habit: Learn It and Use It for Life* (New York: Simon and Schuster, 2003), 165.

210 *"The only true joy is self-possession":* Boethius, *The Consolation of Philosophy,* trans. Richard Green (Indianapolis: Bobbs-Merrill, 1962), 27.

210 *Fortune is fickle:* Ibid.

211 *The ability to find pleasure independent of:* Mary Catherine Bateson, *Composing a Life* (New York: Grove Press, 1989).

211 *"Authentic happiness is always":* Epictetus, *The Art of Living: The Classical Manual on Virtue, Happiness and Effectiveness* (New York: HarperOne, 1995), 26.

212 *"Creative decisions are more likely":* Sharon Begley, "Brain Freeze," *Newsweek,* March 7, 2011.

213 *"The art of being wise":* William James, www.brainyquote.com/quotes/authors/w/william_james.html

216 *Because too much input:* John Freeman, *The Tyranny of E-Mail: The Four-Thousand-Year Journey to Your Inbox* (New York: Scribner, 2009).

216 *According to Nicholas Carr:* Nicholas Carr, *The Shallows: What the Internet Is Doing to Our Brains* (New York: W. W. Norton, 2009).

9: Creativity and True Connections

223 *"When you choose your friends, don't be short-changed":* Somerset Maugham, www.brainyquote.com.

223 *Showing the True Self enhances relationships:* Hara Estroff Marano, "Clues to Character," *Psychology Today,* June 2011.

224 *Research has shown that friendships can help us recover:* K. Orth-Gomer, A. Rosengren, and L. Wilhelmsen, "Lack of Social Support and Incidence of Coronary Heart Disease in Middle-Aged Swedish Men," *Psychosomatic Medicine* 55, 1 (1993): 37–43. See also Tara Parker-Pope, "What Are Friends For? A Longer Life," *New York Times,* April 20, 2009; Candyce H. Kroenke et al., "Social Networks, Social Support, and Survival After Breast Cancer Diagnosis," *Journal of Clinical Oncology* 24, 7 (2006): 1105–11.

224 *In another study, students asked to climb a hill:* Simone Schnall et al., "Social

Support and the Perception of Geographical Slant," *Journal of Experimental Social Psychology* 44 (2008): 1246–55.

224 *When women experiencing stress seek solace from friends:* Shelley E. Taylor et al., "Biobehavioral Responses to Stress in Females: Tend-and-Befriend, Not Fight-or-Flight," *Psychological Review* 107, 3 (2000).

224 *According to Ethel Person, MD:* Ethel Person, "Creative Collaborations: Writers and Editors," *Psychoanalytic Study of the Child* 54 (1999): 1–16.

226 *"Social connection helps push":* Stephen Ilardi, *The Depression Cure: The 6-Step Program to Beat Depression Without Drugs* (Cambridge, MA: Da Capo Press, 2009), 191.

228 *"A relationship is a physiological process":* David Servan-Schreiber, *Instinct to Heal: Curing Depression, Anxiety and Stress Without Drugs and Without Talk Therapy* (New York: Rodale, 2003), 169.

231 *As Freud said, when we do not remember:* Sigmund Freud, *Remembering, Repeating and Working Through,* in in *The Standard Edition of the Complete Psychological Works of Freud,* trans. James Strachey (London: Hogarth Press, 1995).

235 *D. W. Winnicott coined the term "holding environment":* D. W. Winnicott, "Ego Distortion in Terms of True and False Self," in *The Maturational Processes and the Facilitating Environment* (Madison, CT: International Universities Press, 1960).

239 *New research shows how the Internet encourages fabrication:* Elias Aboujaoude, *Virtually You: The Dangerous Powers of the E-Personality* (New York: W. W. Norton, 2011).

239 *Without authentic expression, we can become depressed:* Sherry Turkle, *Alone Together: Why We Expect More from Technology and Less from Each Other* (New York: Basic Books, 2011).

239 *According to recent research, there are circumstances:* Katelyn Y. A. McKenna, Amie S. Green, and Marci E. J. Gleason, "Relationship Formation on the Internet: What's the Big Attraction?" *Journal of Social Issues* 58, 1 (2002): 9–31. See also Nicole B. Ellison, Charles Steinfield, and Cliff Lampe, "The Benefits of Facebook 'Friends:' Social Capital and College Students' Use of Online Social Network Sites," *Journal of Computer-Mediated Communication* 12, 4 (2007): article 1; James R. Baker and Susan M. Moore, "Distress, Coping, and Blogging: Comparing New MySpace Users by Their Intention to Blog," *CyberPsychology and Behavior* 11, 1 (2008).

242 *Dr. Rita Charon, pioneer of narrative medicine:* Rita Charon, *Narrative Medicine: Honoring the Stories of Illness* (New York: Oxford University Press, 2006).

242 *Setting is important for conjuring up:* Louise DeSalvo, *On Moving: A Writer's Meditations on New Houses, Old Haunts and Finding Home Again* (New York: Bloomsbury, 2009).

246 *Some researchers have explored the idea of laughter:* Michael Miller, "Laughter Helps Blood Vessels," University of Maryland Medical Center, March 7, 2005, www.umm.edu/news/releases/laughter2.htm.

10: Creativity and Identity

255 *"That is happiness: to be dissolved":* Susan Lacy, *American Masters: Willa Cather: The Road Is All* (Thirteen/WNET, 2005).

262 *"We are what we repeatedly do":* Aristotle, quoted at liberty-tree.ca.

263 *"royalty doesn't rush":* Merrill Ashley with Larry Kaplan, *Dancing for Balanchine* (New York: E. P. Dutton, 1984).

Recommended Readings

Herbert Benson. *The Relaxation Response*. New York: HarperCollins, 1975.

Boethius. *The Consolation of Philosophy*. Translated by Richard Green. Indianapolis: Bobbs-Merrill, 1962.

Boethius lived between AD 475 and 524 and wrote about self-possession as a way to endure the unendurable.

Andrew Brink. *Creativity as Repair: Bipolarity and Its Closure*. Hamilton, Ontario: Cromlech Press, 1982.

A psychoanalyst and literature professor describes the relationship between creative processes and self-repair.

David Brooks. *The Social Animal*. New York: Random House, 2011.

The story conveys how relationships, community, and character are sound routes to contentment.

Julia Cameron. *The Artist's Way: A Spiritual Path to Higher Creativity*. New York: Tarcher/Putnam, 2002.

Cameron leads you through a process that can help you to express yourself and uncover creative impulses.

Matthew Crawford. *Shop Class as Soulcraft: An Inquiry into the Value of Work*. New York: Penguin, 2009.

This book shows how working with the hands may bring more satisfaction, creativity, and intellectual fulfillment than cerebral pursuits.

Louise DeSalvo. *On Moving: A Writer's Meditations on New Houses, Old Haunts and Finding Home Again*. New York: Bloomsbury, 2009.

A writer with a keen understanding of creative processes and troubling feelings describes how setting influences mood, mind, well-being, and creativity.

Ralph Waldo Emerson. "Self-Reliance," in *Emerson's Prose Works*, volume 1: *Essays*. Boston: James R. Osgood, 1875.

   It is comforting to read this classic.

Mark Frauenfelder. *Made by Hand: Searching for Meaning in a Throwaway World*. New York: Portfolio, 2010.

   This is an inspiring book on the value of doing it yourself.

John Freeman. *The Tyranny of E-Mail: The Four-Thousand-Year Journey to Your Inbox*. New York: Scribner, 2009.

   You are not alone in feeling swamped. This book poses concerns and questions about being overrun by technological minutiae and how we might combat this.

Terry Gross. *All I Did Was Ask: Conversations with Writers, Actors, Musicians and Artists*. New York: Hyperion, 2004.

   These interviews offer interesting insights into the minds of established creators.

Stephen Ilardi. *The Depression Cure: The 6-Step Program to Beat Depression Without Drugs*. Cambridge, MA: Da Capo/Lifelong Press, 2009.

   This book suggests practical, well-researched methods for changing your lifestyle to help you feel better.

Samuel Johnson. *The History of Rasselas, Prince of Abissinia*. London: Penguin, 1976 [1759].

   A short tale about how the journey can offer more than the destination.

Kelly Lambert. *Lifting Depression: A Neuroscientist's Hands-On Approach to Activating Your Brain's Healing Power*. New York: Basic Books, 2008.

   This book has many interesting ideas, and it outlines research about depression, the current culture, and use of the hands.

Anne Lamott. *Bird by Bird: Some Instructions on Writing and Life*. New York: Anchor Books, 1995.

   Lamott is an engaging, empathic writer who can make you feel a whole lot better about your "shitty first draft."

Richard Louv. *Last Child in the Woods: Saving Our Children from Nature-Deficit Disorder*. New York: Workman, 2005.

   This expert offers solid evidence on how nature is essential for well-being.

Sonja Lyubomirsky. *The How of Happiness: A Scientific Approach to Getting the Life You Want*. New York: Penguin, 2008.

   The writer offers scientific explanations for processes that lead to happiness.

John Ratey with Eric Hagerman. *Spark: The Revolutionary New Science of Exercise and the Brain*. New York: Little, Brown, 2008.

   If you ever needed convincing that exercise is good for you and can improve your mood, this is it.

Twyla Tharp with Mark Reiter. *The Creative Habit: Learn It and Use It for Life*. New York: Simon and Schuster, 2003.
    An illustrious choreographer explains how habit is the essence of her creative success and how habit can help you, too.
Henry David Thoreau. *Walden*. Princeton, NJ: Princeton University Press, 2004 [1854].
    The classic on what nature can do for you.
Booker T. Washington. *Working with the Hands: Being a Sequel to "Up from Slavery," Covering the Author's Experiences in Industrial Training at Tuskegee*. New York: Doubleday, Page, 1904.
    This book illustrates the power, pleasure, dignity, and loftiness of handwork.
Lee and Bob Woodruff. *In an Instant: A Family's Journey of Love and Healing*. New York: Random House, 2007.
    Lee and Bob will let you know that you can survive.

Recommended Sites for Handwork

American Craft Council, www.craftcouncil.org

American Quilter's Society, www.americanquilter.com

American Sewing Guild, www.asg.org

The Knitting Guild Association, www.tkga.com

American Welding Society, www.aws.org

Recommended Groups

A self-help group for any ailment you may have; this fosters
   True Connections

Any group that shares your interests, either online or in the flesh

Writing groups or classes in your area

Meditation classes or yoga classes

Athletic or intellectual teams for group competitions

A gym (joining will help motivate you and help you feel part
   of something)

Church, synagogue, or spiritual congregation

Community activities, such as your PTSA or volunteer corps

Charities and nonprofits that share your values

Index

Index

Creative Capacity (*cont.*)
    starting a project to awaken, 74
    stress reduction and, 170
    True Self and, 17–18, 19, 58
    willingness to explore, 22–23
Creative Hour, 164–65, 190, 219, 253, 256
Creative Self
    characteristics of, 18
    Creative Capacity leading to, 18, 255
    definition of, 55
    description of, 17
    5PP process to promote, 33
    Movement and, 260
    projects and, 256
    psychological clutter and, 85
    self-mastery and, 194, 195
    self-possession and, 211
    True Connections and, 224, 237, 238
creativity
    artists and depression and, 15
    body involvement in, 38–39
    changing inner states using, 12–13
    character and, 195, 200, 215
    "closeted creatives" and need to
        express, 2
    concerns over artistic ability and,
        22–23, 45
    contentment and, 20–21
    Creative Capacity and, 11
    definitions of, 13–14, 196–97
    eminent, 14–15
    engagement and peak moments with, 25
    everyday, 14, 15
    hands-on work and, 12, 13, 138, 139
    happiness related to, 1, 2, 20, 258
    humility and, 205–6, 208
    importance of, 20–21
    inhibition and, 53, 75
    mental health and, 16–19
    nature and, 168–70
    personal and community relations
        and, 26
    play and, 17, 168, 169
    professional prowess and, 25
    reasons on essential aspects of, 24–26
    resilience and, 113, 131
    self-mastery and, 195–97, 200
    self-possession and, 24
    self-reliance and, 13
    soul satisfaction and, 24
    source of ideas in, 14
    types of, 14–15

Creativity Cure
    concerns over artistic ability and, 22–23
    description of, 10
    development of, 11
    examples of people who changed,
        26–27
    happiness and, 10, 11, 12
    how it works, 15–16
    self-reliance and, 12
    twofold approach of, 15
    unconscious mind and, 10–11
    understanding changes after complet-
        ing, 255–57
    whatever works mantra in, 76
criticism, fear of, 72–73
critique, constructive, 73
crocheting, 80, 158
Cropley, Dr. Arthur, 16
Csikszentmihalyi, Mihaly, 16, 21, 47
Cunningham, Merce, 27
cutting and pasting, 46, 81, 111, 135

dancing, 27, 40, 67, 79, 110, 133, 152, 163,
    188, 191, 217, 235, 252
daydreaming, 20, 41, 42, 80, 155, 163, 169
decorating, 81, 111, 135, 189
decoupage, 46
deep breathing, 163, 189
defective, feelings of being, 99–103, 109
delayed gratification, 94, 209, 219
depression
    creativity and, 12, 15
    Creativity Cure for overcoming, 10
    exercise for, 39, 177–78, 180, 260
    exposure to nature and, 171
    False Self and, 56
    feelings of being defective and, 102
    group activities and, 149
    hands-on work and, 12, 45, 141, 142,
        149, 157–58
    loneliness and, 224
    medications for, 8–9
    meditation and, 42
    overstimulation and, 8, 9, 216
    passivity and, 127
    positive outlook for decreasing, 49
    procrastination and fear of starting
        and, 74, 98
    self-mastery and, 198–99
    sources of, 19
    struggles with, 3
    symptoms of, 5–6

Index

Index

Index

Movement and, 259
nature's benefits for, 169, 170–72
self-reliance linked to, 13
Hephaestus, 12
Heraclitus, 200
holding environment, 235–37
home-focused projects, 12, 14, 45, 46,
    111, 135, 145, 146, 154, 212, 235
horticultural therapy, 148
hostility, feelings of, 61–62
humility, 71, 123, 198, 261
hurting others, fear of, 63–65

identity, and True Connections, 223, 229
Ilardi, Dr. Stephen, 178, 180, 226
imagination, 60, 168, 169, 202
improvisation, 11
independence
    do-it-yourself projects and, 146
    fear of, 65–66, 77, 82
    self-reliance and, 211, 212
indirect attention, 143
inhibition
    creativity and, 53, 75
    examples of people who changed,
      56–58
    families and, 59
    5PP for, 76, 77–82
injuries
    5PP for, 132–36
    lack of hands-on work and, 141
    resilience after, 119–20
inner compromise, 197, 201–4
inner conflicts
    change from facing, 56–57
    creative acts in working through, 13
    fear of pleasure and, 69
    feelings of being defective and, 99
    5PP for working through, 33
    True Self and facing, 54, 57
innovation, 25
Insight, 29
    combination of steps with, 31–32, 76
    creative process and, 196
    daily time commitment for, 31, 50
    definition of, 34
    description of, 34–38, 262
    exercise and, 187
    hands-on work and, 161
    inhibition and fears and, 77–78
    importance of, 35
    journal for, 35, 47, 50, 109

order of steps performed in, 31
process and change using, 32
psychological clutter and, 109
required action for, 34–37
resilience and, 132
self-analysis using, 35
self-mastery and, 216–17
suggestions for, 38
True Connections and, 252
writing process in, 35–37, 48, 50, 76,
    77–78, 109, 132, 187, 190, 216, 252
internalized relationships, 241–42
interruptions, managing, 69–70
intimacy, fear of, 239
inventiveness, 25
irrational critic, 86–87, 90, 91, 93, 97

James, Henry, 242
James, William, 48, 50
Jamison, Kay Redfield, 15
jogging, 174, 178, 188, 217
Johnson, Samuel, 130
journals, 35, 47, 50, 109

Kahn, Dr. Peter H. Jr., 170, 185
Kaluli people, 142
Keats, John, 159
Kellert, Dr. Stephen R., 168
Kelly, Sean Dorrance, 182
King, Stephen, 119–20, 182
Kirsch, Irving, 8
knitting, 46, 80, 81, 100, 111, 135, 142,
    144, 147, 151, 288
Kohut, Heinz, 198
Kotz, Deborah, 170
Kuo, Frances, 168

Lambert, Dr. Kelly, 12, 44–45, 141–42
Lamott, Anne, 25
Laski, Marghanita, 169
laughter, 246
learning
    critiques and, 73
    exercise and, 177, 179–80
    forming friendships and, 224–25
    hands-on work and, 141, 219
    natural spaces and, 168
    self-mastery and, 261
    small steps in, 45–46
Lehrer, Jonah, 41
leisure, 130–31
"less than," feelings of, 99–103

Index

Index

Index

About the Authors

DR. GRACE CAROLINE (CARRIE) BARRON is a board-certified psychiatrist/psychoanalyst on the clinical faculty of the Columbia College of Physicians and Surgeons and at the Columbia Psychoanalytic Center, where she has taught writing to clinicians and psychotherapy to psychiatry residents in training. She has a private practice in New York City. She has published in peer-reviewed journals, won several academic awards, and presented original works at national meetings of the American Psychoanalytic Association and local meetings. She is a member of the American Psychiatric Association, the American Psychoanalytic Association, and the Association for Psychoanalytic Medicine. For twenty years she was a classical singer and performer. Dr. Barron created and conducted a series of panel discussions on the creative process for the RiverArts Council in Westchester County, New York.

DR. ALTON BARRON is a board-certified orthopedic surgeon who specializes in problems of the shoulder, elbow, and hand. He is a fellow of the American Academy of Orthopaedic Surgeons and the American Society for Surgery of the Hand as well as the American Shoulder and Elbow Surgeons. He is currently the president of the New York Society for Surgery of the Hand. He is in an academic private practice in New York City. He has been a treating orthopedic surgeon for the New York Philharmonic Orchestra and Metropolitan Opera for more than a decade and has treated many other professional artists and musicians. He has also been a team doctor for Fordham University athletics for many years. A clinical faculty member of Columbia College of Physicians and Surgeons, he teaches and speaks regularly at national meetings. Dr. Barron is a consultant for CBS and has appeared on the *CBS Early Show* several times. He has also written for the *New York Times,* was listed in the *New York Times Magazine* as one of the "Super Docs," annually since 2009 and has published extensively in multiple peer-reviewed journals. He is an accomplished athlete and marathon runner.

THE BARRONS HAVE been married for twenty-three years and are the parents of three children.